# Praise for *Twice Blessed*

"What makes *Twice Blessed* unique and important is how Stefanie, Claire, and Stan's individual experiences and perceptions create a fulsome, complete narrative. Each of us should play a significant role in the forming of a family. *Twice Blessed* sheds light on the equally significant roles that trust, patience, endurance, and love play. A truly worthwhile read!"

—**Ronald E. Richter**, CEO & ED, JCCA | Repair the world, child by child

"This is a wonderful story about love, loss, and commitment. Stan and Claire's unwavering support of Rosa and their unconditional love for Stefanie are testament to how family can be found in unexpected places, and it can blossom regardless of race, ethnicity, religion, and all the things that we mistakenly believe define our lives. Stefanie's strength and resilience in the face of all her early losses and suffering are a tribute to the power of love."

—**Lilliam Barrios Paoli**, Former New York City Deputy Mayor for Health and Human Services

"Adoption always begins in tragedy. And the Altmans' story is no exception. But the story of Stefanie, Claire, and Stan is much more. It is the story of a dying mother who gets to choose how her daughter will be raised. It is the story of a couple past their childbearing years who learn to be the parents a little girl needs. It is the story of a girl's resilience through devastation and instability. It is the story of a maddening journey through family court. Most of all, though, *Twice Blessed* is the story of a family forged through love."

—**Naomi Riley**, Senior fellow, American Enterprise Institute, and author of *No Way to Treat a Child*

# Twice Blessed

# TWICE BLESSED

## A Story of Unconditional Love

### Stefanie Mercado Altman,
### Claire Altman, and Stan Altman

**EMPIRE STATE EDITIONS**

AN IMPRINT OF FORDHAM UNIVERSITY PRESS

NEW YORK 2026

Permissions:
Lyrics from the song "Suddenly" from the musical *Les Misérables*
Music by Claude-Michel Schönberg
Lyrics by Herbert Kretzmer and Alain Boublil
Music and Lyrics Copyright © 2012 by Alain Boublil Music Ltd. (ASCAP)
Mechanical and Publication Rights for the U.S.A. administered by Alain Boublil Music Ltd. (ASCAP) c/o Spielman Koenigsberg & Parker, LLP, Richard Koenigsberg, 1675 Broadway, 20th Floor, New York, NY 10019,
Tel 212- 453-2500, Fax 212-453-2550, ABML@skpny.com
International Copyright Secured. All Rights Reserved. This music is copyright. Photocopying is illegal. All Performance Rights Restricted.
Reprinted by Permission of Hal Leonard LLC

Cover art: Pastel drawing by Rosa Mercado

Fordham University Press has no responsibility for the persistence or accuracy of URLs for external or third-party Internet websites referred to in this publication and does not guarantee that any content on such websites is, or will remain, accurate or appropriate.

Fordham University Press also publishes its books in a variety of electronic formats. Some content that appears in print may not be available in electronic books.

Visit us online at www.fordhampress.com/empire-state-editions.

For EU safety / GPSR concerns: Mare Nostrum Group B.V., Mauritskade 21D, 1091 GC Amsterdam, The Netherlands, gpsr@mare-nostrum.co.uk

Library of Congress Cataloging-in-Publication Data available online at https://catalog.loc.gov.

Printed in the United States of America

28 27 26   5 4 3 2 1
First edition

*To*
*My Mom Rosa,*
*I want to remember you as your paint brushes,*
*as your easel, and as the paintings you created.*
*Your art was the liveliest part about you.*
*I want to embrace your memory in a kaleidoscope of*
*colors and shapes.*
*Love, Stefanie Rosa*

# CONTENTS

# FOREWORD

THIS HUGELY IMPORTANT chronicle takes us on a years-long journey with a mother (Claire), a father (Stan), and a now adult daughter (Stefanie) as each gives individual voice to the ways in which a complex legal process of adoption brought out their resilient best and made them into a family of deepening love. Through all the obstacles they successfully resolved, the reader will experience compassionate and renewed confidence in an ancient and respected practice established in the very earliest codes of law going back to that of Hammurabi (Stone 7), the first king of the Babylonian Empire (present day Iran) nearly 4,000 years ago. It has long survived as the most successful and ubiquitous solution worldwide to raising children whose biological parents for one reason or another wish to freely relinquish them or who have passed away. In these pages, the reader will find the highest modern conceptualization of adoption at its best as "the act of taking a child into your home and heart by choice"—an act that has flourished in the contextual blend of "various styles of family units" and that "has existed since the dawn of time."

But fasten your seat belts, because at the deepest level, this is a book about pure unlimited love. Claire and Stan Altman are our teachers as they underscore that "what remains at the heart of this new adoptive family unit is love, unconditional love and a determination to give that child love and a nurturing safe home." This is not just another book about the ethics of adoption in theory, but it is rather a powerful narrative that everyone ensconced in an adoptive family or with interest in adoptive families should read to celebrate the victory of adoption in a family struggle for completion. This is a book for social workers, lawyers, judges, philosophers, historians, and for those who know that spiritual practice and helping others can allow inner peace to arise and make the most of adversity.

As a professor of family and preventive medicine at the same university where Stan Altman once taught years before my arrival, I hope that all physicians will read this book. Parents should always want to raise a kind and caring child, and most ask of them at some point "Could you have been a little kinder?" Claire and Stan Altman apply wise and effective love—the best kind—to overcome the stiff and even threatening resistance from Stefanie's mother's partner and one of Stefanie's kin relatives. They tell us, "This is our story of how we, Stan and Claire Altman, fell in love with a little girl named Stefanie Mercado, long before any legal documents came into play and while her birth mother was still alive to love and make plans for how to raise her. It is our journey through formal adoption and how we have grown together as a family." It becomes vividly clear that the court system certainly around this specific case of adoption leaves much room for improvement, but in the Altmans' case, parental heart conquers all and thank heavens. Gandhi remarked that love is a virtue for the courageous.

The narrative of courage in this book makes it a breathtaking and even suspenseful masterpiece. I have studied adoption and the family for more than thirty years, and this is the most unique and fully engaging genre I have yet come across. Reading will make anyone more empathic and compassionate as it will expand their awareness of a whole range of human experience and emotion.

███

Significant criticism of adoption has dominated the literature since the 1970s and has obscured its immense value when conducted in such a way as to respect the autonomy of the infant-relinquishing birth mother. True, in worst cases, there may be an exploited birth mother who was forced by circumstances economic or social to "give up" a beloved infant. As a senior medical ethicist active in hospital consultations, I have seen a major sea change from the 1970s, when departments of obstetrics always asked birth mothers if they would prefer relinquishment to abortion. But after the 1973 Roe v. Wade Supreme Court decision permitted abortion, the very mention of the adoption option began to disappear in all but Catholic

Hospitals. I make a point to always bring "relinquishment" up in passing in the clinical setting.

The Altmans were highly respectful of the autonomy of Stefanie's birth mother, Rosa Mercado. In fact, they were adopting at Rosa's appreciative request. Claire led the development and opening of a residence in 1991 for homeless people in the wake of the AIDS epidemic. The first two residents were Rosa, a Puerto Rican mother who was living with AIDS, and her lovely infant daughter, Stefanie, was then just three months old. By 1995, when Rosa's health was failing rapidly, she needed loving guardians for Stefanie, by then four years old. Rosa asked the Altmans to become those entrusted guardians. It is in honoring the spirit of freedom that this story of love commenced with the free will request of a dying mother seeking a loving family for her only daughter. The way Claire and Stan lived their spiritual lives to become the parents and persevering people of love they had to be to succeed with adoption makes this book doubly interesting. They both had to grapple with deep and even disturbing adversity to gain the outcome desired and needed; they were strengthened along the path by mindfulness, meditation, and compassion training that served them well.

███

In 2021, Stan, Claire, and Stefanie decided to write this story with equal space for each one's distinctive voice. I have never read a book as well structured as this one is, with three voices independently addressing the topic of each chapter. One thing is clear, the three authors were synergistic as they grew in love for each other, overcoming challenges unveiled throughout these pages. As they state, they felt ready to tell their individual and collective stories, to share many intimate experiences, and to offer thoughts about how they found the strength to carry on. There is a major drama that arises from Rosa's partner, who wanted to lay claim to Stefanie. Stan and Claire were at first merely Stefanie's legal guardians, albeit handpicked by Rosa for a much greater role. For years, the unpredictability for the Altmans of seeking sole custody of Stefanie in court kept in place a contentious joint custody arrangement with the mother's partner, who insisted on a complicated and coercive shared parenting arrangement. For six years, Claire and Stan lived with this contentious arrangement fearing how the Family Court would respond to their request for sole custody of Stefanie. An unexpected event led the Altmans to finally go to Family Court seeking sole custody. Then, after eight tortuous months of a Family Court trial, the case ended when the birth mother's partner suddenly died.

This is a peerless book on the kindness of and for strangers that goes far beyond any existing work on adoption for its clarification of how complicating policy and law can be experienced at the deepest personal levels by those whose lives are adversely affected. It is a book about how a little girl was saved by adoption. This is a practice that John Eastburn Boswell, the great historian of the family and the ways of family formation in the West through the Renaissance, sums up as follows: "Society relied on the kindness of strangers to protect its extra children, a kindness much admired and prominent in the public consciousness" (John Eastburn Boswell, *The Kindness of Strangers: The Abandonment of Children in Western Europe from Late Antiquity to the Renaissance* [New York: Pantheon, 1988], 433). Europe, he shows, relied on "a panoply of formal and informal arrangements" (417) for providing a family for children in need. In Christian ethics, all believers are, as St. Paul stressed, "adopted" into Christ. At the deepest level, no one "possesses" a child or another human being. God alone possesses. Even biological parents are nothing more and, importantly, nothing less than caring stewards with the primary task of being good role models for loving-kindness.

I have known Claire and Stan Altman over the years, and can point to them as exemplars of what Boswell described as the "ideal of nonbiological, fostering love" (239). I offer this foreword with gratitude for what they have done to bring this form of love to life.

Stephen G. Post
Founding Director, The Center for Medical Humanities,
Compassionate Care & Bioethics
The Renaissance School of Medicine, Department of Family,
Population & Preventive Medicine
Stony Brook University

# PREFACE

FAMILIES ARE CREATED in a myriad of ways, most often with one or more biological parents as part of the family unit. At other times, one finds a number of variations with widowed or divorced adults becoming parents to their mate's children from previous unions. Sometimes the family is created by careful planning, often by a surprise pregnancy, and occasionally by tragedy or happenstance.

Adoption, the act of taking a child into your home and heart by choice, is in the middle of all those various styles of family units, and it has existed since the dawn of time. Adoption was an informal system of parenting centuries before it became a formal legal process. Children have been parented, taken in and raised by individuals who held no biological connection to them—close and distant relatives, neighbors, and friends—for reasons too numerous to mention. Sometimes they were orphaned, abandoned, purposely put into the care of the state, some person or another family. In the best of all worlds, what remains at the heart of these new adoptive family units is love, unconditional love and a determination to give that child love and a nurturing safe home.

This is our story of how we, Stan and Claire Altman, fell in love with a little girl named Stefanie Mercado, long before any legal documents came into play and while her birth mother was still alive to love and make plans for how to raise her. It is our journey through formal adoption and how we have grown together as a family.

Our story starts in the late 1980s when the HIV/AIDS epidemic was ravaging many urban communities in the United States. Gay and lesbian individuals, intravenous drug users and their partners, and those with hemophilia were the primary initial groups infected with the HIV/AIDS virus. Eventually, as the world learned more of its transmission, it became clear that no one was immune from the disease. It spread to heterosexual people and others became infected via blood transfusions and the accidental transmission of bodily fluids. Secret lifestyles became public as more and more people became infected by a disease that initially had almost a 100 percent mortality rate.

The human immunodeficiency virus (HIV) targets cells of the immune system. It does not always develop into AIDS and can take a decade or more to do so. Acquired Immune Deficiency (AIDS) is the late stage of HIV infection when the body's immune system is badly damaged because of the virus.

One consequence of the AIDS epidemic was its impact on the most vulnerable of our population: children of adults with AIDS. There were those who were orphaned and others born with the disease via their mother's transmission of it to them. Stan, a professor at the State University at Stony Brook, New York, was immersed in leading a research project to determine the housing needs of people living with AIDS. Stan found himself raising funds to create housing for persons living with the disease. His study concluded that there would be a small number of persons with AIDS who would survive and require supportive housing. When Stan's efforts to lease housing for people with AIDS failed, due to the public's fear of AIDS and opposition to housing this group in their neighborhoods, he donated to Claire's not-for-profit organization the $10,000 he had raised to create a residence for persons with AIDS.

Previously, most housing efforts had focused on the gay and lesbian population. But given that the percentage of newborns in the Bronx, New York City's poorest borough, born with the HIV/AIDS infection was 2 percent, Claire and her organization decided to create a residence in the Bronx for parents living with AIDS and their children.

In 1991 Claire led the development and opening of this residence, which became home to Rosa Mercado, a Puerto Rican mother, and her daughter, Stefanie, who was then three months old. By 1995, when Rosa's health was failing rapidly, she started arranging for loving guardians for Stefanie, then four years old. Rosa didn't want to die leaving her daughter an orphan of this crisis. Rosa asked us to become Stefanie's guardians and that is how the story of our family began.

In 2021, we decided to write this story of how the three of us, with our different backgrounds and perspectives, came together to create what many thought of as an uncommon family. We discovered an unconditional love for each other as we have overcome many challenges that we encountered on this journey. We felt ready to tell our individual and collective stories, to share many intimate experiences, and to offer our thoughts about how we found the strength to carry on.

We decided to tell our story in three voices. The authorship of each section of the book is denoted by the author's name (Stefanie, Stan, Claire).

We hope that this book will help people recognize and realize the joy that comes with being part of families whose members come from very different backgrounds who love and trust one another so that the barriers that might have kept them apart are bridges to bring them together. We applaud especially adoptees, adoptive parents, the many professionals involved in the health care and child welfare fields who facilitate adoptions, as well as members of the general public who recognize adoptive families as natural families.

# Twice Blessed

# PROLOGUE

It is the night of November 19, 2001, in Manhattan. New York City and the world are still reeling from the tragedy of 9/11. The lives of three people—Claire Altman, her husband Stan Altman, and a ten-year-old girl named Stefanie Mercado—have changed dramatically in the last few years. Their lives are about to change even more when the events of this night unfold.

Claire and Stan have been raising Stefanie, a child they love and very much consider their daughter, for five years now. Stan and Claire are Stefanie's legal guardians, handpicked by Rosa, Stefanie's mother, to perform that important role. But they have been in a contentious joint custody arrangement with Rosa's former partner Angela and, by default, Stefanie's uncle, who adds another complicated element to this shared parenting arrangement.

This November night will end Stefanie's divided time for the past five years between these two very different home environments.

The drama unfolded after a series of bad choices by Angela and the uncle, designer clothes, a knock on the door, a sting operation, half-finished science homework, a telephone call, Stefanie's rescue chariot in the form of Stan's blue Honda Civic, and Stefanie grabbing the dog right before her exit.

It's the story of several lives, coalesced in these three people—Stan, Claire, and Stefanie—in a rather incredible, fortuitous way with a very happy ending.

**1**

```
🁢
```

# Who Are Stan and Claire?

OUR STORY BEGINS by introducing ourselves and explaining who we are and how our individual journeys led us to meet and eventually adopt Stefanie.

### Stan

I was born on September 11, 1940, in a private maternity hospital located in the West Bronx. My mother had been warned that having children might kill her because she had an enlarged heart, a consequence of having had rheumatic fever as a child. I remember during my first five years my mother was often away, either because she was hospitalized or sent to a convalescent home to regain her heath. No one ever told me why my mother was gone. I was just sent to live with my maternal grandparents or with my mother's oldest sister, Betty. When I was about two years old, my mother was taken seriously ill while at home. When I tried to see her, my mother's other sister Esther stopped me and said, "It is your fault your mother is so sick. You should never have been born. You will kill her." I burst into tears, frightened by the thought I would be responsible for my mother dying.

In addition to my mother's poor health, it was the war years, and times were difficult for our family. Three of my uncles went to war. Getting work became difficult for my father, who worked as a plumber. When he could not get a job in New York City, he took a job in Virginia to support our

3

family. I so missed my father. I cherish the memories of his coming home from work and whistling below our kitchen window to let me know he was home. I would run into the hall, and when he got to our landing, he would pick me up and hug me. I felt loved and safe. Then he would be gone for several months.

I am sure that these early chaotic years contributed to my being withdrawn. Every place I was sent to live had different rules and routines, which created a merry-go-round that left me confused about how I should behave.

In addition, while my mother and father were both born into Jewish families, their families were very different. My father's family was Ashkenazi, typically Jews from Eastern Europe, and my mother's family was Sephardic, part of fifty families who immigrated to the United States from Ioannina, Greece, at the turn of the twentieth century. As I would learn later in life, some Jews were referred to as Ashkenazim to distinguish them from Sephardim_(Spanish rite) Jews. Ashkenazim differed from Sephardim in cultural traditions, in synagogue chanting, and especially in synagogue liturgy.

All of my maternal aunts married sons whose parents were from Ioannina. My mother broke the rule by marrying my father. He did not speak Greek, and for a long time he was the outsider, as my mother's family would often speak Greek when he was around. It stopped when my father demanded they speak in English.

As a result of my father not being Greek, I was often referred to by my maternal family as the "half-breed." I was the different one, impure, given the outsider label, which I never overcame. To make matters worse, I was the only grandchild who did not speak or understand Greek.

My family spent a lot of time with our Greek relatives. Until the age of fourteen, my maternal family and several of the other families from Ioannina spent summers in Rockaway Beach in Queens. From the end of June through Labor Day, we all lived together in a communal housing arrangement. There were dozens of cousins of all ages. I loved the beach and the freedom of playing with my cousins.

I was also a very curious child, always wanting to know what made things tick. My energetic behavior often got me in trouble, and I also could be quite stubborn. This often led to punitive measures by my mother, often with no warning. As a result, I felt isolated and alone.

Given this chaotic, unpredictable environment at home, by the time I entered kindergarten I began to stutter. By the first grade, my stuttering increased. I often felt depressed, and I had difficulty reading and pronouncing words. As a consequence, I was afraid to speak in public and felt worthless. I was put into a special remedial reading class and learned little about reading. But I learned a lot about the cruelty of other students who enjoyed teasing me and making fun of my stutter and difficulty reading. The rage and anger that I carried with me came out as I got into fights both in and outside of school. I was labeled a problem child, which led to the administrators calling my mother frequently to come to school and meet with my teachers because of my disruptive behavior.

I also got sick often, and I had all the standard stuff: measles, mumps, whooping cough, and who knows what else. I was so sick in the fourth grade that I missed classes most of April, May, and June. I think some of my illnesses were a defense mechanism for dealing with a difficult home situation. I could not be hit with a strap if I was sick.

One of the few adults I felt I could trust was my father's youngest brother, Seymour. He took me with him to the movies and the zoo, and he even let me hang out with his friends in their clubhouse. I thought he would always take care of me, but I felt betrayed one day when he and his new girlfriend, Dorothy, announced they planned to get married. I felt that he no longer loved me. I was abandoned again. I screamed that I would not go to their wedding. I did not go because I willed myself to be sick.

It was when I was in college and working for my Uncle Seymour Saturdays in his electronic store that I realized the false assumption I made that night. I had convinced myself that he could only love one of us, and he was picking Dorothy over me.

My inner rage often reared its ugly head, resulting in my taking two steps forward and one step backward. I felt I was living in a world full of nightmares and not connecting to what was happening around me. The summer before my thirteenth birthday, I woke up in the room we rented in Rockaway Beach and saw myself in the mirror. It felt like I had woken up from a long sleep, and for the first time I became aware of myself.

Reaching one's thirteenth birthday is a significant milestone for a Jewish boy because he makes his Bar Mitzvah and the transition into adulthood and religious responsibility. One attends Hebrew School to prepare for reading a passage from the Torah, the heart of the Bar Mitzvah ceremony.

I had spent four years attending Hebrew School, and in all that time I never learned to speak Hebrew or understand the Hebrew text. None of the rituals had any meaning for me. Although my family was Jewish and observed the holidays and Sabbath, they did so in name only. For example, during the high holy day of Yom Kippur they would find ways for us to watch the World Series even though we were supposed to spend the day in prayer and atoning for negative deeds during the past year.

For my Bar Mitzvah, there were two ceremonies I had to perform in Shul. First, I had to do the morning prayer, which involved me wrapping leather straps to hold a tefillin, or a prayer box, around my arm. Since we were in Rockaway, my grandfather took me to the local Sephardic Synagogue, where the morning prayer was conducted differently from what I had learned in the the Ashkenazi Hebrew School near my home. I was unprepared and was lost trying to follow the service. I struggled the entire hour we were in synagogue. My grandfather was angry and told me how ashamed he was of me. While my grandfather ultimately realized what happened, it did not change the hurt and feelings of rejection and isolation I felt that day. I swore to myself that I would do a flawless reading of the Torah at my Bar Mitzvah. I practiced so hard that I memorized the entire reading and when the time came, I delivered on my promise.

For me, completing my Bar Mitzvah was freedom, because I would never have to go through the charade of being a practicing Jew when the rituals had no meaning for me. Nonetheless, I had a deep sense of a higher being, whom I sometimes referred to as God or Father. I believed in the power of prayer, as one Saturday when my father was working in the middle of a tropical storm, I prayed to bring him home safely. The nearby clock read 3:00. When my father returned home, he told me that a gust of wind had blown his truck from the right lane to the left lane just as a large neon sign crashed into the right lane. He remembered that the time was 3:00 p.m.

Junior High School was different. I found myself in a leadership position within days of school starting. My older cousin was a senior and was on the school's election committee. As part of the committee's succession planning, they were recruiting seventh graders like me. Two days after my appointment, my cousin and his friend resigned, and they urged me to resign as well. When I refused, my cousin and his friends beat me up. I convinced the teacher in charge that I could handle the elections, including recruiting a new team. He agreed, and the annual elections went smoothly during the three years I attended junior high school.

I am not sure why, but I got involved in many other activities, including becoming a member of the school chorus and often serving as the MC of a performance. We earned points for services we performed. I earned sufficient points to make the school honor roll. Again, I became my own worst enemy. Being a school leader meant that I drew attention from my teachers. Given the way I was treated in elementary school, I did not know how to deal with this new recognition and attention. My position went to my head, and I began to show off in front of other students. I did this in part because I wanted other students to be my friends and partially because I did not know any better. I did not have anyone I felt I could trust with my feelings of inadequacy over not knowing how to behave in these situations. I could not talk to my father, and I did not trust my cousin to respect my feelings. This ultimately led to me making poor decisions and behaving in ways that resulted in my being reprimanded by teachers I respected.

When it was time to go to high school, I wanted to get away from the pattern of fighting and street life that I had grown to despise. So I applied to Science High School in the Bronx, one of New York City's special public high schools. While I did not get a high enough grade on the special entrance exams for Bronx Science, my score was high enough for me to be admitted to Stuyvesant High School in Manhattan.

The decision to go to Stuyvesant was a turning point in my life, although I was unaware of the significance of my decision at that time. I completed high school without many incidents, and I discovered my love and talent for solving mathematical problems. I graduated with an average of around 85 percent, good enough to be admitted to City College of New York. While at Stuyvesant, I also discovered I had a photographic memory. I could recall portions of a book or anything else I read. This ability saved me more than once while taking exams.

I uncovered a whole new side of myself at City College. I decided to major in electrical engineering. My strengths were mathematics, sciences, and problem solving. My weaknesses were the liberal arts and humanities, in part because I was still a poor reader but also because I did not trust my ability to give "the right answer." I avoided speaking up in class, and my written work was often confused and superficial. However, there was always a single right answer in my other subjects. I excelled academically in my engineering courses, and I was elected to the electrical engineering honor society ETA Kappa Nu, where I held several offices including the presidency the year I graduated.

I completed my degree requirements in January 1963. After finishing my last final examination, I got married to Loren, whom I had been dating for two years. We were both young. Loren was nineteen, and I was twenty-two. We both brought issues to our marriage resulting from childhood traumas that made it impossible for us to be fully trusting and open with each other.

The day following our wedding, we set off on a seven-day road trip to California so I could begin my job at an aerospace company in Downey, California. This was a difficult time for Loren, as she left college one semester short of graduating and was unable to find a job for months. All our friends worked, leaving her alone most days.

The company had promised me the opportunity to go to graduate school at the University of Southern California (USC). I quickly discovered that they meant the USC extension division, which only offered night classes. I dropped out of the first class I took because I found it impossible to balance work, school, and family life. After working at the company for six months, I decided to pursue a master's degree.

Before graduating from college, I had been approached by Purdue University in Indiana to apply to their graduate school. I decided to accept Purdue's offer and started my graduate work in September 1963. I excelled in my classes and did research on the early application of Artificial Intelligence (AI) to large industrial systems. However, my wife did not want to remain in Indiana, so we returned to New York. After earning my master's degree in the summer of 1964, I transferred to the Polytechnic Institute of Brooklyn (now NYU's Tandon School of Engineering) to complete my Ph.D.

That spring, we became parents to a baby boy—Jeffrey. It was a defining moment in my life to hold my son and immediately wish for him a life of joy and promise.

In my last year at Brooklyn Polytechnic, I joined the City College electrical engineering faculty as an assistant professor. Throughout graduate school, Loren and I were able to live on my scholarship income, but now I needed a real income since our first child had been born the previous April. I didn't feel like there was much growth opportunity for me at City College. So when a former classmate from City College approached me about applying to Princeton, I did just that and was hired by the electrical engineering department starting in the summer of 1968.

The department chair I met with when I arrived at Princeton informed me that I was on probation and had to prove myself by doing research and getting grants. I worked hard, and my research efforts were rewarded with a large National Science Foundation (NSF) grant. Three months after arriving in Princeton, our son David was born. Sadly, with all of my attention focused on proving myself in my work, I had little time for the children. Like many workaholics, years later I would regret having not established a more balanced home and work life.

By the end of the first year, I accepted a summer position at the RAND Corporation in California. When we returned to Princeton at the end of August, I met with the chair of the department again. I asked him for an assessment of my work the previous year. He responded, "If you have to ask, you should get another job." And I did a year later at Stony Brook University.

During my second year at Princeton, I had agreed to co-edit a special issue of the professional journal *IEEE Transactions on Systems Science and Cybernetics*, focusing on the application of a systems approach to addressing urban problems. This decision was a result of my growing interest in the delivery of public services, particularly in urban settings like New York City. Within a month of the special issue being announced, my co-editor resigned, leaving me to deal with the issue. My initial reaction was panic, as I feared the humiliation of failing to produce the special issue.

I procrastinated for months until March when I realized I could not keep putting off the decision. Either I had to cancel the issue or do it. I decided to go forward and do the best I could. I solicited articles from practitioners and academics. I edited several submitted papers, and by early May 1970 I had a draft of the special issue. Next, I needed to write my introduction to the issue. As always, I tried to find the perfect first sentence. Rather than staring at the paper for hours, I heard my inner voice say, "Don't worry, you will write the editorial when you are ready." I stopped, put my pen and paper away and one week later I wrote my introduction in less than thirty minutes. The words and thoughts just came to me. This experience was the beginning of my overcoming my fear of writing, even though I felt like I had avoided a catastrophe. My editorial suggested that systems thinking would play an important role in addressing the delivery of public services and a glimpse into my long-term professional interest.

I wrote, "It is important that we begin to understand the nature of societal problems. We begin to achieve this objective by encouraging and soliciting technical papers from those active in the field. We can use our strength as an interdisciplinary group to provide a forum for interaction among sociologists, technologists, politicians, and economists. We must begin to address the total problem from its definition to the implementation of its solution."

In the fall of 1970, I joined the Stony Brook University faculty as the education director of a new master's program called Urban Science and Engineering. Stony Brook is the flagship campus of the State University of New York (SUNY) system of sixty-four campuses, located fifty-five miles outside of New York City.

I saw my work shift from computer engineering to improving government operations. The program had received a major grant from the National Science Foundation (NSF), which required faculty in the program to work with New York City government agencies. For the next three years, I worked closely with NYC's commissioner of sanitation and developed a reputation as someone who "was good at creating and implementing productivity improvement programs" in New York City agencies. I was receiving the recognition for which I had long hungered.

Despite all that I had accomplished professionally, I was emotionally immature and overly sensitive to what people thought of me. I never lost the feeling that having successfully concluded one project, I would not be able to repeat my success on a different problem. I suffered from "imposter syndrome." In retrospect, I believe I threw my myself into my work as a way to avoid my sense of inadequacy and fear that at any moment I would be abandoned by people I believed to be my friends and colleagues. I felt like I was always on guard to avoid being hurt. One wrong word or action and I was likely to never speak to the person again. I was not very present in my marriage or my family. I had this overwhelming feeling that a voice inside me was trying to tell me something important, but I did not understand what it was.

## My Crisis Flashback

By January of 1973, the pressure from being incapable of dealing with the emotional crises in my personal life led to a feeling that I was drowning. My troubles at home were compounded by a growing distrust of my boss and his future plans for the program. While traveling on the Long Island Railroad for a meeting in New York City one day, I felt that an inner voice was trying to communicate to me, but I was unable to understand what it was saying. At that moment, I decided to seek help from a therapist. At my first session, the therapist asked why I had come to see him. I said, "I need help understanding what I am trying to say to myself."

Several months into my therapy, I had an experience that shocked me to my core. While lying on the therapist's couch, I saw myself as a child, about four or five years old, huddled in the door of a building. It was cold and dark, and it was raining. I was sobbing and saying, "They are trying to take my soul. I am losing who I am. They want me to be someone else." I repeated this over and over while shivering when I heard a second voice. It was a male voice I never heard before, and he said, "I will protect you and never let anyone hurt you again."

I felt that he would shield me from the outside world, but his voice was cold and dispassionate. I felt like my feelings and emotions were being buried deep inside of me where neither I nor anyone else would ever find them again. My mind suddenly became the filter through which I interacted and perceived the world—cerebral and emotionless.

As I sat looking at that boy huddled in the doorway, I was reliving my childhood traumas. "They" were my parents, particularly my mother. The wall symbolized the emotional hurt and rejection I endured as a child. This experience was overwhelming. I did not fully appreciate the significance of what I had just gone through and how profound an explanation it provided for what I was undergoing. My alter ego had protected me by suppressing my feelings and emotions. It gave me an insight into why I operated from a place of rational and logical thinking, excellence in mathematics and science, and the ability to work well on specific tasks. Yet I feared exposing myself to humiliation by risking rejection of what I had to say or thoughts I put to paper. The result was that I had buried my feelings and emotions and constructed a view of the world where feelings and emotions did not exist.

Through March and April of 1973, my personal life continued to fall apart, and by May my wife and I had separated. The breakup of my marriage was traumatic, but the worst part was seeing the fear and confusion on my two sons' faces as I drove away from our home. Jeffrey had just turned seven, and his brother David was four years old. The looks on their faces as I drove away shocked me to my core. I was so overwhelmed by my emotional reaction that I almost blacked out while I was driving. Looking back at that moment, I think I relived the sense of abandonment I experienced as a child. I felt like I was a failure as a parent and father.

In May 1973, I had an opportunity to travel to Greece. I wanted to understand where I came from. The timing of the trip came after my separation from my wife and kids. It was an incredible trip. I was worried about being in a country whose language I did not speak or understand. However, as soon as I arrived in Athens, I felt free. Even though I did not speak Greek, communication was not a problem. I rented a car and drove down to Vouliagmeni Beach for a few days. Then I drove to Delphi, the home of the Greek Oracle, and I spent five days on the Isle of Mykonos returning to Athens for a few days before returning to New York City.

During my time in Greece, particularly while on Mykonos, I had time to reflect on who I was and what I was doing with my life. I wanted my life to have meaning, but I had no clue how to achieve this. I pondered what name I would have given myself, given the choice. I had no answer. I never identified with my name being Stanley, as I would shorten it to Stan. A month later, I was signing a wedding shower card, and I wrote Stefan, not Stan. Stefan felt right, and it became my name to all my friends. The Mykonos experience was other worldly. I would watch the sunset and feel I could step into another world away from the craziness of my life. I felt an inner calm for the first time I could remember.

I returned to New York City at the end of May. I had rented an apartment from a colleague for a few months, as I did not plan to move back to

Stony Brook. I had taken a leave without pay from Stony Brook to direct a project involving rating the cleanliness of city streets. It was named Project Scorecard, and the office would be housed at a local foundation where I would work and be paid as a visiting scholar.

A few days after returning to the city, I interviewed the New York City sanitation commissioner as part of a National Science Foundation (NSF) funded project to learn about their management practices and experiences leading city agencies. Jeanetta, one of the people from the foundation, was also at the interview.

When we concluded, Jeanetta introduced me to her friends and invited me to join them at their meditation class that night. I agreed more out of curiosity than any real interest. The class was led by Rev. Ellen Resch, who wove together life lessons and spiritual philosophy and practice. Her meditation class consisted of her giving a lesson on living a meaningful life followed by individual messages to those at the meeting. Ellen was psychic, and the message she gave me about my work at the foundation came to pass one month later. I felt that her lessons spoke to the inner turmoil I was dealing with, giving me the feeling that someone understood what I was struggling with. I connected with the community of diverse individuals who studied with Ellen. It was the first time in my life that I felt like I belonged and was accepted for who I was. The following Saturday, I remember rushing to Ellen's meeting and arriving five minutes late. My experience at this meeting was even more profound than the first one. From that moment on, I studied with Ellen until she passed away in July 1990.

One theme through all of Ellen's lessons was the importance of serving others, of living a life where service to others gave one meaning and purpose. Support of the work of the Dalai Lama and the Tibetans in exile in India were two of our areas of service. Feeding New York City's homeless was another.

For the rest of the summer, I felt like I was speeding and living in a new world with people who understood and cared about me. I terminated my therapy sessions, falsely believing all my problems were solved. As I was to learn, my problems were still my problems, and I was simply deluding myself into thinking otherwise.

In September 1973, my wife and I agreed to get divorced. I hired a lawyer, and the negotiations between my lawyer and my wife's lawyer continued until January 1974 when our divorce was approved. I was emotionally drained by the process of dissolving almost ten years of marriage, and the realization I was leaving my sons. Although I had shared custody and faithfully saw them regularly, it was not the same because the pain of leaving them made me delude myself into thinking I did not care.

Ellen never let me forget my responsibilities for my two sons. She helped me experience how much I loved them and cared about them.

It was being part of Ellen's group that I met Claire, though it took me five years after she started studying with Ellen before I took the time to get to know her.

## Claire

Growing up in Tennessee, my early life was fenced in by the culture of my religious upbringing, the segregation of the deep South that was still alive and well in Memphis in the 1960s, and the general view that one grew up, went to college in Memphis or nearby, married, and stayed in the South.

When I was born, my parents and I lived in a small town with 3,000 residents in eastern Arkansas. My father was a traveling hardware salesman. His customers were small hardware stores and farmers. Most of the town's families lived on and worked their farms. There were a few families like us who were "town" families. In short order, my sister and brother were born. My mother stayed home and ran a nursery school in a room my dad had added to our house.

I began school in a two-room Catholic school—four grades in a class. Our classroom had grades one through three, plus the sixth grade. Since I was tall, even as a six-year-old, I was placed in the row with the sixth graders. That meant that for the entire first grade I had no idea what was being taught. By the second grade, I was with students my age, but learning was still limited. Since most of the students were from farm families and had to work on their family's farm, the school year began when the crops had been harvested and ended when it became planting season in the spring. Some years, we never even opened the books for some subjects. The nuns who were teaching us would say, "Well, we didn't get to history (or whatever subject we hadn't touched) this year."

I think my parents realized that my brother, sister, and I weren't going to get an education this way. My dad's hardware business was not good, so he managed to get a job selling life insurance in Memphis, Tennessee, across the Mississippi River from our home in Arkansas. We moved to Memphis, at that time a town of 500,000 residents where the schools were better. Once again, my brother, sister, and I were enrolled in a Catholic school, with mostly nuns as teachers. I don't remember much about elementary school, which seemed uneventful. I do remember taking piano lessons, and by the time I was about twelve I was teaching piano to neighborhood children. Growing up, we did many of the usual kid things—swimming in the summer, scouting, some family summer vacations when my parents could afford it, and fairly frequent visits to my grandmother and aunts (on my father's side of the family) who lived in Memphis. My mother had converted to Catholicism when she married my father, and she was a devout Catholic. So we went to church every day Monday through Friday during the school year, and Saturdays and Sundays with my parents. I never understood the Mass, which back then was in Latin, nor the meaning of most of the rituals.

I'm not sure what my dreams and aspirations were until I went to high school and found my voice. But that voice wasn't always in sync with the wishes of the nuns. On several occasions, the nuns called my father to come to the high school, where he was met with their complaints that I hadn't followed their rules. My biggest offense was sending an article that a classmate had written for the school newspaper, of which I was the editor, to a competition. But I hadn't asked their permission to do this. My classmate's article won first prize in the competition, but that was beside the point to the nuns.

When I was approaching graduation from this all-girls Catholic high school, I wanted to find my own life, not the one that was expected of me. I had an interest in politics, but didn't see myself running for office, but maybe the Foreign Service or the law. I knew I wanted to explore paths beyond the confines of a conservative southern town where the majority views were opposed to my own. New York City was my goal, but I didn't know yet how I would get there. My parents had placed a 300-mile limit on the distance between the college I would attend and Memphis, figuring that that's how far they could drive in one day to "rescue" me from the evils of college life.

I decided I wanted to attend Vanderbilt University in Nashville, 200 miles from Memphis. Vanderbilt was the "Ivy League" school of the South, and I figured I would get a top-drawer education there. I applied to Vanderbilt, as well as to St. Louis University, a Jesuit college 300 miles north of Memphis. I received a major scholarship from St. Louis University, which I promptly filed away as the ticket to my "safety school." When the April date for college announcements of admissions or rejections came and went with no word from Vanderbilt, I called the admissions office of Vanderbilt to inquire about my status. I was told that while Vanderbilt had planned to admit me and give me a full scholarship, the nuns at my school had refused to send Vanderbilt my transcript, so they had given my scholarship to someone else.

When I pleaded with my parents to intervene with the nuns at my school, their response was, "The nuns probably know best. After all, they work for God. There's nothing we can do."

That September, I took my first plane trip, this time to St. Louis, Missouri, where I entered a totally new world. To me, St. Louis was a big city, 1.8 million people, as opposed to Memphis with 650,000 residents.

As it turned out, St. Louis U. was a radicalizing influence on me. While St. Louis U. was a Catholic college, religion was not at the center of the academics or college life. One of the most visible Catholic influences were that many liberal seminarians and some priests attended the college, including Daniel and Philip Berrigan, two major US antiwar activists during the Vietnam War, who taught at St. Louis University during my college years. Driving to Washington, DC, for weekend peace and civil rights marches became part of my regular college routine.

During summers at home, I worked with two seminarians at an inner-city church in Memphis, near the Bishop Charles Mason Temple, a Pentecostal Church, where Martin Luther King Jr. gave his "I've Been to the Mountain Top" speech on April 3, 1968, the night before he was assassinated. A year later, I joined the "anniversary" march of the garbage workers that Dr. King had been slated to lead. That day was a defining moment for me. The march organizers put me in charge of leading a group of sight-impaired people and placed us in the front of the march. Within minutes of the march starting, the police began showering the marchers with tear gas. My sight-impaired group panicked as tear gas goes directly to one's eyes. I was finally able to steer my group away from the police and get them to a safe place.

The next day, Memphis's local newspaper *The Commercial Appeal* ran a front-page story on the march. The accompanying picture was of me and the sight-impaired people carrying a banner. At that moment, I knew that I wasn't destined for the exotic life of a Foreign Service officer, but rather I wanted to address social issues here in the United States.

After graduation from college, I married Phillip from New Jersey, whom I had met at St. Louis University. He was involved in some of the same activist activities that I was. Phillip was a medium-height, red-headed Irish Catholic, with no solid career ambitions other than settling into a predictable life, probably in a civil service job. His idea of a good weekend was drinking beer with his buddies. We had started dating more out of convenience than love, and never really got to know each other. In those days, in the early 1970s, most of my female friends in college got married the summer we graduated and set about starting a family. I wanted to explore the world and what my options were in it.

After we got married at a small wedding in Memphis, Phillip wanted to return to his family in New Jersey, the neighboring state of my dream destination New York City. With a lead from Phillip's mother, I managed to get accepted into a master's program in urban studies at New York University with a fellowship, which paid me a stipend to do community service.

I had heard about a newly formed not-for-profit organization, the Fortune Society, that helped ex-offenders reintegrate into society. Their mission appealed to me, so I found my way to their office in New York City's Times Square, met the founder, David Rothenberg, a former Broadway press agent turned helper of ex-offenders. I immediately took a liking to David and asked him how I could help. He and I agreed that I had no skills for helping ex-inmates deal with adjusting to life after prison, but I could try to find jobs for them. I began calling employers, interviewing ex-inmates who came to our office, and trying to match them with jobs. I was pretty successful, mostly because the men (and a few women) who came to our office were very motivated to succeed, and they worked hard at getting and keeping jobs.

Four years later, I was hired at the Vera Institute of Justice to work on creating job opportunities for ex-offenders, with a focus on creating small businesses that employed people coming out of prison. The Vera Institute of Justice had been founded in 1960 by philanthropist Louis Schweitzer and a young journalist he hired, Herb Sturz. Mr. Schweitzer wanted to make societal changes that ensured people's rights were protected. Their first initiative had been bail reform.

My husband worked for a while as a teacher and then got admitted to New York University's Law School, leaving me as the breadwinner. Innocently, and without much thought, I guaranteed his law school loans. I had decided that a law degree would be a helpful credential for me, especially in my work in the criminal justice system. But to pursue my dream of going to law school, I had to continue to work during the day and attend law school at night. I was accepted into Fordham Law School in New York City as a night student and continued to work at the Vera Institute of Justice in the criminal justice field.

When I joined Vera, they were seeking ways to help ex-offenders after release from prison or jail. So I designed and led one of the first of these enterprises: a paratransit service for elderly and disabled persons staffed by ex-offenders. By 1990, this had grown to be a New York citywide operation, and our "company," which we called EASYRIDE, handled the service in Manhattan. That paratransit operation, which New York City renamed Access-A-Ride, continues today to serve persons with disabilities.

In the late 1970s, I launched an ex-offender construction company called the Neighborhood Work Project. It provided day labor opportunities for persons just released from prison. This enterprise grew to a 200-employee operation with crews working all over New York City and continues today as the Center for Employment Opportunities.

While I was successful in my professional life, I knew my marriage wasn't what I wanted it to be. Phillip and I and shared few interests. I wanted to create a family, but not with him. After six years of this non-working marriage, I told Phillip I wanted a divorce. He agreed, and in 1976 we were divorced.

When I graduated from law school a year later, I had spent enough time in the criminal courts as part of my work that I knew my original law school goal of criminal defense work was not for me. Rather, I wanted to continue to work for the Vera Institute to help ex-inmates make it back into society, principally helping them get jobs. While this was meaningful, something was missing from my life, but between working and going to law school at night I had no time to figure out what was missing. I was living in my head, not in my heart.

After I finished law school, I was able to arrange a three-month break to work in the Vera Institute of Justice's London office. I returned to New York City on New Year's Eve, 1977, and came home more determined than ever only to spend time with people who shared my values. A few days after my return, a friend asked me if I'd like to join him at a meeting with his spiritual teacher, Ellen Resch. I attended that first meeting with my friend and was drawn to Ellen's peaceful approach. I had just turned twenty-nine and was searching for meaning in my life. Ellen's messages, drawn principally from Tibetan Buddhism, resonated with me. I began to attend her weekly meetings regularly, which had a profound impact on me. I had finally found a spiritual home where I could be comfortable, explore my spiritual nature, and get answers to questions that had seemed unfathomable.

Stan had joined Ellen's group several years earlier, and we knew each other professionally. Yet we had barely spoken to each other. In the summer of 1981, Stan and I ran into each other when we both registered for a retreat that the Dalai Lama was giving in Madison, Wisconsin. We said hello at the registration table and went our separate ways. We then spent the next three days in a large tent on the grounds of the University of Wisconsin listening to the Dalai Lama's teachings. It was a transformative experience being in the presence of such a global figure as His Holiness the 14th Dalai Lama, the Tibetan Buddhist monk who is the spiritual and temporal leader of the Tibetan people, exiled from his homeland since 1959.

When we connected a year later, little did I know that my life was to be forever changed in ways that I could never imagine.

# 2

###

# Our Surprising Romance
# and Marriage

## Stan

The glow of moving to New York City in the summer of 1973 faded as the reality of being divorced sunk in. I wanted to lose myself in the community I found in Ellen's group, but I also wanted to maintain a connection with my two sons. After my divorce, this meant commuting to Cambridge, Massachusetts, every other weekend where my ex-wife had relocated. I was not very good at managing my time with my sons on weekends, running Project Scorecard during the week, and my life in Ellen's spiritual group.

I was exhausted. My mother came with me to Cambridge one weekend and could see the strain I was under. She suggested I fly my sons from Cambridge to New York on the Eastern Shuttle. This made a huge difference, and by the summer of 1974 my life was less chaotic. That fall, I returned to the Stony Brook faculty but continued to live in New York. By now, I was living on the westside of Manhattan and the daily commute to Stony Brook was almost two hours each way.

In 1975, I was living with Jeanetta, the woman who had introduced me to Ellen Resch's spiritual group. We got married in the spring of 1975. I continued to work at Stony Brook University, but I found the commute exhausting.

Jeanetta decided to pursue a law degree and enrolled full-time in a law school in New York City. As the sole wage earner, I felt a lot of pressure to

19

bring in additional income. I was supporting my sons, bringing them back and forth to New York, and maintaining a home with Jeanetta.

In 1974, I had formed a not-for-profit research institute that by the summer of 1975 was being awarded grants that provided me with the additional income I sought. Even though both Jeanetta and I studied with Ellen, we began to grow apart. By 1979, we divorced.

I lived with someone for the next three years, which was a rebound situation for fear of being alone. It was not a healthy relationship, and from 1981 to 1982 I was depressed and in a dark place. I was lost and no longer knew who I was.

In the summer of 1982, a photographer friend who did travel brochures for American Express was hired to take pictures of the maiden voyage of the recently refurbished SS Norway of the Norwegian Cruise Line. He hired me to model for his photo shoot. The last day of the cruise was a stop on a private island. I decided to walk alone on the beach and to examine my life. I realized how unhappy and depressed I was. I was tired of trying to please everyone by being someone other than myself. In trying to please the women in my life, I had compromised my needs and feelings to be the person they wanted me to be.

Each relationship had had its own challenges. In one, it was the issue of earning more money; in another it was a lack of interest in being around my children; and in another it was a lack of shared spiritual beliefs and the complaint that I worked too much. I told myself that I was the father of two sons. That was not negotiable. My spiritual beliefs and practices, as well as my work, were important to me.

By November 1982, I had decided that I would only have a significant relationship with another woman if she accepted me for who I am, and we shared common spiritual beliefs. I thought about the women in Ellen's spiritual group. No one stood out. "Oh, well," I thought, "it's time to get on with living my life."

The night after Thanksgiving I organized a small dinner party to introduce my older son Jeffrey to a few kids his age. He was sixteen and was beginning to spend more time with me in New York City. I reached out to friends in Ellen's group. One friend Tamara had a daughter I thought might introduce Jeffrey to her friends in SOHO (South of Houston Street). I also invited a few other friends. On the spur of the moment, I invited Claire who was Tamara's close friend.

Claire had joined Ellen's group five years earlier. During those five years, we had rarely spoken to each other. I knew very little about her. People were to arrive for dinner at 8:00 p.m. At eight o'clock sharp, Claire flew into my apartment full of energy. For the first time, I recognized she had frizzy blonde hair. For the next thirty minutes, we talked about several topics. Claire talked mostly about her work, and I talked about cooking and the dinner I had made that was getting cold. I was surprised at our conversation, because most of my friends accused me of being a workaholic. I didn't mention my work at all. Claire was the first woman I ever met who seemed to think about work more than I did. For those thirty minutes, it felt like Claire and I were the only people in the world. This is not what I had expected. At exactly 8:30 p.m., all of the rest of my guests arrived. To this day, I wonder if this was planned or a coincidence.

Throughout the evening, I was aware of Claire in ways I had never been before. I found myself studying her. I was so taken by my awareness of Claire that I decided to invite her out for a cup of coffee a week later. We were both scheduled to attend a dance performance organized as a benefit by mutual friends to raise money to support Tibetan refugees living in Dharamshala, India. It was to be held in Riverside Church on the Upper Westside of Manhattan.

Claire showed up after the performance had already started. Both of my sons were with me, and it was impossible to chat with her until the performance was over. Claire joined the after-performance reception as did my sons and myself. David was, and to some extent still is, a shy kid. He had just turned fourteen and often appeared uncomfortable around new people. He rarely had much to say, and it was a challenge for me to engage him in conversation. That night, every time I tried to approach Claire, David urgently needed to talk to me about something or the other. I still do not know how he sensed my intentions, but for about twenty minutes he managed to steer me away from Claire.

Finally, concerned that she would leave before I could issue my invitation, I told David to cool it. I got up my courage and asked Claire if I could take her out for a cup of coffee after the reception, and she accepted. We dropped my sons off at home, and Claire and I went to Tribeca for coffee at what came to be our favorite place, Capsouto Freres. It was a French restaurant and late-night hangout for artists in the downtown Tribeca/SoHo neighborhoods of Manhattan.

We sat for over three hours talking about ourselves, who we were, and what was important to us. Claire told me that she had recently decided, as I had, that no relationship was worth it if it compromised her values or dreams. By the time the evening was over, I realized that my preconceived opinions about Claire were breaking down along with the walls I had built around my feelings. Claire listened to me in ways that I couldn't remember others doing. It was as if she really cared about who I was.

A week later, I was invited to Tamara's annual birthday party for the first time. Claire was also there. We spent the entire evening talking to each other, and our friends kept reminding us that we were at Tamara's party and not on a date. Their teasing was lighthearted, and I sensed that our friends were enjoying our budding romance.

Tamara's party ended around 3:00 a.m. I dropped Claire off at her apartment and headed home. I went to bed, but three hours later I was wide awake and feeling like a lovestruck nineteen-year-old. I couldn't believe how agitated I was. What was happening to me? I couldn't stop thinking about Claire. It was December 12th and only two weeks had elapsed since the dinner party for my son. I found myself chain smoking, a practice I reverted to when I was very anxious. I had decided to call Claire at 9:00 to see if I could figure out what was going on. My call woke her.

"It was an interesting evening last night," I said when Claire answered the phone, referring to my inability to sleep.

"Yes, it was," she responded, probably thinking I was talking about the party.

"No, I don't mean the party," I continued. "I feel like a nineteen-year-old, and I don't understand why."

She asked if I wanted to join her for breakfast. I said I would be downtown to her apartment in twenty minutes. I give her credit for being so cool about meeting me again. I was dressed, and my car was ready to go, so I arrived in the promised twenty minutes. When Claire opened the door to her apartment, we embraced and then spent the entire day together at her apartment before taking a long walk along the Hudson River waterfront. It must have been below zero with a cold wet wind blowing, but it did not matter since I found myself enveloped in an endless conversation with her about what I remember not. It was early evening by the time we returned to Claire's apartment to retrieve my car so we could attend Ellen's regular Sunday night spiritual meeting.

As Claire and I entered the meeting hall, every pair of eyes and ears seemed to fix on us. All our friends sensed that things were no longer the same between us. Given the way we had been carrying on during the last two weeks, it was no surprise that our friends reached this conclusion, although we thought we were being circumspect.

For New Year's Eve that year, we decided to dress formally for Ellen's group's New Year's Eve party. Claire and I agreed that she would get dressed, and then we would go to my apartment where I would get dressed. As I began to walk up the four flights of stairs to Claire's apartment, she appeared at the top of the landing dressed in an incredible navy blue satin gown styled along the fashion lines of the 1920s and 1930s. As soon as I saw her, my knees went weak, and I fell to the floor.

A few weeks later, on a freezing Saturday afternoon in January, Claire and I drove to Connecticut to have lunch with an old college mate of Claire's and his wife. After a delicious lunch of pasta and wine, we drove back to New York City. I began to feel sleepy and pulled over to the side of the road. I told Claire I was going to get out of the car and have a cigarette in the hopes that the cold air would wake me up.

"If not, I'll ask you to drive the rest of the way home," I said to Claire.

I got out of the car and so did Claire. I told her to get back in the car, but she refused. I could not believe she intended to endure the cold as long as I did.

When we returned to New York City, I had not planned on what followed. The experience of standing in the cold with Claire triggered some deep inner feelings. Within a few minutes of our arriving back at my apartment, I said to Claire:

"I love you, and I want to marry you. Will you marry me?"

She did not say a word. I drove Claire home that evening not knowing what she would do. There was a part of me that believed I might have offended her by proposing. To my great relief and delight, she accepted my proposal the next day.

The next three months were a whirlwind. I proposed to Claire on January 12, 1983; we became engaged on February 12; and we were married on March 12. In the three months, I received two significant messages from my inner voice. First, shortly after we began to date, I had heard my inner voice warning me not to try analyzing what was happening with Claire because "this relationship was different and nothing like I had experienced before, and if I persisted in analyzing it, I would screw it up." The second message occurred about a week before I proposed. We had gone to a movie and had come back to my apartment. We were playing music and dancing when I heard my inner voice saying to me, "Your relationship with Claire is a special gift and one that, if you are lucky, occurs once in a lifetime. Appreciate what is being given to you."

Our wedding was held in a friend's loft that easily accommodated our 100-plus family and friends who attended. Our group friends (as we called our friends from Ellen's group) handled the catering and music. Our friend Tamara designed and made Claire's sheer lavender silk wedding gown. Standing at the altar, I saw Claire in the back of the room walking toward me. I was overwhelmed with how beautiful she was. At that moment, I experienced how much I loved her. Like on New Year's Eve, my knees gave way, but this time my best man grabbed me before I hit the floor. Ellen married us. The celebration was a grand party. My son David and our nephew Sascha filmed our wedding. Jeffrey could be found on the dance floor most of the night.

I was blessed in having Claire as my partner, who has always had my best interests in mind. Whether it involved Claire's support when my oldest son came to live with us when he turned eighteen and we had only been married a year, when I found myself unable to deal with a highly charged emotional situation at work, or when I became ill, Claire took care of me and always stepped in to make sure I was supported, understood, and loved. No task was too great for her if it helped me. I have come to realize that Claire loves me unconditionally, a truly rare gift.

## Claire

The weekend after Stan proposed to me, he decided to take Jeffrey and David to dinner and tell them our news. I had first met Jeffrey at the small dinner party Stan held, and I had met David the night we all attended the dance benefit in early December. Now it was mid-January, and we were to be married in mid-March. Jeffrey and David lived on Long Island with their mother, which was on Stan's route back into New York City from Stonybrook University. Stan called them that Sunday evening and asked if they were free for dinner the following night. They said yes, and Stan planned to pick them up for dinner and tell them our news.

Later that night, close to midnight, David called and asked, "Dad, is what you're going to tell us good news or bad news?"

Stan responded, "I think it's good news."

David's response was, "I thought you were going to tell us you were going to die."

"No, no, I think it's very good news," Stan responded.

The next evening, Stan picked up David, and they met Jeffrey at a local Chinese restaurant.

Stan began making small talk.

"How was your day? What do you guys want for dinner?" he asked.

Jeff interrupted and said, "Look, Dad, just tell us what it is. I can't stay. I have to meet my friends. Are you going to tell us you're buying us a new computer or are you marrying Claire?"

"Yes, Claire and I are getting married March 12th."

"See, I told you, David. We're not getting a new computer. I've got to run. See you later, Dad," Jeff said.

Thus, began the discussion of our wedding with Jeffrey and David. David was excited and wanted to film the wedding. At fourteen, he was an aspiring filmmaker and had made several slapstick films in his high school film class. He had a super-8 camera and was ready to go. We agreed that this would be great. David announced he wanted to wear a tuxedo to the wedding and asked Stan to take him to get fitted. We were both happy that David shared our excitement about our wedding. Jeffrey had a less overt response, but he enthusiastically volunteered for a behind the scenes role in putting together the music for the reception. Jeffrey had assisted a friend of ours in assembling play lists for parties, so he was prepared to organize the music for our wedding.

Over the next two months, I got to know Jeffrey and David more. They would spend every other weekend with us; so, on those weekends we'd plan a family activity, often a movie and dinner. I learned a bit about both of them but, as is often the case with teenaged boys, they were not long on conversation. They shared a bedroom in Stan's apartment. On Sunday mornings, Jeffrey and David especially looked forward to Stan's famous pancakes.

A few weeks before the wedding, when Stan picked them up to come to his apartment for the weekend, Stan told them that on our wedding night they would go home with their grandparents.

David voiced his objection "Why should we do that? I thought we were going to be a family. We should all go home together."

Stan relayed this to me, and I readily responded that I agreed with David. They would come home with us. Nothing else would make sense.

When our wedding day came, David filmed it from beginning to end with his nine-year-old cousin Sascha as his assistant, carrying the cord and helping to set up the shots. The filming went well and didn't end when we came home to our apartment. David announced to Stan that he'd have to carry me across the threshold. The only hitch was that Stan had to do this about five times before he got it right. Each time, David would find something wrong such as, "Dad, you didn't put the key in the lock, let's do it again."

Finally, Stan got it right, and we all tumbled into the apartment. David fell back in a chair, taking off his bow tie and commenting, "Filmmaking is exhausting. I could use a glass of champagne."

I opened a bottle and poured each of us a glass. David took one sip and spat it out saying, "I don't know how adults drink this stuff."

Everyone was very relaxed. We enjoyed being a family.

In our first few years of marriage, both David and Jeffrey were in high school. We spent a couple of weekends a month with them and also spent some vacations together. This was a period of getting to know each other. There was one memorable event early in our marriage as Stan, Jeffrey, and David welcomed me into their family.

### Return of the Jedi

In April of 1983, a month after we were married, David called Stan one night saying,

"I have a problem. You know, Dad, that the *Return of the Jedi* movie is going to premiere in May of this year. I saw an ad for a program called "Make a Wish," and I wrote to them asking for four tickets, you, Jeffrey, myself, and my mother. But I didn't know you were dating Claire at the time, so I didn't include her. What should I do?"

"Why don't you send them another letter explaining that your dad has now remarried, and you'd like to include your stepmother," Stan replied.

"OK, that sounds good," David said.

Stan relayed this conversation to me. I wished we could make his dream come true. The following Sunday, I saw an ad in the *New York Times* selling tickets for the *Return of the Jedi* premiere, which was to be held on May 25, 1983, in New York. That weekend, Jeffrey and David were both at our apartment, and I shared with them and Stan this ad and said,

"Why don't I buy tickets, and we can all go to the premiere?"

David said, "You don't have to do that."

But I ordered the tickets right away. When they came in the mail a few days later, I shared the news with my new family. Everyone was ecstatic. David, Jeffrey, and Stan were all major *Star Wars* fans. I had seen none of the *Star Wars* movies, knew little about the series, and realized I had some homework to do.

May 25th came. Stan picked Jeff and David up after their school day ended on his way back to Manhattan from Stonybrook. We had a quick dinner at our apartment and took a cab to the Loew's Theater Times Square, which was only ten blocks from our apartment. When we walked into the theater, Stan immediately recognized the emcee for the night, Carter Bales, who was in front of the stage testing the microphones. In addition to the film, the starring actors were also scheduled to be present. It turned out that this premiere was a benefit for the American Cancer Society, of which Carter was its president that year. Both Jeffrey and David knew Carter from camping trips that Stan had taken them on with Carter. That night, it was starting to feel like things were falling into place. The movie lived up to their expectations. I was too new to *Star Wars* to have any expectations. But it presaged what was to be an important part of our shared experiences.

When the movie ended, we scrambled down from our balcony seats to the front rows to see the stars, Mark Hammill and Carrie Fisher. David met them and collected their autographs. We left the theater on an exuberant cloud.

It made me very happy to see how I could connect with Jeffrey and David on their terms. I knew nothing about being a stepmother, except that I figured I should just do what my instincts told me were things that would be important to the boys. They were fairly independent, so I had to listen carefully for cues to learn what would be important to them.

Over the next few years, we took David and Jeffrey on summer vacations and traveled with them to St. Croix (where we had honeymooned), Miami Beach (where we had bought a small apartment when I started doing consulting for Dade County), Puerto Rico, and other vacation spots. All of these trips brought us closer together as a family. We realized that shortly David and Jeff would be off to college and then on their own, so we tried to take every opportunity we could to include them in our lives.

By 1990, both Jeffrey and David had graduated from college. Jeff continued at Stonybrook and earned a master's in computer engineering. David had graduated from SUNY New Paltz and began his career working in retail sales in Manhattan. They were both leading busy lives, but we managed to have dinner when we could and always got together for birthday and holiday celebrations.

Stan's and my professional lives were busy. Stan had become the deputy to the president of Stony Brook University, which meant in many ways that he was essentially Stony Brook's chief operating officer. I was consumed with launching Housing and Services, Inc. (HSI), the not-for-profit housing development company that I had founded. HSI was built on the strong belief that "the homeless problem" that was gripping New York City in the late 1980s could be solved if the city supported the construction of permanent housing for homeless people. After all, many homeless people had become that way because psychiatric institutions were closed and residents put on the streets with few if any supports.

Previously, New York City had relied on a large stock (over 100,000 units) of single room occupancy (SRO) housing to provide inexpensive accommodations to people who became homeless. But by the mid-1980s, the real estate industry recognized that many of these SRO's were ripe for conversion to middle-income housing. So, the SRO tenants were illegally evicted, the properties converted, and they became housing for the middle class. The City of New York had done nothing to prevent these illegal evictions. As a result, homelessness became a growing problem.

At the same time that I was consumed with homelessness and other social issues in New York, Stan and I were enjoying our life together. We shared our spiritual lives together and supported each other's work lives. We enjoyed similar social pursuits, the theater, traveling, and getting together with friends.

From time to time, I would ponder the idea of children—our own or adopted. Two things held me back from advocating for the idea of having children. The first, and probably most powerful, was that I had a deep-seated fear that I couldn't be a good mother. I had no role model for good mothering. My own mother was cold and self-absorbed in her own way. When she got angry at me, my sister, or brother, she would often work herself up into a state where she would faint. As the oldest, I experienced this more often than my siblings did, and believe I was affected more than they were. Her other tactic when she became angry was to drive by the local Catholic orphanage and threaten to leave us there. My mother had lost both her parents by the time she was sixteen, and she and her siblings were farmed out to be raised by three different aunts and uncles. When my mother and father married, they had a child eleven months later. The child had a congenital heart defect and died within a year of his birth. I don't believe my mother ever dealt with this traumatic event. I think all her losses affected how she raised me and my siblings. Thus, I grew up with a perpetual fear that I could never be a good mother.

My second reason for avoiding this subject was one that Stan and I talked about. I knew he had reservations about additional children, as he had raised two sons under difficult circumstances. We both told ourselves that our work projects were our "children." I don't think I realized until we got involved with Stefanie years later how deeply we had buried all these emotions.

In 1992, I was asked by a member of the Miami-Dade County Board of County Commissioners if our organization, Housing and Services, Inc., would work with them to develop a plan to provide permanent housing for homeless individuals and families, of which there were growing numbers. I agreed and soon found myself commuting to Dade County, Florida, at least once a week to move this project ahead.

Initially, I stayed with our good friend Camila, a native of Brazil and a dear friend from New York City. She had owned a thriving men's club wear and design studio in New York, serving largely the gay population but also creating costumes for many stars in the music business. As the AIDS epidemic grew, Camila lost many of her staff members and good friends to AIDS. She wanted a change of scenery, and so she had moved her business to Miami Beach in 1990.

When I started commuting to Miami, Stan and I bought an apartment in her building. A few years later we, along with Camila, bought slightly larger apartments further up South Beach. By that time, Stan had considerable independence at Stony Brook University and could work via early internet connections from anywhere. He took advantage of our Miami Beach apartment and would coordinate coming down there for long weekends to accommodate my work schedule.

With both our sons out of college, we enjoyed a fairly carefree lifestyle in Miami, in which I worked during the day on addressing homelessness in Dade County, and Stan worked from the beach on his computer. We spent our evenings enjoying relaxing dinners and walks on the beach. Stan always said it reminded him of his youthful summers on Rockaway Beach in New York City where his family spent every summer.

We had managed to ease into a very tranquil lifestyle on Miami Beach, enjoying time with Camila and other friends we met. This was especially welcome given that it allowed us to avoid the cold winter months in New York. But life soon had other plans for us.

###### ▰▰▰

# Creating the Highbridge-Woodycrest Center

## Claire

After Stan and I were married in 1983, I continued to work at the Vera Institute of Justice. In 1987, I had begun to consider the need in New York City for a not-for-profit organization that would buy buildings, renovate them, and rent them to formerly homeless and low-income individuals and families. The homeless population in the city had been growing rapidly, and there was a great deal of pressure on the city government to provide shelter beds for them. I viewed shelters as only a stopgap measure. While I knew very little about real estate finance or development, I had gleaned a fair amount of practical knowledge from operating the Neighborhood Work Project, the ex-offender construction project I had started ten years earlier. In managing that project, I witnessed the fact that the City of New York had seized tens of thousands of apartment buildings due to the owners' failing to pay property taxes; most were sitting empty. In my role as an associate director of the Vera Institute, I was charged with coming up with ideas for projects aimed at solving social problems in New York City.

It seemed to me that these empty city-owned apartment buildings presented an opportunity to create affordable housing. I consulted with a member of Vera's board of directors about possible financing sources, and I put together a plan on how to assemble financing and renovate buildings for low-income populations. I met with some resistance from New York City officials, as this was a new model for them, but I finally got them to agree to work with us. The Vera Institute board of directors supported my idea and helped to set up a not-for-profit organization, which we called Housing and Services, Inc. (HSI). Its purpose was to acquire and develop vacant properties as permanent housing for low-income people.

The Vera Institute agreed to support this effort for two years while we started this new venture. Our first project was a vacant single-room occupancy building, the Cecil Hotel, in New York's Harlem neighborhood. The Cecil Hotel had been a single-room-occupancy hotel from the time it was built in 1902 until the owner lost it to the city in the 1970s for failure to pay taxes. This building had formerly housed individuals in single rooms with shared kitchens and baths. I knew that this would be a cost-efficient type of housing to bring back into the marketplace, and that there would be a large demand for it if it were managed well.

A Harlem-based New York State agency agreed to purchase the building for HSI and lease it back to HSI through a long-term lease. This agency collaborated with HSI in convincing the city to make a low-interest loan to the nonprofit for the cost of renovations. Thus, I learned about housing development by doing it—working with architects and contractors and building local community support. The renovated Cecil Hotel opened after an eighteen-month renovation period, and HSI quickly rented the 100 rooms to homeless individuals who used their welfare, disability checks, or other minimal income to pay rent.

This formula had promise, and HSI began to offer its services to other not-for-profits that wanted to follow this model of developing low-cost housing in their neighborhoods. I led the fundraising efforts to cover the operational costs of HSI, and in 1989, Housing and Services, Inc. became its own legal entity. Over the next fifteen years, HSI went on to develop another twelve properties with a total of 3,500 units valued at about $300 million.

Each project was unique. For some buildings, HSI retained ownership and managed them. Others were owned by the not-for-profit for which HSI served as the developer. HSI arranged financing that was largely equity or loans with 1 percent interest rates so that the property would not be burdened with loan repayments.

## Stan

In 1981, physicians and nurses in New York City and San Francisco had begun to see a new strain of pneumonia called pneumocystis carinii pneumonia (PCP). They also noticed a spike in cases of Kaposi's sarcoma (KS) among gay men in New York. Health officials were alarmed about these outbreaks of both PCP and KS, which were rare, deadly diseases associated with immune suppression.

By 1982, this "new" disease had been named Acquired Immune Deficiency Syndrome or AIDS. Initially, AIDS was seen only in the gay community. However, cases of AIDS began to appear among hemophiliacs, and it was discovered that AIDS could be transmitted through blood transfusions. Treatment of AIDS was limited to using traditional antiviral medications, but these were not very effective. Many local residents feared that AIDS was transmissible through the air and wanted to exclude those living with AIDS from their neighborhoods.

My earlier work with the sanitation department sparked my interest in measuring the performance and productivity of public agencies. In 1974, I formed a not-for-profit corporation, the Institute of Public Service Performance (The Institute) as a vehicle for pursuing my interest in improving government services. The institute began its first project in 1975 with a grant from the Russell Sage Foundation to study performance monitoring systems. I worked on a range of problems with funding from federal, New York State, and New York City governments, as well as a number of foundations. The projects focused on the use of technology and data analytics, which often involved improving management of public agencies. In 1985, when I found myself working on a project about the housing needs of people dying of HIV/AIDS, I was amazed to reflect on how my work at the institute from a decade before helped with analyzing this new housing crisis.

To respond to the AIDS health crisis, in 1983 the New York State Department of Health (NYSDOH) had created the AIDS Institute. The AIDS Institute's mission was to gather information and to develop programs to serve people with HIV/AIDS. In early 1986, Claire received a call from the director of the AIDS Institute asking her to take on a research project to assess the housing needs of persons with AIDS. Claire declined the offer, indicating that Housing and Services, Inc. did not conduct research. She suggested that "The Institute" could do the study.

Shortly thereafter, I received a letter from the director of the AIDS Institute inviting me to submit a proposal for assessing the housing needs of persons with AIDS. The Institute was awarded the contract. I took a year's unpaid leave from Stony Brook in order to work full time directing this project.

At the time, HIV/AIDS was still concentrated within gay communities, primarily in New York City and San Francisco. A close friend, Scott Zeldin, who was one of the leaders of New York's gay community, agreed to chair the project's advisory board and help me recruit members of the gay community to staff the project. As a result, our research efforts became well known in the gay community as we worked to assess the housing needs of people with HIV/AIDS.

About six months into the project, two men walked into my Institute office creating quite a scene. One of them was dressed formally in black tails. I had never met either one. The one in formal tails introduced himself as Mitchell Braverman.

"My colleague and I are theatrical producers. We would like to produce a play to raise funds for an AIDS housing project, but we need the help of the Institute to serve as a sponsor for the project. We do not expect the Institute to pay any of the costs of production. But if the Institute sponsors the play, we can rent costumes and secure donated theater space at a not-for-profit rate, a substantial discount from the price normally charged for commercial productions."

My first reaction was quite negative. I was thinking who are these guys? Are they for real or is this a swindle? I had no idea what I would be getting the Institute and myself into if I said yes. I responded to Mitchell,

"No, I don't think we want to do this."

Mitchell and his colleague left my office. A few days went by, and I began to think that Mitchell's proposal might be a good idea. I discussed it with Claire and decided to accept their proposal on a handshake. I had taken a leap of faith in agreeing to participate, overcoming my fear of being made a fool. Little did I know the impact this decision would have on my life and professional career.

The play was titled *Let's Misbehave*, a gay romantic comedy, based on a 1927 Cole Porter song that had been sung in numerous movies. Mitchell invited us to the opening night at an off-off-Broadway theater on Manhattan's Upper West Side. The house was filled on opening night, with a mixture of single people and couples, mostly from the neighborhood. Just before the curtain closed, Mitchell introduced me and explained the project and our need to raise funds. He also said Claire would be waiting at the door with a bowl for accepting donations as people left the theater. Claire and I were surprised, but we did our bit. I talked about the project, and Claire found a jar and started the collection with her own $20 bill. We thought this was a one-night-only performance for us, but we soon learned the cast expected us to appear at every performance. For the entire month's run of the play, Claire and I arrived each night at the play just before the curtain went down, and I would go onstage and make a short speech asking for donations to support the Institute's effort to raise funds for housing for people with HIV/AIDS. By the end of the play's run, we had raised $3,000. Mitchell suggested a fundraising dinner and promised that the opera singer, Jesse Norman, would attend. Jesse Norman did not attend the dinner, but we raised an additional $7,000 that evening, mostly from HSI's generous board member Helen Vanderbilt.

My efforts to lease a building as a residence for people with HIV/AIDS on Manhattan's Upper West Side collapsed when local residents demonstrated against people with HIV/AIDS moving into their neighborhood for fear that they would contract the disease. This controversy brought out the worst "not in my back yard" sentiments in people. That ended my discussions with owners about leasing the Institute a building as an AIDS housing project. At that point, I told Claire that the Institute would donate the $10,000 raised to HSI, if it developed a supportive residence for people with HIV/AIDS.

The need for such a residence was reinforced by the New York City Health Department's preliminary research finding, which indicated that a small percentage of those with AIDS would survive. This was contrary to the prevailing belief that AIDS was a terminal disease. This finding, coupled with the research the Institute had done, suggested people with AIDS would need supportive housing that included such services as accessibility features, social and health services on or near the residence, and access to healthy foods,

The year I spent leading the AIDS Project was emotionally challenging. I met many individuals who were involved in serving those dealing with HIV/AIDS and living with it themselves. They would shop for those unable to shop for themselves, take them to medical appointments, advocate for increased support from local and federal government agencies, while at the same time coping with their own cases of HIV/AIDS. Five months into the project, individuals I had come to respect and befriend suddenly died. Death became a daily fear as I felt the loss of those around me. When I lost a dear friend and colleague, I grieved for months. Even as I write this thirty-five years later, I remember the dark feeling in the pit of my stomach when I heard he had died.

At the start of the AIDS epidemic, there were very few intravenous (IV) drug users with the disease. By 1986, the United States Centers for Disease Control and Prevention (CDC) reported that African Americans and Latinos were disproportionately affected by AIDS, especially those who were IV drug users. AIDS had become a social stigma, as was cancer in the early 1950s. Many doctors did not want to treat people with AIDS based on the unfounded fear of contracting the disease.

Claire decided to develop a residence for families and individuals with AIDS and found a vacant building in the Highbridge neighborhood in the Bronx that HSI could develop. On behalf of the Institute, I donated $10,000 for the project as promised. From that moment on, my role was to support Claire's efforts through HSI to secure the building and the financing to renovate it. I contributed in small ways, such as helping with constructing proformas for the financing of the Highbridge Woodycrest Center, "Woodycrest," as the project became known. It was amazing to watch Claire put together all the pieces that led to the opening of Woodycrest. My wife had taken on the monumental task of making this dream of opening a residence for people with AIDS come true.

## Claire

In 1986, while Stan was leading the Institute's pioneering project to study the housing needs of people with HIV/AIDS, I was leading HSI and had two projects in development. My staff urged that HSI consider developing a residence for families living with HIV/AIDS. At that time, the neonatal infection rate with HIV for infants born in the Bronx was 2 percent of all babies born there. I agreed HSI should think about how to do this, but I had put it on the back burner. As Stan got deeper into his study of housing needs for people with HIV/AIDS, I began to think more about HSI doing such a project.

Once Stan committed his Institute's $10,000 donation to HSI that had been raised through the Institute's AIDS Housing Project's fundraisers, HSI's board and staff supported us moving forward with the development of such a residence. I began to look for an appropriate and affordable site. I had learned from my brief experience in the affordable housing world, with two projects under my belt at that time, that it was easier and less costly to renovate an existing building than to build a new one. I put out feelers with brokers and my network to find the perfect site for this project in the Bronx, because the greatest need for supportive housing for people with AIDS was in the Bronx, New York City's northernmost borough.

I was not having much luck finding a building through my sources. But one Sunday, as Stan and I were having our coffee and reading the Sunday *New York Times*, I scanned the real estate ads at the back of the *Times* Magazine. One ad caught my eye. It was a photo of a beautiful Beaux Arts mansion-like building with the caption "Great Manhattan Views." To have a view of Manhattan, I knew the building had to be in the Bronx.

I called the number listed in the ad, got the address, and drove to the Bronx to find the building. It was tucked away on Woodycrest Avenue, a residential street in the South Bronx just behind Yankee Stadium, "the home of Babe Ruth." It was a beautiful but foreboding building with most of the windows broken, the copper gutters missing, and the yard overgrown with weeds. Still, I was intrigued by the prospect of a building that appeared to be abandoned, yet was in a location perfect for our project. It was large enough to house one hundred people, the number we thought would be needed to make the project economical. Despite its rundown condition, you could see that it was once a stunning structure.

I rang the sellers of the property, who were not the owners but were in contract to buy the building from the then current owners. I arranged to meet the sellers the following week. In the meantime, I did a little research and learned that the building had been an orphanage built in 1902. It was designed by the architect of Carnegie Hall, William Burnet Tuthill, and operated by the American Female Guardian Society. The Society was a prototype of civic improvement associations and a pioneer in saving children. Incorporated in 1849, it operated until approximately 1941 rescuing homeless children, securing adoptions, and providing shelter for indigent women, helping them find employment.

I was leading the development of other buildings built around the turn of the twentieth century and was fascinated by the history of these buildings. Architecturally, the buildings constructed in that era were usually very solid. A lawyer friend of mine from Washington, DC, Robert Blanton, was to be in New York City the day of the scheduled visit and had expressed interest in investing in this project, so I asked him to join me. Stan had just been appointed as the deputy to the president of Stony Brook University; he was spending full time on the campus in eastern Long Island and could not always accompany me on these "adventures." Some of the people selling these buildings did not look like very savory characters. I felt that I needed someone to go with me to meet the sellers in my newfound role as a low-income housing developer.

Robert and I met the sellers at the building and went inside to find the building full of pigeon nests and falling plaster. However, the hallway floors and staircases were of solid marble, and the massive wooden front doors were in decent condition. This told me that the building had "good bones" and that much of it could be reused during renovations. We climbed to the roof and had a magnificent view of Manhattan and into Yankee Stadium. I was convinced that this was the right building for our project, but I knew it would not be easy to deal with these sellers. Robert and I made our way down to the front of the building, and I told them I would be in touch.

I went back to the office and began to work with my staff to see if this would be a feasible site based on the amount of square footage, the number of residents who could be housed, and whether it could accommodate a medical clinic. We figured out that this sixty-thousand square foot building was large enough to house about one hundred residents, mostly in apartment style living for families and in single rooms for individuals. I went back to tour the building several times with an architect and contractor with whom I had worked previously. We calculated the cost of renovation and backed into a purchase price offer.

I felt an urgency about buying this building that I had not felt before, nor since. It seemed that there was a strong reason that HSI needed to buy this building, but I had no idea what that was. So with no idea how I would finance the purchase and renovation of the building, I called the sellers and told them that HSI was prepared to buy the building for a price of $1.5 million, with a refundable $10,000 deposit. To most sellers, this would have been a preposterous offer. It was to these sellers as well, but they had had no other offers for months. They finally agreed.

With a lot of tenacity on our part and support from Mayor Koch, his deputy mayor, and his housing commissioner, HSI secured a bridge loan from the City of New York and closed on the purchase of the building in November 1989. HSI formed a separate not-for-profit affiliate organization, Highbridge-Woodycrest Center (Woodycrest), to own and operate the project, with HSI serving as the developer of the project.

We named the project the Highbridge-Woodycrest Center for two simple reasons: The building was located in the Highbridge section of the Bronx and was on Woodycrest Avenue. The name was neutral; it did not signal this was a residence for persons with HIV/AIDS. We had quietly built good relations with the residents of the surrounding neighborhood. Many had members of their families living with HIV/AIDS. A number of Latina grandmothers in the neighborhood had grandsons who were gay and had contracted the disease. The grandmothers wanted their grandsons to live nearby so they could help support them through their treatments. Most of these grandmothers wanted the proposed use of the building to be kept quiet.

Now that Woodycrest owned the property, it could apply for a license as a nursing home, which made the project eligible for Medicaid reimbursement from New York State for the operation of the building.

As Woodycrest was going through the licensing process, there were many naysayers who objected to a residence for families and single individuals with HIV/AIDS. Fortunately, there were also some very strong supporters who helped us get past many huge hurdles that arose during the completion of this project. Woodycrest had been championed by then New York State Health Commissioner Dr. David Anderson. He supported licensing this unique residence with apartments for the families, a learning center for the children, an on-site clinic, and all in a home-like atmosphere. Dr. Anderson was aware that neither HSI nor Woodycrest had any experience in operating a health facility, but he believed we would get experts to help us do it right. He was a man with a great deal of faith. Sadly, two months before the Woodycrest opened, Dr. Anderson had a massive stroke. We lost one of the first strong supporters who was to make this residence possible.

### Stan

In the middle of this period in 1990, while the Highbridge-Woodycrest Center was under renovation and when I turned fifty, Claire organized a real vacation for us to Paris to celebrate my birthday. She managed to make all the arrangements while managing the complex project of opening the Highbridge-Woodycrest Center. For my birthday lunch, we dined at the Eiffel Tower. We saw the sights of Paris and then traveled to the Loire Valley for a few days enjoying the food and wine.

To thank Claire for arranging this amazing trip, I planned a special surprise at a well-known restaurant. I practiced ordering our meal in French. That evening nothing went as planned. My French was poor, Claire changed her mind about the menu, but to my surprise it made for a wonderful evening. By the end of our trip, I realized how much I loved Claire and how easy it was to travel with her. It was at that moment that I decided to quit smoking. I knew I didn't want to leave Claire before my time.

Shortly after our return to New York City, we had the rare opportunity to meet with the Dalai Lama, who was receiving an honorary degree at Stony Brook University. We brought a silk khata, a Tibetan ceremonial scarf, to give to the Dalai Lama. I also brought a copy of his book *Freedom in Exile*. Afterward, we gave him the khata and I asked him to autograph my copy of his book. What follows is the English translation of what the Dalai Lama inscribed in my book.

*Stan and Claire*

*As a token of close bond and with my prayers for your longtime happiness.*

*HH (His Holiness)*

The Dalai Lama handed me the book and then took Claire's and my hands and wrapped the khata around them and gave us a deep warm smile, his eyes full of love. Claire and I felt blessed. The trip to Paris and the meeting with the Dalai Lama were an incredible way to celebrate my fiftieth birthday.

## Claire

The renovation was completed in a record fifteen months, and the next two months were spent hiring staff and equipping the residence with everything required from medical equipment to food, and planning for the Department of Health's stringent pre-opening survey. On May 1, 1993, the Department of Health survey team showed up to do their review. Staff were primed to answer all their questions and to show them every nook and cranny of the residence. We passed the survey with flying colors.

Woodycrest was taking on the full health care responsibility of very ill people with a disease for which there was no cure. Looking back, I realize I should have found this undertaking daunting, but if I did, I buried this feeling and carried on. I was so excited that we were offering mothers and their children, as well as some single men and women, the opportunity to live with dignity in a beautiful building. They would be in a home-like environment and receive health care and other services on-site. By opening day, we had had a number of applications, and the staff had screened all the people referred to us. If they met our criteria, the staff had scheduled dates for them to move in. I felt confident we could provide the services our residents would need.

While I continued to lead HSI, I was also the unpaid chair of the Highbridge-Woodycrest Center. I spent most of my time the week before opening day meeting all the staff, checking the readiness of the facility for the first residents, and making sure all the departments had what they needed. Opening day, May 3, 1991, was a sunny, but cool, brisk spring day. Staff were all ready for residents to move in, including the kitchen staff who were making lunch for the day. The smell of roasted chicken and vegetables floated up from the kitchen to the first floor. Six or eight new residents were scheduled to move in that day. I had a desk in the office of the executive director/administrator with windows facing onto Woodycrest Avenue. I peeked out of the window every half hour or so to see if any residents were coming in. I was anxious.

# 4

### ⬟

# Claire Meets Rosa
# and Stefanie Mercado

## Claire

Woodycrest was on a hill, and its front entrance was flanked on both sides with wide grand marble staircases. On the day we officially opened, May 3, 1991, around noon, I looked out of the front window and saw a small woman carrying a baby wrapped in a pink blanket trudging up our front stairs. I knew that they must be the prospective residents, Rosa Mercado and her three-month-old daughter Stefanie, who had been scheduled to move in that day.

The nursing director and I went to the front door to greet them. As Rosa came through the grand front doors of the building, the nursing director greeted her with, "You must be Ms. Mercado. We are so glad that you've chosen to come live here with your daughter."

I followed up by saying, "You and your daughter are very special. You are our first residents. It's noon time, why don't we all go downstairs to the dining room for lunch. Then we can take you on a tour of the residence and show you your apartment."

Rosa was very thin, short in stature, and seemed timid about taking the step to come to a new place like Highbridge-Woodycrest, but she broke out into a broad smile when we greeted her.

"Lunch is a great idea," Rosa said. "I haven't eaten all day."

When we entered our bright sun-filled dining room, Rosa's eyes popped wide open. She said, "I've never seen so much food before," as she surveyed the steam tables and counters laden with a variety of fresh, tasty-looking dishes. Our chef brought out a bottle of baby formula for Stefanie, and we all sat down at one of the communal tables to chat over lunch. We had designed the dining room to accommodate both residents and staff to support the family atmosphere we were trying to create. Pretty soon, we were calling each other by first names.

Rosa kept repeating that she had never seen so much delicious-looking food. She ate a substantial lunch, and Stefanie seemed satisfied with her bottle of formula. Rosa explained that since she left the hospital three months earlier with Stefanie, they had been living in an abandoned building, which was the only housing she could find. Stefanie had slept in a cardboard box.

Rosa continued, "When the social worker I see at the hospital told me about this place, I felt that maybe this was our chance for a better life. So, I called to see what it was about. I am so grateful to have this opportunity to live in a safe place and bring up my daughter. I've dreamed of a place like this, but never thought we would have the good fortune to find one."

And just like that, Woodycrest once again became what it was originally. Rosa and her child were the first residents to move into a building constructed in 1902 to care for children in need and women down on their luck. Highbridge-Woodycrest would take its place as one of the earliest such residences in New York City to help deal with what was steadily becoming one of the worst health care crises the world had faced.

When we took Rosa and Stefanie upstairs, Rosa was astounded. We had assigned them to a "suite"—two adjoining rooms with a bathroom in between. Stefanie's room was outfitted with a crib and a dresser with a pull-down changing table. A rocking chair sat in the corner. Our staff had equipped each child's room with stuffed animals and mobiles hanging over the crib. Rosa's room was cheery with a single bed, dresser, small table, nightstand, and side chair.

Rosa hardly said anything. She just held onto Stefanie tighter. We then went down to the childcare center. We had created a large space so we could provide infant care to the moms during the day as they participated in group discussions about child development, overcoming their addictions, and how to live with HIV/AIDS, which we were convinced would eventually become a chronic disease.

One of our goals at Woodycrest was to help these mothers, and some fathers, prepare to live as well as possible for whatever time they had. But we also believed at that time that AIDS was a terminal diagnosis, so we needed to help the parents plan for their children's futures if they died.

Primarily, we focused on helping them find a standby guardian, someone they could appoint while they were healthy to become their child's guardian if they became too ill to take care of the child or if they died. The mothers also needed time to get medical treatment, which we provided on-site unless they needed scans or higher-level treatment. In that case, they went to the hospital for an outpatient visit.

Woodycrest had staff who could serve as nursery school/kindergarten teachers for children two to six years old. Rosa was very impressed that everything she would likely need would be at her fingertips. We wrapped up the tour with the staff helping Rosa and Stefanie get settled in their apartment and talking with Rosa about what a typical day was like at Woodycrest. I gave Rosa a hug.

"Why don't you and Stefanie get settled, and I'll see you tomorrow, Rosa," I said. "I start most of my days here at Woodycrest to make sure everything is running smoothly."

Driving back downtown to my office, I could not stop thinking about Rosa and Stefanie.

The dream of this residence, which had begun three years earlier, was now a reality. Woodycrest was responsible for these families and individuals, and we had to make sure we did everything possible to help them live well. While many friends of Stan's and mine had died of AIDS over the past decade, this was the first time I had met a mother with AIDS and her child. I realized that this child would most likely grow up without her mother, and I wondered what would happen to her.

As it turned out, I had little time to ponder such questions. Shortly after we opened, with Dr. Anderson no longer serving as the commissioner of the Department of Health, the director of the AIDS Institute began to raise questions about what we were doing at Woodycrest. He asked whether we should be housing men, women, and children in the same building. He stated that he wanted to close Woodycrest. He did not think Dr. Anderson should have approved it, and he began a summer of assaults on Woodycrest, sending survey teams each week to interview every resident and staff member about what they thought of the residence and its operations and to read every resident's chart. They inspected the residence from top to bottom.

I ended up spending most of my days at Woodycrest, as the executive director was not used to dealing with such opposition from the same government agency that had licensed our operation. As chair of the board of directors, I needed to serve as the executive director's shield against undeserved bad publicity.

The residents were solidly in Woodycrest's corner, supporting the operation of the residence to the surveyors, being helpful where they could be to our staff, and conducting themselves like "star" residents.

Rosa Mercado emerged as the leader of the residents' committee. The other residents trusted Rosa to speak for them as she was very forthright and honest. Rosa had never finished high school, but she exhibited a great deal of common sense and urged the residents to support the leadership of Woodycrest.

"If we do not make it clear to these people from the Department of Health that this residence is what is keeping us alive, they will try to close it down. I do not want that to happen, do you?" she asked her fellow residents.

Word got around in the health community that the New York State Department of Health was surveying Woodycrest weekly, an unheard-of move. Many assumed that we must be doing something wrong. We had the support of many staff members in the Health Department, but none of them were willing to speak up on our behalf, so the rumors grew. Reporters called and came to the residence "to see what was going on." They interviewed me as the chair of the board of directors and wanted to interview a "resident leader." Rosa volunteered and was supported by her fellow residents as their spokesperson. Rosa and I were asked to do television interviews as well. As she and I spent more time together, I got to know Rosa as a person, not just as one of our residents and to feel a camaraderie with her.

Rosa was born in Puerto Rico and immigrated to the US when she was about ten years old. She shared with me that she had been abused by men in her family, and that her mother had become a heroin addict when she was very young. Her father had died before they came to New York City. By the time Rosa was fifteen, she recounted that she was living on her own, mostly on the streets. Rosa said she had tried to resist becoming part of the drug culture but had seen no way out. However, when she was in her early thirties and became pregnant with Stefanie, she was determined to find a way out of the world of drugs and violence. Rosa began to live to provide a good life for Stefanie and to raise her the "right" way, which was not how she had been raised.

Interviewed by Mireya Navarro for a *New York Times* story that appeared on October 20, 1991, Rosa said she could not think of better living quarters for her eight-month-old daughter and herself. She called Woodycrest heaven and said she felt secure. She told the press that she was not bothered by the presence of single men.

"The men that I know here are all so polite and respectful," Rosa said. "We have support groups together, and they have gone through a lot of pain, just like me. They are still human beings, and they have the right to be here just like us. I came to Woodycrest, because I knew I needed a safe place to raise Stefanie," was Rosa's frequent refrain.

My explanation of what we were doing was usually, "Rosa, as our first resident, immediately understood what we are trying to do in creating a drug-free healthy residence for people living with AIDS. We had a sense that there would be a survival rate, and they needed help to get better in all aspects of their lives."

"The way Claire welcomed Stefanie and me when we first came here makes me feel like she's a second mother to me," Rosa often said.

Rosa and I had an easy way of talking with each other, despite our different backgrounds and our eleven-year-age difference. We were brought closer by working together in this struggle to keep Woodycrest open.

I came to love both Rosa and Stefanie. As soon as she could talk and walk, Stefanie was quick to speak up about what she wanted to do. "I'd like to read this book now," she'd say. She was very confident walking around Woodycrest, usually at a pace that was brisker than the staff member who was walking with her.

By the end of the summer, the entire staff and I were exhausted as we had worked hard to take care of all of the usual challenges of opening a new residence, as well as dealing with the weekly Department of Health surveys. We needed to close the chapter on what seemed like harassment so we could get on with the work of caring for our one hundred residents. I made a trip to Albany to see the new acting commissioner of health and pled with her to put an end to this endless process of checking on how we were doing.

She formed a Blue-Ribbon Committee composed of the presidents of eight New York City hospitals and assigned them the work of spending a week at Woodycrest. They were tasked with assessing our operations and reporting back to her on their findings. These eight hospital presidents gathered at Woodycrest on a Monday shortly after the acting commissioner had appointed them as members of this committee. They spent eight hours a day for five days at Woodycrest looking into every aspect of our operations. At the end of the week, they produced a report that said that "this residence for persons with HIV/AIDS and their children which houses men, women, and children has created a 'normalizing' environment and that it was healthy to live in a 'normal' environment." The acting commissioner accepted this conclusion and gave the word to the AIDS Institute to cease their weekly surveys. We were permitted to go back to normal operations. This acting commissioner was another strong supporter who helped the project keep going.

## Stefanie

In May 1991, when I was three months old, my mother had bundled me up as best she could against the early spring chill. She carried me the ten blocks from the abandoned apartment where we had been living ever since I was born to a place she had heard of that offered housing to women living with HIV/AIDS and their children. My mother told me that she cried when we were taken into the dining room for lunch, and they offered her a bottle of baby formula for me. She said that she had never seen so much food and had never been welcomed to any place as warmly. That day we moved into our three-room apartment. I had a crib, instead of a cardboard box, to sleep in. There was a nursery on the ground floor where my mother would take me in the mornings while she was in "group." There were about ten other infants and toddlers like me. We played and slept, and then in the afternoons we went "home" with our moms. I never knew this was not a normal way to grow up.

When I was later told about the "birth" of the Highbridge-Woodycrest Center, I learned a lot about synchronicity and the role it would play in my life. Woodycrest was created by the couple who became my adoptive parents, but in 1991 neither I nor they knew how our lives would become intertwined. My father, Stan, is an electrical engineer who has devoted his life to improving metropolitan public services and "solving problems."

As I later learned, the state's health commissioner at the time, a forward-thinking compassionate doctor named David Anderson, understood Woodycrest's vision and told his staff "to get out of their way and let them do what needs to be done." The concept of housing families with both infected and uninfected children in a nursing home setting was not the norm.

This vision materialized through Woodycrest's small board of directors, which included its board chair and my future mom, Claire. The man who would become my "godfather" Bob, as well as a psychiatrist friend of my parents, Dr. Michael O. Smith, were also on the board. With Stan's $10,000 charitable donation from his institute, the board later leveraged this to raise $16 million from a New York State bond issue. They were then able to buy and renovate this "white elephant" of a building in the shadows of

Yankee Stadium. My biological mother, Rosa, and I were the first family to move in.

Over the next few months as the Woodycrest family grew, my mother became a leader. This was not something she had ever done, but it was clearly in her DNA. My mom, as the head of the residents' committee, and Claire, as the chair of Woodycrest's board of directors, bonded. As I've heard the story, Dr. Anderson, the champion of Woodycrest, had a massive stroke just before Woodycrest opened. Many of his staff didn't share his vision for this atypical nursing home. Shortly after opening, the Department of Health started making weekly survey visits, interviewing all the residents and staff and reviewing all the charts looking for something amiss.

The press picked up on this controversy, and Rosa and Claire became the spokeswomen, even sharing makeup before a TV shoot. The Body Shop cosmetic company made a video about Woodycrest to show in their stores during AIDS Awareness Week. My two mothers and I star in this video.

Back in 1991, I don't think Claire or the staff at Woodycrest knew what palliative or hospice care was, even though that was essentially the role Woodycrest filled. These terms had not become commonplace, though Dame Cicely Saunders had founded the first hospice program in England a few years earlier. Claire and her colleagues simply created a unique livable and supportive community. They believed that one day HIV/AIDS would be viewed as a chronic, but not necessarily a life-threatening, disease.

In the early days of the AIDS epidemic, most infants were presumed to be infected with the HIV virus. The thinking was that those infants, born of HIV-infected mothers, carried the virus in their blood until they were about fifteen months old. My mother later told me that the happiest day of her life was when I was about fifteen months old, and the doctor at Woodycrest did an HIV test that came back negative for the virus. Other infants born back then weren't so lucky, and many died after brief lives.

When reporters asked my mom, Rosa, how she thought I had "dodged the bullet" of HIV, I'm told that she said she knew exactly how this had happened. "The love at Woodycrest has bolstered Stefanie's immune system." She always said that that was true. My mother was always there for me. Sometimes her sickness would flare up and she couldn't take care of me, but the staff jumped in, like lots of aunts (and a few uncles). For me, it was one big extended family.

When I was about eighteen months old, Mayor David Dinkins came to Woodycrest for a ceremony. They were dedicating the garden to

Dr. Anderson, the health commissioner who had died. My mother had dressed me in a frilly pink dress for this August day, and we were proudly sitting in the front row on the terrace. The mayor had come to this corner of the South Bronx and was addressing a crowd of mostly HIV-positive people. I remember Claire, whom I thought of as the tall blonde giant, greeting everyone and introducing the mayor. It was a very special occasion. My mom was one of the speakers that day and was seated in front with Mayor Dinkins, the Bronx Borough President Fernando Ferrer, Claire, and key members of the staff. I'm sure my mother never imagined that she would be with these dignitaries, but that's what happens when a place like Woodycrest is created with love. The residents, staff, and board all played parts in creating a real home for all of us.

When the mayor started to speak, I wanted some attention as well, so I slipped from my mother's lap and walked in front of the podium. Finally, after I had distracted the audience's attention, the mayor picked me up and gave the rest of his speech holding me in his arms. I guess even at eighteen months old, I wanted to be noticed. *The Daily News* printed a picture of me with the mayor the next day. The caption read, "Stephanie Mercado, who is HIV positive, points out a thing or two to Mayor Dinkins yesterday at Highbridge-Woodycrest Center in the Bronx." The press made an incorrect assumption that all the children were HIV positive. The writers got it right, however, when they quoted Mayor Dinkins, who said that "families coming together, coping with HIV disease, and living drug-free is what Woodycrest is all about."

## Claire

Mayor Dinkins's remarks summed up how building communities like Woodycrest is transformative, changing the quality of life for everyone involved. This is what we had set out to do, without a roadmap, but with the strong conviction that these families living with HIV/AIDS deserved to have a real home. And it was not just providing a home. It is hard to describe the fear that many people lived under in this earliest period of the AIDS epidemic when there were still wild rumors and misinformation spreading about how easy it was to transmit the disease. Our staff treated the residents with dignity and respect, coming in close proximity to them and providing counseling and support through a traumatic time in their lives.

It feels now that our work to create this "home" brought with it special blessings for Stan and me in that we met Rosa and Stefanie. And then a few years later we were asked by Rosa to step in as Stefanie's guardians, which led to our becoming her adoptive parents. We would never have predicted this path, but when it was offered to us, we knew it was the journey we were destined to take.

## 5

**☷**

# Steps to Becoming Stefanie's Guardians

## Stefanie

Childhood memories are often fuzzy, especially when a child tries to disassociate herself from pain and loss. For me, unfortunately, I went through a lot of pain and loss until age eleven when I was blessed twice over with a chance to become part of a new family. Here is the beginning of my story. With my account, interwoven with that of my mother and father, Claire and Stan Altman, our collective memories are braided together in this story.

I was born in the Bronx, New York, at Lincoln Hospital. My birth mother, Rosa Mercado, brought me into this world on February 10, 1991. I cannot fully recall my earliest childhood experiences, but as I have come to understand at my birth our circumstances were not supportive of raising a healthy, well-rounded, confident child.

My mother was born in Mayaguez, Puerto Rico, and came to New York City when she was ten. My mother had few supports when she came to New York City, and the schools were not particularly welcoming to children moving from outside the fifty states. So my mom dropped out of high school and drifted; essentially, she became homeless. The late 1980s and 1990s will always be thought of as the era of the HIV and AIDS epidemic, as well as the war on drugs. There were three primary ways to contract the disease: sexual activity, blood transfusions, and intravenous drug use with addicts sharing needles. My mother was the product of her time, fell in with the wrong crowd and started using drugs.

It was when I was born that she beat her addiction and stopped using heroin. A child can do that, make you see the world in a different way and reassess how you want to live your life and what you hope for them.

For the first couple of months of my life, my mother and I were homeless, as my mother had been living on the streets since dropping out of high school. She knew no other way. We illegally squatted in abandoned buildings in the Bronx. I have no idea how we ate. I did have my mother's family, her siblings, mother, and grandmother, but I guess we couldn't count on them. I never knew my father.

Though I was a baby at the time, in later years I came to understand that it was not until we entered Woodycrest that we had the semblance of a real home for the first time. Housed in a beautiful, refurbished orphanage built in 1902, Woodycrest provided us a feeling of home and hope. My mother and I were the first family unit to climb the front steps and request admission. My adoptive mother, to this day, says that the instant she met my mother was the day she felt she had found a sister in her and a daughter in me. My mother and Claire connected easily, despite the huge differences in their backgrounds.

While my memories have started to become a little clearer, there are still gaps in them. I remember being a child of the clinic. Woodycrest had a clinical yet hopeful atmosphere. I remember sessions with my mother when she received medications through an intravenous drip. The beeps, the clear tubes, the pokes, and prods signaled the ongoing evaluation and monitoring of her condition. My mother and I lived in our own small apartment in the residence that we called our own.

Claire would often come to the childcare center when my mother was in group therapy or at a clinic visit. Claire would sit on the floor with me and my toddler friends and read to us, or she would pick me up and show me the latest toy that had been purchased for the center. I began to think of Claire as a second mom. She may not have felt it at the time, but she was. I remember she was striking. I was born during the Clinton administration, and when I was older and saw pictures of Hillary Clinton, I thought Claire reminded me a lot of her. Claire had short cropped blonde hair, blue-green eyes and wore dignified pant suits. She always looked put together, as if she were about to take on the world one pant suit at a time. I called her the "Blonde Giant" because from my vantage point of the world, she was extremely tall and towered over my mother by five or six inches. Claire was full of love and grace. On days when my mother's condition became worse, and she had to go to the hospital, Claire always stepped in. I had loving arms that embraced me at Woodycrest, but this lasted only for a while.

When I was almost three years old, my mother met her girlfriend, Angela, who had also been a drug user and had contracted HIV and Hepatitis B. I do not recall how they met, but then I had three mothers, although Angela felt more like a stand-in or pseudo caretaker. Shortly after my mother and Angela met, my mom asked that we be transferred to a two-bedroom apartment on East 176th Street and Prospect Avenue in the Crotona-West Farms neighborhood of the Bronx. This was one of many apartments that Woodycrest rented for "graduates" of Highbridge-Woodycrest Center and other families with HIV/AIDS who were able to live independently. I was never told, but I came to understand that my mother and Angela wanted more independence than living in a clinical residence like Woodycrest.

When we moved there, it was the first time I noticed that my mother's condition was beginning to get worse. I had my own room that became my safe haven; a room adorned in pink and purple, filled with a Fisher Price kitchen, toy cars, and Barbie dolls. I was able to find my refuge in the worlds of make-believe. My mother loved to paint realistic figures with acrylics on canvas. A lot of her images were scenes of Puerto Rico, of animals or cartoon characters. I can recall sitting by her and trying to paint what she was painting. I was learning brushstroke by brushstroke, canvas by canvas. But soon, the paint dried up and she no longer bought canvases for her art. When she stopped painting, I knew something was very wrong.

## Claire

My full-time job as the president of Housing and Services, Inc. (HSI) continued to be very busy, but Woodycrest still demanded a lot of my time. We had weathered severe start-up storms in launching Woodycrest. Given the seriousness of AIDS and the challenges of helping people to live well when they had a terminal illness with no cure in sight, I was spending at least several hours a day at Woodycrest in my capacity as the board chair to help manage this complex operation. I was making sure senior staff positions, such as the medical director, were filled with qualified people, and that our affiliated hospital was caring for our residents well when they had to be admitted to the hospital. I was also working to ensure we received the proper payments from the Medicaid program, to name a few of my primary responsibilities.

After Woodycrest had been open for about three years, Rosa, Stefanie, and Rosa's girlfriend, Angela, moved to one of HSI's "scattered-site apartments" in the Bronx. We had no way of knowing then, but Angela would come to play a significant role in our lives.

The next year flew by. In the summer of 1995, when Stefanie was four years old, I got a call from Lisette, the social worker at HSI's scattered-site apartments program in which Rosa and Stefanie lived.

"Claire, I knew you would want to know that yesterday Rosa was admitted to Beth Israel Hospital in lower Manhattan for pneumonia," she said. "Her condition is steadily getting worse."

"Thanks, Lisette, for letting me know. I will go to see her tomorrow," I responded.

I did not usually visit residents of Woodycrest in the hospital, but given the close relationship I had developed with Rosa, I wanted to see if I could help her. I took the subway downtown to the hospital the next day and walked into Rosa's room. Immediately, I saw how much she had deteriorated since I had last seen her about a month earlier. Rosa was lying in bed, looking pale and very fragile. She was always thin, but now her face signaled to me that she had lost more weight. Yet there was still a sparkle in her eyes.

"Rosa," I said as I leaned over and hugged her, "how can I help you?"

"I need you to help me find a guardian for Stefanie," she replied. "It can't be Angela. I don't trust her."

"Of course," I said. "I understand. I will do whatever you need."

Rosa and I chatted about her all-important request, but Rosa did not elaborate on why she didn't trust Angela. I assumed it might have something to do with Angela being friendly with Rosa's brother. Rosa was adamant that she wanted nothing to do with her brother and didn't want him around Stefanie. I had learned that Angela was friendly with him and would often slip him money out of their ground-floor window, as Rosa wouldn't permit him to come into the apartment. I didn't think more about Rosa's comment at the time.

As I left, I said to Rosa, "Let me see who I can think of to serve as Stefanie's guardians. She is so adorable that I know we will find the right person or couple."

I hugged Rosa before I left, trying to hold back my tears. When I got home, I shared Rosa's request with Stan, but we did not think that becoming Stefanie's guardians was something we could do. I knew that I had trepidation about becoming a mother given that my own mother and I were so distant, and she had never understood me. I was afraid that maybe I would be that kind of mother. Stan had made it clear early in our relationship that he was not warm to the idea of our having children, given that he felt that he had faced real challenges in fathering his sons, Jeffrey and David.

So I put the idea of our becoming Stefanie's guardians aside. Over the next couple of months, I helped Rosa connect with several couples, both heterosexual and gay. They would take Stefanie to their homes for the weekend as a trial. But after every one of these weekends, they would bring Stefanie back to Rosa, shaking their heads and saying, "No, we don't think we can do this."

We did not see Stefanie after these "weekends," so we did not see her reaction, but Rosa told me that Stefanie was crestfallen. The summer went by quickly, and then the Thursday before Labor Day, Rosa called me and asked if I would come up to her apartment the next morning. I agreed. Then I called Rodney, the property manager for our company, to ask if he knew what was up. He said he had no idea but informed me that Rosa had also asked him to join us. The next day I drove up to the building where Rosa, Stefanie, and Angela lived.

When I rang the bell for their apartment, Angela answered the door and invited me in. I saw Rosa, Angela, and Stefanie all looking somber. They had kept Stefanie home from nursery school that day so she could join our "meeting." She was all dressed up in a navy jumper and skirt. Rosa and Angela were dressed in slacks and shirts, not jeans. Their choice of clothing signaled an important meeting.

We all sat down, and Angela started, "Rosa has something she wants to ask you, Claire."

Then Rosa got right to the point, albeit with a tremble in her voice.

"Would you and Stan be willing to become Stefanie's guardians?" she asked.

I was taken aback. I had spent months trying to help Rosa find a guardian for Stefanie and had resisted the thought that Stan and I might fill this role.

A month earlier, a friend and neighbor, who was about to adopt an infant from Russia, had suggested to Stan and me that we step in as Stefanie's guardians.

"No, that's not for us," I replied. But, when Rosa asked, I said, "I need to talk with Stan, but we will think about it."

We had developed a policy at Woodycrest urging our residents who were parents to develop a plan for the future care of their children, since AIDS was then viewed as a terminal illness. We assisted our residents in their daily living activities, taught them about independent living, cooking, taking care of an apartment, as many of these mothers had lived in shelters and other group living situations. We helped them learn how to take care of their children.

But the sad reality was that we knew for many of them the day would come before their children grew up when they would not be able to care for them, and they would eventually die. We learned that the best way to encourage these parents to plan for the future care of their children was by identifying someone or a couple to be a standby guardian for each of their children and secure the formal guardianship agreement with the person. Then, within sixty days of the parent becoming disabled or dying, the standby guardian would go to court to have the agreement officially recognized.

When Rosa was living at Woodycrest, she and I talked about this, but Rosa had been reluctant to develop a standby guardianship agreement. When I had asked her about living relatives who might take care of Stefanie, she said that Stefanie's father was not on the birth certificate and had never been in the picture. Nor did she have any living relatives who she thought would be able to take care of Stefanie. Rosa had now come to the conclusion that the only people she felt were appropriate to be Stefanie's guardians were Stan and me.

After about an hour, I reiterated to Rosa that I would talk with Stan about becoming Stefanie's standby guardians, and we would get back to her quickly. I hugged Rosa. Stefanie had been very quiet during our whole meeting, mostly standing by the chair in which her mother was sitting. I am not sure how much of what we said Stefanie understood, but she looked as if she was taking in the gist of what we talked about. I bent down and hugged Stefanie, and then Angela escorted me and Rodney to the door. I shook Angela's hand.

I left their apartment trembling. Was becoming Stefanie's guardians what Stan and I should do? What about our reluctance to become parents—for me, the first time, and for Stan, again? Filling the role of stepmother to David and Jeffrey had been meaningful and heartwarming. But their mother was alive and well, whereas this would place me legally and emotionally into the direct role of a little child's mother.

I realized that our becoming Stefanie's guardians might not be a rational path for us to take, but I had been touched by Rosa and Stefanie since that day over four years ago when they first came to Woodycrest. As much as I tried to put the guardianship question out of my mind after Rosa had asked me whether Stan and I would consider this back in July, I couldn't stop feeling that Stefanie needed us, and that this is what we were meant to do.

I didn't think too much about what our being Stefanie's guardians would mean to Stan and me. I knew our lifestyle would change, but I felt we were ready to bring a child into our lives, not just any child, but Stefanie. I felt strongly that Stefanie was meant to be with us, and we were meant to be with her.

While I had respected Rosa from the day we met, I had new respect for her now. She knew she didn't have long to live, and she wanted to make sure that there was a solid plan in place for the right people to become Stefanie's guardians and to hopefully adopt her one day. Rosa didn't want to leave it to chance that the right people would come along to become Stefanie's guardians or that the wrong ones might be given her care by default. She knew Stefanie was her legacy, and she wanted to protect her and ensure that she had loving parents who would raise her daughter the way she wanted her to be raised. Rosa wanted to protect Stefanie at all costs.

I thought about how strong a mother Rosa was to make sure that one of her last actions in this life was to protect her daughter while she could. I quietly applauded Rosa for her courage and forethought, but most of all for her unconditional love for Stefanie.

## Stan

It was Friday, September 1, 1995, and Claire and I flew down to Miami for the Labor Day weekend. I felt carefree for the first time I could remember. David and Jeffrey had graduated college and were on their own. I had greater flexibility in my job and was beginning to work remotely, making it possible to spend more time on Miami Beach. A typical day was working from home for a few hours, spending the afternoon on the beach, and then Claire and I would have dinner with friends at the growing number of new restaurants opening.

I knew Claire had met with Rosa before we left New York, but I was unaware of the reason for the meeting. The next morning as we were walking along the beach, Claire raised the issue of us becoming Stefanie's guardians. I thought that she was kidding at first, since it was hard for me to conceive of raising another child, and a little girl at that. I had met Stefanie and found her adorable, but I was about to turn fifty-five and Claire was forty-seven. While I knew that Stefanie was important to Claire, I was shocked and expressed my disbelief by saying that this was a ridiculous idea. Claire was quite hurt by my response and became a bit sullen. She raised the subject on a number of occasions over the next two days, forcing me to step back and examine my strongly negative reaction to her request.

As we continued to walk along the beach, I began to realize how strong Claire's love for Stefanie was and her desire to protect the child by our becoming her standby guardians. I had a subconscious fear of the changes in my life that becoming Stefanie's standby guardian would bring. I was confused and unable to reconcile my love for my wife and my fear of losing her if we didn't become Stefanie's standby guardians, which I knew would eventually lead to adopting her. Was I prepared to parent Stefanie considering I did not think I did a great job parenting David and Jeffrey? For days, I felt paralyzed and unable to understand what I was going through.

Was my reluctance to become Stefanie's standby guardian due to a fear of losing Claire's love, or did it stem from a deeper emotional fear of opening my heart to another person only to be hurt again? I now believe it was the latter because Claire was always there for me. But I had buried my feelings so deeply that overwhelming emotional situations resulted in my denying my feelings and freezing. The ability to trust another person, particularly a woman, resulted from my unresolved anger and deep-seated rage at my mother because of the way she had treated me. However, Claire was different, and I had learned to trust her because she accepted and loved me for who I was.

As I was thinking about my negative reaction to becoming Stefanie's standby guardian, I asked myself the key question: "What does it mean to be in it together?" You see, Claire and I often agreed that a key part of our relationship was being in it together, having each other's back and always being there for each other. I realized that if I truly believed what I had been saying about our relationship since we married in 1983, then shouldn't I make Claire's feelings and needs a priority in this situation?

The more I thought about this question, the more I realized I was approaching the question of Stefanie from the wrong perspective. Rather than focusing on the logical and rational reasoning for not becoming Stefanie's standby guardians, I should look at the situation with my heart and through my feelings for Claire. Once I viewed the situation from Claire's perspective, it became clear that I needed to support her by agreeing to become Stefanie's standby guardian. When I told Claire of my decision to support her, I also confessed that I had no idea what was involved in parenting a girl. I told her my concern that I would probably "screw this up" and that she would have to be patient with me. Claire simply smiled.

You might wonder why "being in it together" was so important to me. Simply put, it meant I was not alone. It was knowing that my partner, friend, and lover would never hurt me and always had my back. It was a feeling I had never experienced before.

## Claire

When Stan told me he would agree to become Stefanie's standby guardian, I almost broke down in tears. They were tears of joy, as I knew in my heart this was the right thing to do. I immediately called Rosa to tell her our decision. She thanked me, but then said that another couple who had offered to become Stefanie's guardians earlier, and then declined, had now stepped back into the picture. I was crushed. It had been such a big "lead-in" to raise the subject with Stan and to reach our agreement to say "yes" to Rosa's request.

To be told that the other couple had reappeared was a major blow. I swallowed my own feelings and told Rosa that it was OK, and she should know we were there, if she wanted us to be. We went to Greece a week later and had a glorious time. We walked through little towns, lay on the beaches, and ate delicious Greek food. Still, Stefanie was always on my mind. The bond that had developed between me, Rosa, and Stefanie was real. It felt that Stan and I becoming Stefanie's guardians and, eventually her parents, was what we needed to be doing. But was that now out of the question?

We returned to New York and our regular routines. Still, I could not stop thinking about Rosa and Stefanie. I shared my frustration with a friend of mine who lived in the very private Gramercy Park, an upscale neighborhood in Manhattan. She suggested I bring Stefanie to the Gramercy Park kids' Halloween Party the following Saturday. It would be a good opportunity to spend some time with Stefanie. Rosa had recovered from her illness the previous summer, but was still weak. She was glad to have some childcare relief and readily agreed to our proposal to take Stefanie to the Halloween Party. I invited Stan to join us, but he declined, saying he had work to do. I was disappointed but accepted this. I wanted to keep up a connection with Rosa and Stefanie even if we were not the designated standby guardians.

When I arrived at Rosa's, I was a little apprehensive as I had never taken Stefanie out by myself. I rang the bell. Rosa opened the door and smiled, affirming that my being with Stefanie was a good thing. Stefanie was hiding behind a living room chair. She was adorably dressed in a little Pocahontas outfit. We drove downtown and found the party, which had been moved to the Gramercy Park Hotel because of rain. There were dozens of toddlers and their parents in the ballroom, running around and playing games. Stefanie was too shy to participate but crawled around on the floor, chasing some of the children. She did not say much but was very animated as she crawled around. When the party ended in the late afternoon, I drove Stefanie home. I really wanted to bring her to our house and have her stay there, but that was not possible.

I was sad that Stan had not joined us, but I was glad that I had broken the ice and had begun forming more of a relationship with Stefanie. Stan greeted me at our door and told me that he realized as soon as I had left that he had made the wrong decision. Not only had he missed the time with Stefanie, but also with me. He announced he was "in" on the next excursion.

I suggested that we make these Saturday outings a regular occasion to give Rosa and Angela a break, and Stan quickly agreed. Rosa and Angela were delighted with our proposal as well. It was my way of making sure that we didn't lose contact with Stefanie and Rosa. Something had felt right about spending Saturdays with Stefanie. My whole attention was focused on her, not on my work (which I would have normally been doing on Saturdays). I was beginning to realize that forming a bond with Stefanie was filling a hole in my heart. Long ago, Stan and I had made this logic-based decision not to have children. Yet this little girl had entered our lives not based on clinical analysis or logic. She pulled at a motherly instinct and need to nurture in me that I had either purposely or unknowingly suppressed. She pulled at my heart.

## Stan

The first Saturday we were scheduled to spend with Stefanie, I said I would not be going. I claimed I had a lot of work to do. Within minutes of Claire's leaving the house, I felt a deep sense of loneliness and realized that I had made a big mistake. I had given up time I could be spending with Claire. In that moment, I decided that I would be joining Claire every Saturday with Stefanie.

The routine became us going up to the Bronx every Saturday to pick up Stefanie and taking her to some new activity. Driving to the Bronx brought back my childhood feelings of foreboding, as though some catastrophe was about to befall me. My world felt unstable and unpredictable. I could not wait to return home to the security of the world I had built around me. At the same time, I saw Stefanie as a frightened child who had withdrawn from the world around her. It was common for her to hide under a table or behind a chair. I found myself drawn to her and wanting to engage her and bring a smile to her face. I would make up silly games and sing silly songs. I found ways to make *Blues in the Night* funny and silly, and to this day whenever I want to bring a smile to Stefanie's face, I sing my version of this song. As it turned out, I could be a "girl" dad after all.

Entering Stefanie's and Rosa's world brought back memories of my own childhood, memories that I had spent years suppressing. On a superficial level, I was reliving the experience of the little five-year-old boy in the door of a building crying and fearful that "they" were trying to steal my sense of self and make me into someone I was not. I would relive the experience of hearing the "other" voice saying it would protect me by shielding my feelings and burying my emotions so deeply that I no longer experienced feelings. The uncertainty about Rosa's health, our future relationship with Angela, being involved with Stefanie, and the feelings that this situation evoked in me were way outside my rational construct of the world and how I had come to deal with it. These feelings never left me until the day we formally adopted Stefanie, and she became our child and daughter.

I have said many times that Stefanie never let me close my heart to her. Every time I tried, it was as if she refused to let my heart close, whether through a simple look or an endearing gesture. I couldn't close myself off anyway, because I had come to love her deeply and unconditionally. At the time, it didn't occur to me that I was also filling a role in her life she had never experienced: that of a father.

## Stefanie 1995

So it began that every Saturday and sometimes Friday nights, I spent with Claire and Stan. On one of the very first Saturdays I spent with them, we went to the American Museum of Natural History. I had never been to a museum. I was so excited! Claire and Stan told me that we were going to see dinosaurs. Being five years old, I thought we were going to be walking into a scene of *The Land Before Time*, an animated film I had just seen. I imagined we would be able to meet the gang from the show made up of Little Foot, Cera, Ducky, Petrie, Spike, Chomper, and Ruby.

That Friday night I stayed over at their house, and on Saturday morning I woke up, my body pulsing with excitement. I could not remember ever being so eager before. The room I woke up in was a bedroom in Stan and Claire's house, which was an old limestone townhouse tucked away on East 35th Street in Manhattan. There was a small courtyard in the front of the house with a wrought iron fence and gate next to the sidewalk. In the middle of this courtyard was an old well. There were two red doors on either side of a large arched window in the middle of the building. Their home was on the bottom two floors, and Claire's Housing and Services Inc. (HSI) office was on the top two floors of the townhouse.

I called this little limestone townhouse the "church house." The building had belonged to priests and was used as offices before it was converted into a residence. It was magical, and I said, "I think I am going to like it here." The living room area had a twenty-foot-high ceiling, a huge bookcase that hugged one wall of the main living area, and a staircase with a full stained-glass window that led to the second floor. In later years, after having seen *Annie*, I would liken that first visit to me being little orphan Annie and having walked into my own version of Daddy Warbucks's house.

The next morning, I bounded down the stairs to the kitchen where Stan placed a plate of steaming pancakes at my place at the table. All three of us ate heartily. We fed Sapphire and Gabriel, their two cats, and climbed into a cab to head to the museum.

I do not know if it was the cab ride or my nerves, but I was bouncing along as we traveled up the east side and cut west toward the Upper West Side. We pulled up to the main entrance of the museum, and Stan whipped out his money clip to pay the driver. We all stood staring at the building. It was nothing like I had ever seen. I was used to the rectangular, boring red-brown brick buildings of the Bronx, but the museum looked like a palace. My eyes scanned the grand staircase to the entrance where I knew Little Foot and his gang were going to be.

I practically dragged Stan and Claire up the stairs, grabbing their hands as they tried to control every ounce of bubbling-bouncing energy in me. We entered the ticket area, paid for our admission, and took the elevator to another floor. I was stunned. Little Foot, Cera, Ducky, Petrie, Spike, Chomper, and Ruby were skeletal! I looked up at the towering skeletons of the dinosaurs with shock and disbelief. I thought, "Wait, how could this be? Was this some sick joke?" I was seeing only skeletal remains. With absolute crushing disappointment and rage, I exclaimed, "You brought me to see dead dinosaurs?!"

Poor Stan and Claire looked mortified. To get to my eye level, they both knelt to hold me, look me in the eye and explain that no museums housed live animals and that we'd have to go to the zoo to see those. Most museums were places that taught us history and displayed artifacts from the past. I remember tears welling up in the corners of my eyes. I was expecting to see the *Land Before Time* dinosaur characters because, after all, this was my first time going to a museum, and I thought I would see some semblance of life.

My four-year-old heart was crushed. After Claire and Stan helped me calm down from my sudden hysterical moment, we continued on to see the displays of the different kinds of dinosaurs and learn about the range of species. "How cool it would be to see actual dinosaurs?" I thought. For the next couple of hours, we wandered through the other halls of the museum. I enjoyed the taxidermy displays with the various species of animals depicted in carefully constructed scenes of North America and Africa. I had always loved animals and felt a special attachment to them. Then we walked into the immense Hall of Ocean Life.

The room was even grander than the main entrance hall, a life-size model of a whale was suspended from the ceiling. As if frozen in time while swimming in the embrace of the ocean, I later learned that this model was first constructed in the mid-1960s and was based on photographs of a female blue whale found dead in 1925 off the southern tip of South America. We made our way through the different oceanic displays of colored fish and underwater sea plants. I felt my inner Ariel start buzzing with excitement. *The Little Mermaid* was another favorite Disney classic of mine, and here I was a part of her world.

The three of us had lunch on tables set up next to a food counter in the Hall of Ocean Life. After lunch, Stan and Claire asked if I wanted to ride the carousel horses in Central Park. *Wait, what? Horses lived in Central Park!* I did not know this! I had no idea what a carousel was, so I imagined it was where the horses lived. I eagerly nodded my head and said, "Yeah! Let's go," because I knew this time, I was going to see the real thing. We entered Central Park across the street and followed a winding path to the carousel.

I was crushed again when I saw colorful mannequin horses on poles swirling to carnival music. *Why were Stan and Claire lying to me?*

"You brought me to see dead horses!" I said, my disappointment palpable. I am sure now that Stan and Claire were beginning to glimpse the side of my personality that was very literal.

Stan and Claire apologized for the misunderstanding and asked me if I would like to ride one of the horses. I shrugged my shoulders and begrudgingly said "yes." They lifted me onto the cold hard surface of the horse, strapped me in around my waist, and my horse moved up and down as I watched the wintery blur of Central Park go by.

Stan and Claire helped me off my horse, and I thought *That was pretty fun, but not as much as seeing real live dinosaurs and horses.* Then, they asked me if I would like to take a carriage ride through Central Park before we headed back home. Cautiously, I said yes. Was it going to be some motorized form of carriage riding? All three of us walked 20–30 minutes to the southern edge of Central Park. There they were: a line of real, live, breathing horses hitched to carriages! *FINALLY!* I thought, *here we go!*

I jumped up and down. The horses were so beautiful I remember, but I did feel badly for all of them being lined up in a row waiting to haul people through the park. I knew they deserved better, but I hopped into the main part of the carriage like I was Cinderella going to the ball. Stan and Claire sat opposite me in the coach. Ours was a big beautiful brown horse, and we were given red velvet blankets to place on our laps. The driver flicked the reins, and the landau carried us away from Central Park South. The driver periodically turned around to make small talk with us. After we rode for a few minutes, we turned into Central Park. Clopping along the paved tree lined path, I thought, "I like it here." Horses were soon to become a really important part of my life.

## Claire

Our routine of spending Saturdays with Stefanie continued. We also developed a routine of having nightly phone calls with Stefanie and Rosa just to say goodnight to each other. When we would come to pick her up on Saturday mornings, Stefanie would often be hiding behind a chair, just barely poking her little head out. After our outings, we sometimes had dinner back at their apartment. Angela would cook spaghetti with meatballs or chicken, rice and beans. Stan did card tricks and magic tricks to help bring Stefanie a little bit more out of her shell.

When we took Stefanie to the playground, she would profess that she could not do the slide or the monkey bars because no one had taught her how. She was terrified of these "normal" kid activities. Then Stan would urge her to just try, and he would hold her legs as she traversed the monkey bars. After a number of tries, she exclaimed, "I did it." And we said, "Of course you did. We knew you could." Slowly, Stefanie began to gain more self-confidence.

# 6

# Rosa's Decline

## Stan

The day Claire informed Rosa that we agreed to become Stefanie's standby guardians, Rosa informed us that would no longer be necessary. Another couple, Victoria and Virgil, who knew Rosa and Stefanie from when they lived at Woodycrest, had stepped back into the picture to serve as Stefanie's standby guardians.

Although we were not Stefanie's standby guardians, it never occurred to me to suggest we stop involving ourselves in Rosa's and Stefanie's lives. My feelings about the depth of Claire's commitment to Rosa and Stefanie, and my growing love for this little girl, ran very deep. It was not contingent on a legal designation.

The weekend outings with Stefanie would often end by spending time with Rosa and Angela when we brought Stefanie back home. Returning to the South Bronx every weekend, I began to feel the emotion and energy of the streets every time we drove to Rosa and Angela's home. I felt unsafe where Stefanie, Rosa, and Angela lived, sensing hostility because we were not part of their community. I had never been afraid as a kid walking the streets of my neighborhood any time of the day or night, but somehow this was different. Now, I feared violence could erupt and engulf Claire and me at any moment. I never spoke of these feelings to Claire or anyone else.

We continued supporting Rosa and Stefanie and planned ways to include Angela and Rosa's family in our holiday events. Neither Claire nor I wavered in our commitment to Rosa and Stefanie.

## Claire

It was now the fall of 1995. Thanksgiving was rapidly approaching. We invited Rosa, Angela, and Stefanie for Thanksgiving dinner, but they had committed to celebrate Thanksgiving dinner at Veronica and Virgil's house. It was a reminder that they were Stefanie's standby guardians, not us.

"We hope you'll come for Christmas at our house," I said, and they accepted.

One Sunday in early December, while Stan and I were spending a weekend in Miami, I received a call from one of my staff members telling me that Rosa was seriously ill and had been taken to the hospital that morning. We were scheduled to fly back to New York that night, but I felt we had to go back right away. Stan supported my suggestion, so I quickly changed our tickets and within the hour we headed to the Miami airport. With frequent flights between Miami and New York, we were back in the city by late afternoon. We picked up our car at the airport, drove to Manhattan, dropped off our bags at the house, and then drove to Montefiore Hospital in the Bronx.

I felt I needed to be with Rosa, but my thoughts were about Stefanie and who was caring for her with her mother hospitalized. We arrived at the hospital and immediately went to the visitors' lounge outside Rosa's room. We found Stefanie there, crouched in a corner crying. I ran to Stefanie and hugged her. I tried to comfort her, but she continued to cry. I wondered how many of these hospital scenes she had lived through, and she was only four. Angela was there along with Michael, one of my staff members, and Rosa's cousin. It wasn't clear to me what had happened, but I learned that Rosa had contracted pneumonia again. Stan and I stayed for a while, but there was nothing we could do. I suggested Stefanie stay with us, but Angela had already asked Michael, who had a family and a child, to take Stefanie to his house. I remember feeling very powerless as Michael scooped up this weeping little girl and took her away. Stan and I didn't question where all of this was heading. We just knew that we wanted to be close to Rosa and Stefanie, so we went where we felt we needed to be.

## Stan

Soon it was Christmas, and we had invited Rosa, Angela, Stefanie's great-grandmother, and her three cousins to a big family dinner. Our house on East 35th Street had a large living room with a twenty-foot-high ceiling, so we purchased the tallest Christmas tree we could fit through the door. Claire and I thought that this might be Rosa's last Christmas.

On Christmas morning, when I called to arrange to pick Rosa up from the hospital, I was informed by the nurse in charge that Rosa would have to remain there as her discharge papers had not been processed. For Rosa to miss Christmas at our house would have been a great disappointment for all of us. I drove to the hospital and introduced myself as Rosa's brother-in-law. I spoke to the staff about how important it would be for Rosa to be part of our family Christmas celebration. They finally agreed to discharge her, so I drove her home to get ready for the party and then I drove Rosa, Stefanie, and Angela to our house. When I arrived home, Claire told me that I needed to drive back to the Bronx and pick up Rosa's brother who had just been released from jail.

Finally, with my transport duties done, I rejoined our family. We now had a full house with Stefanie, Angela, Rosa's great-grandmother, brother, cousins, and uncles, as well as David and Jeffrey plus assorted friends. We celebrated Christmas as it should be—with a house full of family and friends. We showered Stefanie with gifts, not one or two but over twenty. Everyone enjoyed themselves.

## Claire

As 1996 began, Rosa's health was clearly declining. At that time, there was no treatment available to reverse her deterioration. Stefanie's fifth birthday was coming up on February 10th. We suggested to Rosa and Angela that we throw a party for Stefanie in their apartment and invite her cousins and a few friends who lived in their building. We would bring lunch and a birthday cake. Folks showed up and sat around, barely saying a word.

Stan and I had brought a game, "Twister," which is a heavy sheet of plastic imprinted with footsteps. To play, the individuals walk around touching each footstep with music playing. When the music stops, the player has to have at least one foot on a printed footstep to continue. Stan was the DJ, and within a few minutes, everyone was enjoying the game. Rosa, who was still frail from her recent hospitalization, was an eager player. At one point, she and Stefanie were twisted all over each other on the floor. The kids and adults alike were laughing at their contorted positions as they tried to touch a footstep when the music stopped. There was lots of laughter and pure delight, which we all needed.

Stefanie smiled a lot and came out of her shell. She loved being the center of attention. The kids engaged in games and enjoyed the hotdogs and French fries. Stan and I left Rosa's apartment in the early evening feeling tired, but good. We had put smiles on everyone's faces. I do not remember that we talked much about the party, but we didn't have to. Our hearts were warmed by seeing Stefanie with her mom having so much fun and Stefanie just being a kid. As we would learn later, Stefanie rarely experienced what it meant to "just be a kid."

Rosa's thirty-seventh birthday arrived in late February, and we proposed another birthday lunch at their apartment. Since Rosa was looking more tired, we suggested that just the five of us celebrate together. We took lunch up to their apartment and had a quiet, but enjoyable time. Angela told us that Rosa wished she had a new TV. After lunch, Angela, Stan, and Stefanie walked a few blocks to Tremont Avenue and purchased a TV set to give Rosa for her birthday.

While we were alone, I asked Rosa if she'd like to take a walk to Crotona Park to get some air. She said she would. We bundled up and headed out. As soon as we were on the street, Rosa pulled a certified letter from her pocket and handed it to me. It was from Veronica and Virgil saying that they wouldn't be able to serve as Stefanie's standby guardians. Rosa was furious.

"They didn't even call to tell me," she said.

I was a bit surprised, but not shocked, because they had backed out once before. There was a part of me that never believed they would accept the responsibility of raising Stefanie. I assured Rosa she didn't have to worry because Stan and I still wanted to become Stefanie's standby guardians.

"Are you sure?" Rosa asked.

"Yes, Rosa, we want to do this," I responded.

We hugged right there on the street. I assured her it would all work out. She need not worry. In my heart, I knew Stan would agree.

I said I would return the next day with guardianship papers for her to sign. We could tell Stan, Stefanie, and Angela when we all returned to her apartment. Rosa had gotten much paler in the two weeks since Stefanie's birthday and was much less animated than she had been at Stefanie's party. I felt that Rosa didn't have much time left.

When Angela, Stefanie, and Stan returned with the new TV, Rosa was excited. Within minutes, Stan had the TV connected and working. Rosa's excitement with the TV added an air of birthday celebration to what had become a heavy day with learning about Virgil and Veronica's decision and the way they chose to inform Rosa.

Stan and I talked that night. This would be a major change in our lives once Rosa got sicker or died. The entire period was filled with conflicting emotions for everyone. The somber reality was that Rosa was fading. Yet we tried our best to be a caring support system for her and Stefanie, to bring joy into their lives whenever we could. We had already worked through this decision, so we did not dwell on it. We just trusted that the right thing would happen. I think this approach was the major way we stayed sane during this time. But I was also fearful. What if Rosa died and the guardianship didn't work out? I knew that Stan and I were now "all in" with Stefanie becoming part of our family, but the path to get there was so uncertain.

## Stefanie

It was not long after we moved from Woodycrest to the new apartment that my mother began seeking out guardians who could take care of me when she passed. Close friends of the family offered to take me in, weekends at a time, to see if I was "fit" to be a foster child, or something like that.

I'd walk into these unfamiliar homes with a pink duffel with my pajamas and a change of clothes in it, longing to be in my own home by my mother's side. These visits to different homes remain a blur. I just remember the nights being cold and lonely, without the familiarity of home, the smell of Puerto Rican cooking, the screams of the kids in our building echoing in my hallway, and my mother. The Bronx seemed miles away when I found myself in suburbs and other towns that were not like my home in the Bronx.

I was shuffled from house to house. New faces of potential guardians came and went as the weeks passed. Most of these people I never saw again. I often heard them say to my mother, "No, we cannot take her." I was left wondering where I belonged. Was I *worth* it to anyone? What did this whole process say to me? Did I have to be auditioned, tried out, and tested to see if I was capable of fitting into a family?

The more visits I made to other people's homes, the more resentful I became of my mother. I knew that she was trying to secure my future with people she trusted, but I was the one not being accepted into these families. Continuous rejection stung more each time, especially as I saw my mother getting sicker and nowhere nearer to her goal of finding me a place to live. Her options were dwindling, and my outlook on life dimmed. *Did no one want me?* The "foster care" round of visits damaged me. I was so young, and my childhood home was deteriorating in front of me. I had no idea where I was going to live. My sense of self-worth had been compromised, and my fear of abandonment grew. Only through years of counseling and the amazing guidance of my parents have I been able to gain back the pieces I left scattered in those homes.

Toward the end of my many trial placements, a middle-aged couple, Virgil and Veronica, had expressed interest in becoming my guardians. Even their names sounded like something out of a bad version of an adoption movie, the reckless and heartless adoptive parents. They had told my mother they wanted to become my guardians, but then at the last moment, they pulled out of their commitment. I was devastated. At this point, I did not know how much more I could endure. My run-ins with fallacy and trickery seemed to squash the promise and commitment I thought I had been promised.

My mother's health continued to decline. It was when it seemed that my future would leave me without my mother and no place to live that Claire and Stan stepped in.

As if sent through some divine intervention, I now had two wonderful people who would become my guardians.

## Claire

The day after Rosa's birthday, I drove back to the Bronx with the standby guardian papers for Rosa to sign. I showed Rosa and Angela the papers. The social worker from our program, Lisette, had joined us. Rosa signed the papers and seemed to feel a great weight off her shoulders once that was done.

My next assignment that day was that Rosa had called me earlier asking me to find a new home for Stefanie's pet iguana "Iggy." Rosa was concerned that Iggy was carrying germs that could make Stefanie sick.

I called a few friends and, surprisingly, I found someone who had a house full of iguanas. They would take Iggy. After Rosa signed the standby guardian papers, we hugged. Then I carried Iggy in his cage to the car. I kept my eye on Stefanie, who had come out on the sidewalk with her mother as I loaded Iggy into the car. Stefanie looked so sad at losing her pet iguana, but Rosa was insistent that I take Iggy with me. I moved Iggy to his new home, but I felt badly that Stefanie had not been part of this decision.

That night was our thirteenth wedding anniversary. Stan and I went to a homey French restaurant to celebrate. From the restaurant, we called uptown to Rosa, Stefanie, and Angela. They all congratulated us on our anniversary. It seemed like we were having a celebration with our new family members.

Later that week, Stan and I drove to the Bronx to see Rosa, Stefanie, and Angela. While Angela was putting Stefanie to bed, Rosa, Stan, and I had a chance to talk. Knowing that Rosa did not have long to live, Stan asked her what she wanted for Stefanie. Rosa was very clear. She wanted Stefanie to be brought up in her own religion, the Catholic Church. She hoped Stefanie would have opportunities she did not, especially a good education. Rosa's last request was that she didn't want Stefanie to have anything to do with the kind of men who had abused her so badly.

We understood that Rosa was charging us with the responsibility to help Stefanie live a meaningful and fulfilling life, since Rosa would not be able to make her dreams for Stefanie come true. That was a daunting thought—to be thrust into a child's life when she was age five and her mother was dying. I was overwhelmed, but by this time my love for Stefanie was a foregone conclusion. Her presence in our lives had brought us so much joy, and I wanted the same things for this little girl that her mother did. We never wavered in assuring Rosa we would become Stefanie's guardians and carry out her wishes and more. We had no idea how this uncharted course would work out.

## Stefanie

In March of 1996, my mom developed pneumonia and had to be taken to the hospital. Since her immune system was so weak, the available medicines that were used to treat her were no longer effective. My mother was susceptible to any bacterial or viral infection. It was cold that night, a month after my fifth birthday. For the last couple of weeks, I had seen my mother decline. She was thinner, paler, and sores began to break out on her body. Her cough became more pronounced, and she was having trouble breathing.

Claire had come that night with a colleague of hers, Rodney, from HSI. She told me that she and Angela were accompanying my mother to the hospital. She let me know not to worry that "Uncle Rodney" would stay with me until one of them came back to be with me. Moments later, a gurney was rolled into the apartment by two paramedics. They transferred my mother to the gurney and strapped her in. Wrapped in white bed sheets, my mother was almost too weak that night to say goodbye to me. I watched bewildered, worried, and hopeful as they wheeled her from her and Angela's room, through the corridor of the apartment, and into the hallway, the door shutting behind them.

I saw the swirling red and white ambulance lights outside my window, heard the loud noise of the ambulance siren, and then watched the ambulance pull away.

Uncle Rodney and I played a game or two that night before I went to sleep. Rodney was a very sweet man. With eyes the color of honey and a cartoonish moustache, he was my savior that night. He comforted me as best he could. But my heart was still heavy. I wanted to know more about what was happening to my mother. I remember going to bed that night seeing her whisked away on a gurney and knowing that this might be the last time I would see her. That night I dreamed of her in a white dress sailing away on a boat, going back to Puerto Rico.

## Claire

The day after Rosa was admitted into the hospital, I decided to visit her. I called Stan from work to tell him I would be home later. As I pulled into the Montefiore Hospital parking garage, I was on automatic pilot. I was going through motions, not really thinking about what I was doing. When I entered Rosa's room, I found her grandmother sitting there. Rosa was in bed and looked very weak. I took her hand and told her that Stan and I were sending prayers. She struggled to say that she was glad to see me and asked about Stefanie. I told her Stefanie was being strong, but that she missed her mother. About forty-five minutes later, I offered to drive Rosa's grandmother home, and she readily accepted. I told Rosa I would be back the next afternoon. On the way home, her grandmother told me how much she appreciated Stan and me looking after Rosa and helping with Stefanie. I had gotten to know Rosa's grandmother and Stefanie's four cousins. Rosa's grandmother was raising these grandchildren because their mother, Rosa's sister, had died of AIDS the year before.

The following day I didn't go to work; instead, I drove to the hospital to see Rosa. She was now receiving continuous transfusions because she was bleeding internally. The liver disease that accompanied her HIV had broken down her platelets, so there was no way to stop the bleeding. The doctors said that all her systems were failing. I stayed to talk to her and hold her hand. When the doctors came in, they mostly just looked at the various monitors and left. They did not speak to Rosa or to me, unless I asked a question.

By the afternoon, I realized that I did not know if Rosa had appointed a health care proxy to make decisions for her if she wasn't able to. I asked Rosa about this, and she told me that she had not designated a health care proxy. She asked me if I would become her proxy, and I agreed. The hospital had the form, so I filled it in with my name and took it to Rosa's room for her to sign. Rosa sat up in bed and managed to sign it. This was my first experience as a health care proxy, and I felt the tremendous weight of the responsibility.

Rosa also shared that in early 1995 she had consented to her lawyer obtaining a custody agreement of Stefanie in favor of Angela. While Rosa had mentioned this briefly to me the previous July, I hadn't asked Rosa more about this agreement at that time. Now, Rosa was so weak she could barely speak. All I could think about was that Rosa was dying and how would we tell Stefanie and support her through this tragedy.

The next three days are a blur. I went to the hospital each day and sat with Rosa. She was not able to talk much, but I would tell her how Stefanie was doing and try to make her more comfortable. Rosa was losing a lot of blood. The doctors were giving her more transfusions, but it was clear that these were not sustaining her.

On the third evening, I called Stan and told him I wanted to stay at the hospital with Rosa as I thought she was dying. He said he would go up to their apartment to be with Stefanie so Angela could come to the hospital as well. My heart was aching for Stefanie, but I felt so helpless. There was nothing I could do but be with Rosa while Stan was with Stefanie. The hospital staff came to the door of her room every hour, poked their heads in and left. Stan drove up to the Bronx, and shortly after he arrived at their apartment, Rosa's brother showed up. Angela arrived at the hospital around 10:00 p.m.

I had brought with me to the hospital *The Tibetan Book of Living and Dying* by Sogyal Rinpoche, based on the teachings of Tibetan Buddhism that explores the message of evolution, karma, how to follow a spiritual path, compassion and, importantly, how to care for and show love to the dying. I figured this was at least somewhat appropriate to be reading to a dying person. I continued to read to Rosa from it. I had never had any guidance about being with dying persons. My most recent spiritual experience back then was the teachings of Tibetan Buddhism that Rev. Ellen Resch had shared with us.

Rosa was losing more blood. As soon as one transfusion ended, she needed another. They were not helping her to get better. The doctors could not heal her, so this was their attempt to keep her comfortable.

Around midnight, I asked the doctors to stop the transfusions as it was clear they were not helping her. We prayed for Rosa and held her hands. Around 3:00 a.m., Rosa passed on to a peaceful life. I went to the nurse's station and asked them to send in the doctor. He came and signed the death certificate. I was numb. I asked if Angela and I could have some time with Rosa. We washed her and put new pajamas on her. I called Stan and told him that Rosa was now with her God and that we would drive over to Rosa's apartment shortly. It was about 5:00 a.m. when we arrived.

Stan and Rosa's brother were in shock. Stefanie was sleeping. After an hour or so, Stefanie woke up and stumbled out of her bedroom. We cuddled her and told her that her mother had gone to heaven. She rubbed her sleepy eyes. A few tears rolled down her cheeks. She went back into her room to lie face down on her bed for a few minutes, crying to herself. Then Stefanie got up and said she wanted to get dressed.

"Of course," I said, "and then we'll drive to a diner near our house and have breakfast."

Angela and Stefanie piled into the car. We found a diner and ate breakfast pretty much in silence. What do you say to a little child who has just lost their mother?

We went to our house on 35th Street and began to discuss Rosa's funeral. I made the necessary call to the funeral home, and then Angela and I went to shop for suitable clothes for Rosa. We also got something for Angela and Stefanie to wear to the funeral. It all seemed so surreal. As much as you may think you are prepared for the death of someone suffering from a grave illness, it still stings. And the realities of making funeral arrangements makes one aware that life goes on. Meantime, Stefanie stayed home with Stan.

Angela and I returned to our house in the afternoon. When Stefanie asked where we had been, I tried to gently explain that we'd been shopping for clothes for Angela and her to wear to the funeral. Stefanie did not say much. Understandably, she was in shock. Stan and I did what we could to chat and try to be upbeat, but what was there to be upbeat about? I am not sure what Stefanie was thinking or feeling, but she was clearly very sad.

## Stefanie

It was just another day. I woke up to the hum of passing traffic outside my dimly lit room. The usual comfort of all my stuffed animals was lacking in some way that morning. I felt a strange chill in the air, and I knew that something was gone, missing.

I looked around my room to see if toys had been moved or hidden. I looked under my bed, but nothing was there. The feeling persisted. I rubbed my eyes and then I got up and decided to see what was going on with Angela.

She was sitting at the kitchen table, one hand supporting her head, the other holding a cigarette. The wispy smoke curls looked ghostly as I walked toward her. I was in a movie. I walked the few paces to her, but it seemed like I would never reach her. When I was close to Angela, I just stood in front of her. When she finally realized I was there, all she did was shake her head back and forth.

"What happened?" I asked.

"Your mother . . . ," she said. Then she flicked her cigarette. "Your mother."

She suddenly broke out in tears. Her body rattled with each watery inhale. "She passed away last night, Stefanie."

I had no reaction. I looked at the floor. The something that was missing was my mother. Angela remained at the kitchen table crying. I turned away, needing to understand what I had just heard. I walked back to the cocoon of my room and crawled under the covers on my bed.

An avalanche of sorrow enveloped me. I clawed at my sheets and wrapped myself in them. She was not here to hold me. I knew a part of me had vanished. I remained in the warmth of my bed, wrapped up in darkness and telling myself that none of this was real. My mother would come back, and I'd hear her voice.

I awoke to a nudge on my shoulder. "Stefanie, Stefanie." My eyes welled with tears and sleepy sand, as I attempted to wake up. It was Claire. My head hurt, and I was still sleepy, but Claire embraced me. There, that felt like something that I needed. Claire had come to tell me that she was by my mother's bedside when she had passed. Claire said that she was holding my mother's hand and said she had seen my mother's spirit rise above her body.

I remember that day my mother died. I hid in the closet. I wanted to be in the dark and shut myself away from Angela and thoughts about my mother. Before seeking refuge in my closet, I tried to talk with Angela about what my mother's passing meant and in a bigger sense what death meant. But she did not want to answer my questions. In the haven of the closet, I felt the darkness of the blanket around me. The cluster of luggage, boxes, and shoes provided a little nest for my five-year-old body.

When you are a child and you experience your first death, it does not feel like anything you've ever felt before. I had the notion that my mother was taking a vacation and would be back before I knew it. I made up a time when she would return. As a child, I had no idea what impermanence meant. I knew that material items could be broken and replaced. I did not know this wasn't the case for people as well. I had to face the harsh reality that my mother had departed for good.

A day or two later at my mother's funeral, I felt out of place. Angela had dressed me in a black outfit that I despised. Everyone was wearing black, creating a sea of black pulsating bodies. When we went to the cemetery and I watched her coffin descending into the ground, I asked, "Is she really in there?"

I was stoic that whole day. Family members and friends of the family came over to me and gave me hugs and said they were so sorry. I probably looked at them blankly because that is how I felt inside. My words and feelings froze, and a sense of my own presence on this earth ceased to exist that day. Ironic, isn't it? It was a day to commemorate my mother's death and yet there was a part of me that died too.

I have never gone back to her grave. I did not want to visit her grave and stand there, wishing that she was still with me. I did not want to look at her name on the gravestone and admit to the short thirty-seven years she lived, 1959–1996. I still have never returned, but my feelings have shifted. Before, I just wanted to avoid her grave; but now, I refuse to remember her as a lifeless being whose body is lying in the ground, deteriorating inside her coffin. I want to remember her as her paintbrushes, as her easel, and as the paintings she created. Her art was the liveliest part about her. I want to embrace her memory in a kaleidoscope of colors and shapes.

My mother was so much more than some letters etched into a cold gray gravestone, so much more than the four-letter catastrophe (AIDS) that tried to define who she was.

## Claire

Arrangements had to be made for Rosa's funeral. Stan and I had become Rosa's family and, as part of that, we accepted the responsibility of arranging her funeral. We drove from our house on East 35th Street to the

Crestwood Funeral Home on Spring Street in Lower Manhattan and spoke with the director. He said that he could arrange the wake on the next evening and a funeral and burial the following day.

We hadn't talked with Rosa about what funeral arrangements she wanted. Because she wanted Stefanie raised as a Catholic, we thought she'd want a Catholic burial. We had no idea where a Catholic cemetery was located in New York City or how to buy a cemetery plot. We didn't even know if Rosa was a member of a particular Catholic parish. I didn't know where to start, so I turned to Father Joseph, who was our chaplain at Woodycrest. He had just turned ninety-four and was still going strong. I called him and explained that we were trying to arrange a funeral that Rosa would have wanted.

Father Joseph suggested we buy a plot at St. Raymond's Cemetery in the northeast Bronx. I called them and was told that only Catholics could be buried there. Did we have Rosa's baptismal certificate to prove she was a Catholic? We did not have any of Rosa's documents. I was stumped. I turned to Father Joseph again.

He said, "Don't worry, I'll write a letter attesting that Rosa was baptized as a Catholic. What are they going to do if they find out I've lied? I am ninety-four! The pope will not touch me."

We faxed Father Joseph's letter to St. Raymond's Cemetery and then discussed burial plots. The cemetery director said, "We have a double plot available."

"What's that?" I asked?

"Well, we bury the first deceased, and then when the second party dies, we bury him/her on top," responded the cemetery director.

After we bought the double plot, we reported back to the funeral home, and they confirmed that the wake could be held the following night and the funeral the next day. I made arrangements with the staff at Woodycrest to have the funeral service there.

We planned Rosa's funeral while trying to support Stefanie. I don't remember talking to any of Rosa's extended family, except to let them know about the wake and the funeral. The next evening, Stan and I hosted the wake. Many Woodycrest residents came, as well as Rosa's family, including her mother, Joanna. Sadly, she was still addicted to drugs. As folks were leaving that night, Joanna came up to Stan and me and thanked us for burying her daughter. I could feel tears welling up inside of me. How sad it was that Rosa's mother couldn't be there for her daughter in her final days. Even in her illness, Rosa was the strongest member of her birth family.

Rosa's funeral was held the next day at Woodycrest in the communal dining room, which was also used as the venue for birthday parties and weddings (of which we had six or eight in the first few years). A real community had been created at Woodycrest by the residents and the staff. I presided at the funeral, which felt strange because the night before Stan and I felt like Rosa's parents. Now, I was the officiant at her funeral service. The room was full of Rosa's family, Woodycrest residents and staff, and a few people from the neighborhood. Stefanie sat on the lap of one of the Woodycrest nurses, hardly moving during the service, a quiet five-year-old. Many people shared their thoughts and memories of Rosa; they all loved and admired her. Father Joseph led us in the Twenty Third Psalm. I ended the service with a few words about Rosa.

Then, we all braved the cold March day and proceeded to St. Raymond's Cemetery in the north Bronx. Stefanie rode with her cousins, and Stan and I followed. At the graveside, Stefanie stood off to one side. A single tear rolled down her cheek as she placed a white rose on Rosa's coffin. My heart was breaking that this little five-year-old had to see her mother pass on.

Beneath that one teardrop was a child of great courage. She quietly witnessed all that was going on, and I knew that she was taking it all in.

It is amazing how in times like this you just do what needs to be done. Stan and I didn't speak on the drive back to our house. It seemed we didn't have time to stop and absorb what was happening. We had promised Rosa to take care of her daughter and raise her the way she wanted. So, we instinctively did what we thought was best for Stefanie and hoped that we were right. Notwithstanding that Angela had a prior custody order, we would soon have the Family Court declare us Stefanie's guardians.

In line with doing what needed to be done, the morning after Rosa's funeral, Stan and I drove to the Bronx, picked up Angela and Stefanie and drove to Connecticut for an appointment with Dr. Tom Brunoski, which we had made weeks before to have him assess Stefanie's allergies.

Tom had reviewed Stefanie's blood work and had determined that she was allergic to almost everything, including dust, pollen, grass, cats, dogs, dairy products, and wheat, among many other triggers. Tom advised that she needed to be on a dairy-free and gluten-free diet and needed to take the drops he prepared for her.

We then embarked on what became a two-decade program that gradually helped Stefanie to overcome these allergies. By reducing her asthmatic reactions to several triggers, Stefanie's life was opened up immeasurably. For example, she could now be around dogs and cats, have a pet, participate in sports; and, she would only have to use a nebulizer occasionally. Over time, she would be able to eat almost anything.

The Saturday morning following Rosa's funeral, as Stan and I drove to the Bronx to see Stefanie and Angela. I don't remember if we had a plan for that day. We were all so drained from the week. It was hard to believe that Rosa had died. We just stayed close. That day, we took Stefanie to the local playground, and she practiced doing the jungle gym, which Stan had taught her. In a soft tentative voice, Stefanie repeated, "I can do it." That continues to be her mantra to this day. Stan reminds her when she is faced with a challenge, whether in love or life, that she can do it.

# 7

###

# Guardianship

## Claire

Everything was moving so quickly. In less than a month, we had agreed to become Stefanie's standby guardians, helped Rosa pass peacefully into her next life, made funeral arrangements for Rosa, buried her, and become responsible for Stefanie. Stan and I were feeling emotionally wrenched. I clung to Stan as my lifeline, and I knew that the strength of our own love and commitment was bolstering us both. All the while, I wondered how I would be able to transition into the role of parent, albeit for now a guardian. Yet I had little time to think about how this transition would work because our new responsibilities were very present.

It was only after Rosa's funeral that I had time to follow up on Rosa's reference, made in the hospital just before she died, about Angela's custody order. First, I called our project social worker, Lisette, who had been working with Rosa and Angela since they moved from Woodycrest into HSI's scattered site apartments. Lisette explained to me that in March 1995, an HIV/AIDS advocacy group had suggested that Rosa should grant Angela a custody order so that Angela could take Stefanie to the doctor or to school if Rosa was unable to do so. Lisette also mentioned that she learned that the custody petition should have triggered a criminal records review of Angela as the prospective custodian, which was required by law, but it wasn't done.

The senior staff at Woodycrest was aware that Angela had a criminal record, as she had been released from New York State prison to Woodycrest with the information that she was on parole after her release from state prison.

What I did not realize was that this was just the beginning of legal red tape in which we would become enmeshed as it related to our rights as guardians versus Angela's custody order. HSI's staff member, Lisette, also pointed out to me that in 1995 New York State law did not require that custody petitions be cleared through the New York State Child Abuse Registry, which didn't become law until the late 1990s. This fact was relevant, as Lisette shared with me that Angela had told her that she had three children of her own, before she went to prison. Her parental rights to all three were terminated.

This information was all new to Stan and me.

Stan and I had to go to Family Court within sixty days of Rosa's death on March 26, 1996, to have our standby guardianship agreement with Rosa ratified by the court. We now realized that we would also have to deal with Angela's custody order as well. Our lawyers had advised us that guardianship is a superior claim over custody, so we were confident that the court would agree. However, we had not considered that Angela would make a claim for sole custody of Stefanie. While Angela was not a blood relative of Stefanie, nor was she Latina (her parents were both Italian). Her partnership with Rosa was not a formal civil union, but it didn't occur to Stan and me that the Family Court might consider Angela's custody order a kinship arrangement.

We feared that if we sought to have the family court declare Angela's custody agreement null and void, we might lose everything. We decided to take the conservative approach and try to work out an agreement with Angela for shared custody.

## Stan

The year 1996 was a year in which Claire and I were confronted with one challenge after another.

It was April, and we needed to engage a lawyer to represent us, make all the necessary arrangements as required by the New York City Administration for Children's Services to become Stefanie's legal guardians. Then we had to work out an agreement with Angela on the issue of shared custody.

It seemed like Claire and I were living two different lives: one becoming Stefanie's guardians, which involved Stefanie and the cast of characters in her life, Angela and Rosa's family. The other was our life pre-Stefanie, with ongoing work and social commitments. We never thought about or discussed these dual lives. We had gone through the process of deciding to become Stefanie's standby guardians and our commitment to Rosa to adopt Stefanie. Before she passed away, Rosa had served as the buffer between Angela and her family. Now, without Rosa, the strength of our commitment to Stefanie was being tested by them.

Our first challenge was to find a lawyer to handle the legal issues related to our guardianship and the custody agreement we needed to work out with Angela. We interviewed two lawyers. One of the lawyers proposed a very aggressive approach for us to get sole custody of Stefanie. We were not comfortable with the aggressive approach given that we knew Angela would fight this. The other lawyer, Claudia O'Leary, specialized in family law. She had a much more even-handed approach and made a strong argument that we should negotiate an arrangement with Angela to avoid her contesting our guardianship. We engaged Claudia.

The second challenge was gaining the approval of New York City's Administration for Children's Services, required of all prospective foster parents and adoptive parents. We didn't know what this involved. We were with a group of friends from our spiritual group, and we mentioned our application to get the family court to approve our guardianship of Stefanie. Our friend Susanna, an interior designer, said there were some requirements that our house would have to meet to get approval for us to be Stefanie's guardians. She came to our home and did an assessment of issues we needed to address. She pointed out that Stefanie must have her own room with a door. The refrigerator should be stocked with kid food: milk, eggs, and kid-friendly snacks. We should have child age-appropriate playthings and books in our home.

Fortunately, our living arrangements made this possible. In 1994, the not-for-profit (Housing and Services, Inc., HSI) that Claire had founded was looking for more office space, and so together with HSI Claire and I had purchased a four-story building that had once been part of St. Gabriel's Church on East 35th Street. We converted the building into two condominiums units. Housing and Services took the top two floors of the building, and we occupied the bottom two floors.

Our condominium unit had a living room with a twenty-foot-high ceiling, dining room, half bathroom, and kitchen on the first floor. The second floor was a mezzanine overlooking the living room below, one bedroom with a door, a full bathroom, and a library. To meet the requirement that Stefanie have her own bedroom with a door, Claire and I gave up our bedroom and converted the library into our bedroom. For a short period of time, despite my love for her, I resented having to relinquish the library for Stefanie to be able to live with us. The library had served as my office. But this feeling faded as I began to spend more time with Stefanie on the occasions she stayed at our house. Our emotional decision to parent Stefanie overshadowed any logistical reality of what that meant to our physical space or daily lives.

The third challenge was dealing with Angela. We knew from the start of this guardianship process that Angela was not happy with the prospect of sharing custody of Stefanie, and she took every opportunity to inform us that she was now Stefanie's mother. Angela assumed the relationship would be as it was before Rosa died. But our being designated by Rosa as Stefanie's guardians meant that things couldn't go back to where they had been. We preferred to have sole custody, but we did not think Angela would ever agree to that. There were numerous non-legal issues that we also needed to resolve, primarily our role in raising Stefanie.

After several meetings with Claudia, we agreed it was time to have a meeting with Angela so we could reach an agreement on how all three of us planned to raise Stefanie before going to family court. We had explained to Claudia our preference for sole custody of Stefanie, but we were unsure how the court would decide this, given the order of custody that Angela had obtained in 1995. We discussed with Claudia, before meeting with Angela, that we were prepared to compromise and share custody of Stefanie with Angela.

Angela was resistant to the idea of shared custody, and on several occasions in meetings at our lawyer's office she insisted on sole custody. I had a vision of years in the future Angela passing away and a disturbed child being delivered to our doorstep. I became resolved that we would play no part in that scenario. We made a promise to Rosa, and we would not be able to achieve it if Angela had sole custody. After one such speech by Angela insisting on her having sole custody, I calmly stated in a clear but firm voice, "If we do not share custody with you and have a say in raising Stefanie, then we are walking away from being her guardians. I will not go forward without having a role in raising her only to deal with her after you pass away. We either share custody or you raise her by yourself."

Angela sensed that I was very serious, so she reluctantly agreed to a shared custody arrangement. We agreed that Stefanie would continue to live with Angela during the week and spend weekends and holidays with us.

To help us cope with all of these challenges, along the way we also consulted with Ruth, a friend and lawyer with firsthand knowledge about family dynamics and child development from the hundreds of divorce cases she had handled. Ruth would soon become one of our strongest supporters, as her advice was both compassionate and sage. Ruth advised us to be patient. She believed that jumping the gun and trying to get full custody of Stefanie right away would fail. Rather, we needed to wait until there had been a sufficient *change of circumstances* to argue for sole permanent custody of Stefanie. As we would learn, Ruth was so right. Making a case to the courts for change of circumstances would be a challenge at this point.

## Claire

Now that we had worked out an agreement with Angela on shared custody, we returned to dealing with more mundane matters. We had agreed to give Stefanie the bedroom, and we converted the library to our bedroom. Now, we needed to furnish her bedroom. We decided to take Stefanie shopping and allow her to pick out furniture for her room. At the store, we learned that Stefanie had very good taste and knew what she wanted. She picked out a high-end bunk bed and a desk. She wanted both a desk chair and a side chair because, as she explained, she needed this for her "clients," the owners of pets who would come for her services as a pet psychologist. Then she needed a small tent for her stuffed animals to live in. Within a week, our house was transformed into a child-friendly home. We were ready for the social worker we had selected to do a home study to arrive and prepare her determination as to whether we and our home were suitable. Theresa, the social worker, approved our home and our backgrounds, and she shared with us her experiences in raising an adopted child, as she and her partner had adopted a little girl from China.

The next step was family court. Our attorney set a date for a hearing with a judge in the Bronx Family Court as Bronx County was where Rosa had lived when she signed the standby guardianship papers and Stefanie was still living in the Bronx.

When Stan and I arrived in the Bronx Family Court, it felt as if we had entered a madhouse. Hundreds of parents, children, and lawyers were crammed into a small waiting room furnished with hard orange plastic chairs. Many parents had never met their lawyers; so, there were attorneys yelling out client's names, hoping to connect with them before going in front of the judge.

After several hours, Angela, Stan, and I, along with our attorney, were called into the courtroom. The judge asked Claudia what this case was about. She was eloquent and persuasive, explaining our unusual situation and emphasizing that Stan and I had known Rosa since Stefanie was three months old. Claudia explained that Rosa had developed a common-law partnership with Angela when they both lived at Woodycrest. Claudia recapped that Stan and I held long professional careers in the public sector, had raised Stan's two sons from his first marriage, and were very dedicated to improving the lives of persons affected with HIV/AIDS. By way of background, Claudia explained that, in 1995, Rosa had agreed to give Angela custody so that if she was too sick to take Stefanie to the doctor or be the represented "parent" at her school, Angela could do so.

Claudia continued to explain that in 1996 Rosa had asked us to become Stefanie's standby guardians so that when she passed away, we would eventually adopt Stefanie. Claudia also made clear that we had worked out an arrangement for joint custody with Angela so as not to disrupt Stefanie's current living arrangement.

The judge queried Claudia saying, "This is a very unusual arrangement, Ms. O'Leary. Do you think this will work?"

Claudia told the judge that we had a special relationship with Rosa, and this is what Rosa had wanted. She elaborated on the length of our relationship with both Rosa and Angela and said she was confident that this arrangement would work. The judge then asked Angela to step before him and questioned her as to whether she agreed with the proposed shared custody.

My heart stopped at that moment as Angela remained silent. But a few moments later she voiced her agreement with the arrangement. Following Angela's statement, the judge announced that he approved our becoming Stefanie's guardians and issued temporary papers designating us as her legal guardians. The final guardianship order from the Bronx Family Court would arrive a month later.

We left the courtroom immensely relieved and grateful for the outcome. We could feel that it would not be an easy road with Angela, because she continued to assert that she was Stefanie's mother. Despite her assertion, we had a piece of paper that stated we were Stefanie's legal guardians. Stan and I vowed to carry a copy of our guardianship papers with us at all times.

Our lives were now intertwined with Angela, who had resisted following Rosa's wishes that we become Stefanie's guardians. Although Angela wanted sole custody of Stefanie, deep down we felt she knew that she couldn't take care of Stefanie by herself. We took the approach of surrendering to what was to come and putting one foot in front of the other.

## Stefanie

The Blonde Giant/Claire and her husband, Stan, had become my guardians. I had come to learn that before mommy died the three of them had discussed Stan and Claire becoming my guardians and eventually adopting me. This meant that they were going to play a bigger long-term role in my life as care providers and parents. I still lived with Angela on weekdays, and it was shortly after that that my uncle became a "stand-in" father figure in my life. Weekdays were spent with Angela and my uncle. Weekends I spent with Claire and Stan.

## Claire

After the Bronx Family Court hearing, we felt we were Stefanie's "parents" with all the responsibilities that implied. In addition, we had also acquired a pseudo-stepdaughter in Angela. We tried to help Angela in any way we could. For example, Angela was attending Mercy College and came to rely on Stan to help her with mathematics courses.

Although we usually didn't see eye to eye with Angela on how to help Stefanie pursue things she was interested in, like reading, writing, art, going to musical theater, and learning to play a musical instrument, we tried to build a relationship with Angela for Stefanie's sake.

Another critical challenge we faced with Angela was where Stefanie would go to school. That September she would be in kindergarten. Stan and I had never dealt with the New York City elementary schools. Our two sons had gone to public schools in Great Neck, New York, a Long Island suburb, where they had lived with their mother. We began to research the schools in the Murray Hill section of Manhattan where we lived. The local public school PS 116 was rated as the best in the neighborhood. We arranged for a tour with both Stefanie and Angela. We were all very impressed with the caliber of the teachers whose classes we viewed briefly and with the school's Talented and Gifted (TAG) program. The day of our tour, the students were studying the art of Georgia O'Keeffe and made insightful comments. We were also gratified that the school had a number of Hispanic teachers, since we wanted Stefanie to maintain her connection to her Hispanic roots.

The main obstacle was that Stefanie did not live in the PS 116 district. We knew that the school she would attend if she remained in the South Bronx was no match for PS 116. Also, the apartment in the Bronx that Angela and Stefanie lived in was at least forty-five minutes away from our home. How would we see her frequently? The only solution seemed to be to move Angela and Stefanie to our neighborhood. Another strong supporter dropped into our lives. There were several apartment buildings in our neighborhood designated for low-income families that were owned by a large not-for-profit organization. Elizabeth Simmons was then the chair of this organization. She and I had worked together when she was a high official in the administration of Mayor Ed Koch, so I called Elizabeth and explained our situation to her. She readily agreed to find out if one of the not-for-profit housing buildings in our area had a vacancy. When Elizabeth called back, she said that there was an available apartment in a building on East 27th Street. Because Angela had a disability (HIV/AIDS), she could be given preference and was eligible for an apartment right away.

We called Angela and posed the idea of moving to Manhattan in a subsidized apartment so that Stefanie would qualify to attend PS 116. Angela agreed, as it was in a good neighborhood. She was approved for the apartment and signed a lease effective July 1. On the July 4th weekend, we helped Angela and Stefanie move to their new home. It was a comfortably sized, newly renovated two-bedroom apartment located on the thirteenth floor of a high-rise building. The heavens smiled on us because Jim, the manager of this building complex, was a former employee of HSI, so I knew him well. He had moved up the ladder of property management and was currently attending law school at night. Jim was helpful to us right from the beginning. He was there helping Angela and Stefanie if they needed repairs to the apartment or with anything else as they got settled.

Now that they had moved within the district of PS 116, Stefanie was eligible to enroll in the PS 116 kindergarten class for September. Before school started, we inquired about Stefanie being admitted to PS 116's Talented and Gifted program. The principal told us that we would have to arrange and pay for a test conducted by a private psychologist. It did not seem equitable that parents had to pay $150 for a private test to qualify their child for a program at a public school, but we decided to proceed. She did not pass or fail; she said almost nothing. Even though Stefanie did not get into the Talented and Gifted program, she was admitted to PS 116 for kindergarten that September.

Meanwhile, we needed to consider what Stefanie would do for the summer. These were the functional parts of raising a child that now became a central part of our lives. I had helped Stan raise his two sons, so these dynamics were not foreign to me. But with Stefanie, I felt my role as a mother more directly. We decided to find a day camp for her to attend.

Since Stefanie and Angela had moved to Manhattan and were living near us, we looked for nearby day camps. Going away to camp was not an option, given all she'd been through the past few months. We were fortunate to discover and enroll Stefanie in a Vanderbilt YMCA program called "Performing Arts" that was held at PS 116. Attending this camp would also give her an opportunity to get comfortable with her new school. Stefanie eagerly said she would love to be part of this program, which she called "farming arts." She was one of the youngest students in the program, but seemed comfortable dealing with older kids. The summer project was to put on a production of *Peter and the Wolf*. Stefanie was cast in the role of Peter's dog. A young woman named Carolyn, the program leader, took Stefanie under her wing and made her a realistic brown furry dog costume which Stefanie loved wearing as she crawled around on the stage at Peter's side. The costume still hangs in Stefanie's closet.

## Stefanie

### Life as Seen after Death, by a Child (Aged Five)

My visit to the Museum of Natural History to see the dinosaurs made me feel strangely close to death, but not in a morbid way. Seeing the animals through reconstructed fossil structures and puffed taxidermy animals made me realize that all things, in time, pass on and move on from this earth. I realized that in the same way that dinosaurs and mammoths once roamed the earth, my mother did too. She breathed the same air as they did and lived a life as they did. In some strange way, I was heartened by the natural cycle of living and dying. I remembered Mufasa falling to his death in *The Lion King* and how his son Simba witnessed his father die. I saw the connection between humans and animals, which helped me understand what it meant to live and die.

Another major influence in growing up was that Claire and Stan fostered my love for theater. The theater stimulated me like nothing else. In the summer of 1996, after my mother's death, Stan and Claire enrolled me in a YMCA summer camp. Most days were filled with swimming lessons, crafts, and gymnastics, but I really looked forward to the hours devoted to drama class. I eagerly awaited drama class like a kid waiting to get a new stack of money for their allowance. My brain and emotional body chomped at the chance to become someone else.

That summer I joined the young cast of a junior version of *Peter and the Wolf*, a musical composition with narration that I later learned was written in 1936 by Sergei Prokofiev. The story is of Peter, a young farm boy, who disobeys his grandfather by climbing over the garden wall. When Peter encounters a wolf, with quick thinking and the help of his friends, a bird, a duck, and a cat, Peter captures the wolf, and takes the wolf to the zoo. I played the role of the farm dog and wore my homemade costume, a brown body suit with floppy cloth ears that brushed the floor and a big black eye patch to resemble a spot. We rehearsed the production for eight weeks.

Our final presentation was a major performance on the stage in the school's assembly hall. This first theatrical experience took hold of me. I suppose it was the ability to give "life" and "breath" to a character who did exist and express it outwardly. It was the ability to feel within the confines of that character's inner world. This gave me freedom when I left the characters and their clothes on a hook, tucked away in a dressing room of an old school's theater room, to go home and be me. I knew I could not do the same with real life, and theater gave me both that escape and reprieve. I loved theater and would continue to take drama classes through my elementary and middle school years.

## Stan

I am not sure how the conversation got started. It was a Saturday afternoon, almost eight months after Stefanie's mother had died. Stefanie and I were sitting at the dining table making sandwiches for lunch. Claire was out, so Stefanie and I were alone and had a rare opportunity to talk to each other. I suddenly found myself in a conversation with Stefanie about death and dying. I remember saying that we all will die at some point. It is the cycle of life that we are born, live our lives and then pass away. Even Gabriel and Sapphire, our two cats, will die sometime.

"Are you going to die?" Stefanie asked me.

"Someday. But I will make you a promise that I will give you away at your wedding."

She looked at me and then looked up as one would look to God, and said, "You heard him, God!"

I could feel tears well up in my eyes. This little girl had suffered through the deaths of her mother, aunts, and uncles. Claire and I had avoided talking about death with Stefanie because we were concerned that this topic would bring up memories and emotions in Stefanie that we were not sure we were equipped to deal with. I was overwhelmed with a desire to protect Stefanie and provide her the stability and love she lost with her mother's death. Stefanie had also lacked a stable and loving male figure in her life. She made me feel her fear of loss, but also the comfort and security of my being in her life. And now she was sitting with me discussing a serious subject, yet able to add a bit of humor.

## Claire

That summer we spent a lot of time with Angela and Stefanie helping them get settled in their new apartment and getting to know the neighborhood. In July, Stan and I posed to Angela the idea of an end of summer vacation with Stefanie. Angela was ready for a break from childcaring, and she agreed readily. We planned an ambitious trip with Stefanie, flying to Vancouver and taking the ferry to Victoria, British Columbia. We would then fly to Seattle, Washington, where we would visit my elderly cousins Agnes and Caroline, before returning home. I was particularly eager to have Stefanie meet Agnes, because of their common interest. Stefanie loved her theater classes and, for years, Agnes had led the children's theater program at the University of Washington.

The day we departed, Stefanie was quiet, all packed and ready when we picked her up to go to the airport from Angela's apartment. Stefanie was a great traveler; she had packed her iPad, a book, and a coloring book. She knew I would bring water and snacks, so she'd be all set. She had flown only once when she was about three years old; Rosa had taken her to Disney World in Florida.

After the long flight to Vancouver and the ferry ride to Victoria Island, it was late in the afternoon when we arrived at our hotel and began to settle into our hotel room.

Stefanie took one look at the layout of the hotel room and spoke up.

"Are we going home tonight?" she asked.

My heart sank, I hadn't considered that she had no concept of a vacation in which we would be away from home for a number of days. At age five, it was understandable that she didn't get this. And we couldn't be sure how many memories she had of the Disney World trip. We explained that we would be gone for ten days doing all sorts of activities, then take another plane and return to New York City. We reminded her that when we went home, she would start kindergarten with Ms. Sanchez as her teacher.

Stefanie said, "Ok, I understand."

The next day Stan suggested a nearby Greek restaurant for lunch. As we walked around the block and found the restaurant, Stefanie stopped in her tracks, looked up at the restaurant and said, "Don't tell me you brought me to a restaurant without French fries."

"Of course not, the Greeks make the best French fries," Stan responded. We felt more comfortable joking around with her now.

## Stefanie

The summer after Stan and Claire became my guardians, they took me on my first vacation, to Victoria, British Columbia, and Seattle, Washington. The first part of the trip to Canada was my first time out of the United States. After a long plane journey and rolling up into the hotel room, I looked confusedly at the setup in the hotel room.

"Beds? Are we sleeping here?" I wondered. "Was not this like a trip to a museum where you stay a couple of hours and go back home?" I turned to Claire and Stan, "We are going home tonight, right?" I asked. Claire looked at me with a question mark on her face and sat me down and explained that vacations were a little bit different from museum outings, that we would be sleeping overnight at a place. Now the beds made sense, I thought. My first night in Victoria was hard, I did not sleep well but after that first night I eased into the rest of the trip.

Our trip to Victoria was a leap of faith for me. I inherently trusted Stan and Claire and felt good about them, but there was that edge of leaving what you knew behind. Victoria was also a demonstration for me of how much love and caring they had for me. One of my best memories from this trip was the whale sightseeing tour we took. We had to wake up early one morning and catch the boat. After we boarded, our captain told us we might be able to see whales. These small whales live in families and arrive in Canada in the late summer to mate. After a two-hour boat ride, I was bummed out. I had seen the movie *Free Willy* and was excited but sad that we didn't see whales that day. When the boat returned to the dock and the gang plank was lowered for us to exit, the captain turned to Claire and Stan and apologetically said that he knew how much I wanted to see orcas. He promised that, if he saw any whales, he'd call Stan and Claire so that we could see them another day.

## Claire

We kept busy during the balance of our trip in Victoria hoping for, but not expecting, a call from the captain that he had spotted orcas. One day, I suggested we treat ourselves to high tea at the beautiful historic Empress Hotel.

"No," Stefanie said emphatically, "I want to go to the petting zoo that we saw yesterday at the gardens we visited." Even at such a young age, Stefanie had decided opinions about what she wanted to do or not do and could express herself clearly.

We accepted that we needed to let her choose our activities. She would lead the way following her own inner drummer. So, we went to the petting zoo where she spent the afternoon lying on a bed of sawdust in the goats' pen while the baby goats walked on her back. She was in her "animal heaven."

## Stefanie

Early in the morning on our last day in Victoria, the captain called to tell us that he had seen two pods; he encouraged us to come to the docks quickly. Stan and Claire agreed to delay our departure to Seattle. We hurried back to the docks, parked our car, scrambled down to the boat, and boarded the boat. The crew untied and soon we were cutting through the waves to seek out the orcas.

Excitedly, I looked out over the waves hoping to spy a fin or misty spurt from the top of a whale. I could not see anything yet. The boat continued to chop through the water. The captain and his crew kept scanning in every direction anxious to find signs of a pod.

"Look, right over there!" one crew member shouted.

The captain's dog barked in excitement too! The captain's mate motioned for me to come up front next to her. The captain slowed the boat to a stop. The woman oriented me to the orcas. My eyes moved over the water's surface, and then I saw the black, shiny back of an orca surface and then submerge. We saw puffs of misty blowhole emissions as we admired the beauty and grace of these animals. A mother and her calf moved closer and swam alongside our boat. The orcas glided by with ease. I was transfixed and watched as the whales repeatedly flirted with our boat and then went back down underneath the water's surface. The pod circled our boat and finally swam off into the direction of more open waters.

The captain explained that they had to hunt to survive. I was disappointed that the visit with the most magnificent and majestic creatures I had ever seen had ended; but I understood they had lives to live. We returned back to the docks so that we could head to Seattle. Before leaving, Stan, Claire, and I thanked the captain for his help and guidance. A big smile came to his face. He looked pleased that he could bring joy to us on our last day. He wished us well and told us to have a safe trip back to New York.

The captain gave me a handshake and said that he was glad that I could see the orcas today. I said, "me too" and, with that, our human pod of three drove back to the hotel to pack up our belongings and head on to Seattle.

## Claire

That evening in Seattle, we picked up cousins Agnes and Caroline and drove to Lake Washington. My cousin, Claire, was also visiting Seattle with a friend and they joined us. We shared a picnic of sandwiches and cold salads at a picnic table in the park next to Lake Washington. Afterward, Stefanie offered to perform *Peter and the Wolf*. I did not know what to expect since she'd played the dog with no lines. But given a "stage" on the grassy park, she performed every part, saying the lines of all the characters perfectly while moving from role to role. Forty-five minutes later, we applauded loudly and were amazed at what she'd taken in from her place on the stage floor as the dog. Agnes praised Stefanie and called her a natural actor. Stefanie offered to perform the play again; we had to decline.

## Stefanie

Since this was my first time out of New York that I remembered, I didn't know that there could be cities other than New York. Seattle was impressive! It was a rainy town, clean, spaced out, and more expansive than New York. There was more green space than in New York. The city seemed to have a shimmery hue because of all the rain. One memory I recall from my time in Seattle was when Stan, Claire, and I met up with her cousin, Agnes, and we had a picnic at Lake Washington. Comparable to the Finger Lakes of upstate New York and the Great Lakes, Lake Washington is the largest freshwater lake outside of Seattle. When we met with cousin Agnes, it was a windy-sunny day.

After having finger foods and sandwiches at a picnic table overlooking Lake Washington, I began to get anxious. The adults at the picnic table kept talking and reminiscing about the years past and their families, you know the usual grown-up stuff. My five-year-old self couldn't care less, and I kept glancing over at the waves lapping on the shore. I finally piped up and asked if I could go in the lake. Claire and Stan had suspected that I might want to swim and had brought a fresh change of clothes for me. Given the go ahead, I bounded up from the picnic table and made my way to the lake.

I kicked off my shoes, ripped off my socks and dipped, one toe at a time, into the water. It was cold, but I slowly eased in— ankle deep, then knee deep, finally torso deep. Before the water reached my shoulders, Stan waded into the water and encouraged me to come back closer to shore. I smiled and eagerly paddled out farther; within seconds, Stan's arm was around my waist, reeling me back in. All I can say is that my inner Ariel was emerging, and I had never felt water like this. We eventually returned to shore to dry off and wrap up our day. I headed to the car to change, but Stan did not have a change of clothes. We made our way right back to the hotel quickly, so he could change. Seattle was a fun trip; even so, I have yet to go back as an adult.

## Stan

I watched Stefanie calmly walk toward Lake Washington; the next minute, she was knee deep in the water. I called for her to come back, but she continued to walk farther and farther into the lake. I suddenly feared she would drown. Without thinking, I rushed into the lake. By the time I was in the water, up to my knees, I threw my wallet and watch to Claire to avoid getting them wet. I caught up to Stefanie and brought her back to the beach. We were both soaked.

While Stefanie had a change of clothing in the car, I did not. We headed back to our hotel so I could change into dry clothes. I was a funny sight as we walked into the hotel lobby in downtown Seattle soaking wet and dripping all over the hotel's carpet. While I got strange looks from people in the lobby, I focused on getting to the elevator and our room. All worked out well.

## Claire

Our next animal adventure in Washington State was at Wolf Haven. Stefanie shared Stan's love of wolves. Whether it was their relation to dogs, their familial nature, or their wildness, Stefanie had made it clear she loved wolves. We drove to this wolf sanctuary, located just outside of Seattle, where the owners had rescued wolves who had been hurt or taken into captivity. They had created a sanctuary where the wolves lived until they were released back into the wild. We toured the grounds, saw the wolves in their fenced areas and then were invited to stay for the howling. As darkness set in, we gathered with about twenty-five other parents and children around a campfire. The director explained the meaning of wolf howling, how they do it and why—to indicate their location, warn off enemies, and show affection to their pack. Then he launched a wolf howling contest.

The contestant would howl, and if a wolf howled back, it meant the contestant had achieved a "real wolf howl." After the first couple of kids tried it with no response from the wolves, Stefanie volunteered. Without hesitation, she went to the front of the group and let out a howl that was so real it was eerie. A gray wolf in a nearby pen howled back, and Stefanie howled again. She was communicating as clearly as if she were speaking. Happy and tired, we drove back to town in the pitch-black darkness. Around one turn, our headlights caught a large deer standing in the middle of the road. Stan, being a cautious driver, was driving slowly and put on the brakes. The deer leaped back into the woods. Another animal. There could never be too many for Stefanie.

We flew back to New York the next day. I marveled at how natural it all felt with the three of us traveling together. Stan and I had traveled a great deal on our own and sometimes had taken our sons, most often for weekend business trips to Miami, San Francisco or Phoenix. Traveling with five-year-old Stefanie was a completely different experience, but it seemed so natural. We all seemed to meld easily.

When we brought Stefanie back to Angela's apartment that evening, we were startled to see that another woman had moved in. Angela introduced us to Kate, her new lover. We had not anticipated this, especially so soon after Rosa's death. Why should we be surprised? Angela was lonely and wanted a companion. I don't think Stefanie had ever met Kate before this night. This would be the first of many times that Angela, who had invited Stefanie to share her bed after Rosa died, would uninvite her when there was someone new in the picture. There was not anything we could do but try to be supportive of Stefanie with this new "wrinkle" in her life.

It pained me that night as we left Stefanie at the apartment with Angela and Kate. I just wanted to take Stefanie into my arms to hold her and not have her deal with yet another adjustment in her young life. Our agreement with Angela didn't cover new people moving into the apartment.

Angela had her rights, even though in my gut I did not think this situation was good for Stefanie. There are no rule books for parenting, particularly in complex situations like this one. Who determines what is "in the best interest of the child"?

# 8

**▟▙**

# Kindergarten

After our vacation, Stefanie had a couple of weeks free before kindergarten started. Stan and I took her shopping for school supplies, to a play at TADA!, one of her favorite children's theaters, and to the Bronx Zoo. We began to consider after school programs for Stefanie, as well. The Vanderbilt YMCA, where she had been to summer camp, had an after-school program located at her school at PS 116. We decided to enroll Stefanie into another cycle with the Vanderbilt Y. Everything we did with Stefanie became the subject of negotiation with Angela.

While Angela continued her classes at Mercy College, which we encouraged, she also wanted to pick up Stefanie at the end of the day. So we had that logistical issue as well to work out with her. Looking back, I'm not sure how Stan and I had the patience for all of that negotiating, but somehow, we did. I think we were always on edge, fearful that anything we said to Angela would trigger an argument with her. We knew that had her criminal past been investigated, as it should have been, she would likely not have been granted a custody order. But she now represented a link to Rosa for Stefanie, and we tolerated her constant opposition to us to keep the peace and avoid confrontational outbursts.

The three of us took Stefanie to her first day of kindergarten. She looked so tiny and fragile as we left her with her new teacher, Ms. Sanchez, a warm Puerto Rican woman who had taught kindergarten at PS 116 for at least ten years. She and Stefanie immediately began to chat about what kindergarten would be like, and we knew she was in good hands. However, in the first few weeks, the principal's office called us several times saying that Stefanie was beating up other kids.

One day, the principal called and told me that Stefanie had stepped on a boy's head in the lunchroom. When we confronted Stefanie about this, she was very defensive. Finally, she explained that the boy had brushed against her, and she felt the need to react. We began to realize that she didn't know how to solve disputes with words.

We were not totally surprised about these reports, because we had learned from Rosa that she had received complaints that Stefanie had been pushing and shoving other kids in nursery school. Back then, Rosa had asked us about finding a therapist for Stefanie, and we found a therapy program for children who had lost a parent to AIDS at the North Central Bronx Hospital. I spoke with Ilene, their lead therapist. Rosa and I had an initial meeting with her, and she seemed warm, friendly, and knowledgeable about how she could help Stefanie. Rosa had thought Ilene was a good choice, so we had arranged to take Stefanie up to the Bronx to meet her.

Then, in February of 1996, Rosa, Stan, Stefanie, and I went to meet Ilene; Angela had been busy with classes at that time. Stefanie seemed comfortable with her in that first visit, so we arranged for weekly meetings for Stefanie with Ilene. For the next two years, we took Stefanie on Friday afternoons for the counseling sessions. They seemed to be helpful. When we received reports of Stefanie being aggressive with her kindergarten classmates, we shared this with Ilene.

Ilene joined us in talking with Stefanie about how she could use words to deal with her anger, expressing what she felt, and the fact that physically punching someone was almost never acceptable. One day, Ms. Sanchez told us that some kids had been pushing in line and had begun to push Stefanie's friend Charlotte. Stefanie stepped in front of Charlotte and told the other kids,

"If you want to pick on someone, pick on me."

She was beginning to learn about acceptable ways to deal with disputes, but she was still a little too "streetwise."

## Stefanie

In the fall of 1996, I started kindergarten at PS 116. I had the sweetest and most adorable teacher named Ms. Sanchez. I'm sure she was made aware of the quiet terror I had been in nursery school. Let's just say I was still a child with a lot of unresolved issues regarding my mother's death, and I often outwardly acted out toward others. I was repeatedly sent to the principal's office because I had pulled this one's hair, bit this kid's hand, and hit that one in the face. I made it clear that I was not a girl to be messed with. Even though Ms. Sanchez showed patience when disciplining me, she laid down behavioral rules. So I knew what was and wasn't right. She'll be one of the teachers I'll always remember because of her patience, understanding, and empathy.

## Stan

When Stefanie started school at PS 116, all parents with children in kindergarten were asked to volunteer as lunchroom monitors. I volunteered for Fridays, when I had a lighter work schedule. This gave me the chance to observe Stefanie and see how she was adjusting to school. I noticed that she did not mingle with many of the kids sitting at her table and that she often sat quietly alone through the lunch period. Over time, I got to know many of the teachers and parents assigned to lunchroom duty.

One afternoon, I got a call from the school saying that I needed to come to the principal's office because Stefanie had bitten a teacher. I rushed to the principal's office where the teacher who had been bitten was waiting for me. She explained that Stefanie had been hiding under a table in the lunchroom and had refused to come out. The teacher had knelt on the floor and had reached out to grab Stefanie, when suddenly, Stefanie bit her hand.

Without thinking, I responded, "Why did you put your hand in Stefanie's mouth?"

The principal and teacher were shocked and realized that I was going to defend Stefanie, no matter what. The meeting ended shortly thereafter, with nothing further said. That night, we tried talking to Stefanie about the incident, but she refused to say anything. We continued working with her on overcoming the fears that led to behavior like hiding under the lunchroom table and biting her teacher's hand. We worked to help her replace the survival skills she had adopted in the Bronx to using words rather than physical actions.

## Claire

Stefanie did well in kindergarten. She loved school and told us that school was her own place, where she could be herself and get away from the noise and interruptions at Angela's apartment. When it came to school subjects, Stefanie found her voice in writing. The school encouraged phonetic writing, a new approach for me. Essentially, the students knew their alphabet and the sounds that letters made and would put together words phonetically on paper to tell stories. Deciphering these stories was like reading hieroglyphics. I could barely do it, but Ms. Sanchez could read Stefanie's stories aloud to us. That's when we realized that Stefanie had a vivid imagination and loved to write her stories down on paper.

For the most part, Stefanie was enthusiastic about kindergarten. She loved reading and writing, art, and math. The only thing she didn't like was the after-school Spanish class that we had enrolled her in with Ms. Sanchez. Stefanie resisted learning Spanish. She claimed she had no interest in it and that it was too hard. About midway through the fall semester, Stefanie asked us if she could drop out of the Spanish class. Perhaps she was signaling to us that she wanted no part of her Latin heritage or maybe it was something else. We didn't want to push her since she has always known what she wanted and what felt comfortable to her. We were glad she had a strong sense of who she was.

We continued helping Stefanie explore her interests. On several occasions, we had taken her to gymnastics classes at Chelsea Piers, a major recreational center on the west side of Manhattan. She was a natural at gymnastics. She loved the freedom of jumping into a pit filled with foam blocks and the discipline of working on the trapeze and the balance beam. We found a class at the Sutton Gym and asked Stefanie if she would like to take it. She jumped at the opportunity. We went shopping for leotards and shorts and then took her to the first class the following weekend.

The Saturday morning gymnastics classes became our ritual. Stefanie was always up early to put on her gymnastics outfit and urged us to move along quickly so we would get to her class early. She had a male Puerto Rican teacher who encouraged the girls in constructive ways, always with a soft voice, never criticizing them. Gymnastics was a great release for Stefanie. Afterwards, we would have lunch and go to a children's play or concert. I became the programmer, believing that we needed to keep her engaged.

When she had lived with her mother and Angela, Stefanie had a very sheltered life. Her only interactions with other children were at nursery school and in the local playground. She'd neither had her friends from nursery school over to their apartment for playdates nor had she gone on group outings with other kids to the zoo, the circus, or other kid activities.

Stefanie was always interested in exploring new things, like a new exhibit at the Museum of Natural History or the Bronx Zoo. As soon as we would arrive at one of these places and Stefanie would see a long line to get tickets, she would ask, "Are we members here? Can we join? I see there is no line at the membership desk." She could read well enough to figure out that there was a quicker way to gain admission. It was impressive to witness how, even at this young age, her mind was able to grasp the linkage between what offered better access, a point well taken.

We'd come home after one of these activities on Saturday evenings, have dinner and plan another activity for Sunday, usually with animals, since they meant so much to her. Then late on Sunday afternoon, we'd take her back to Angela's apartment. These partings were always bittersweet. We would miss Stefanie but had concerns. We never knew what to expect from Angela the next time we came for Stefanie. We might find a new guest staying over or Angela might be in a confrontational mood.

A couple of months into kindergarten, Angela signaled to us that she needed help with Stefanie. Every time we'd see Angela or talk with her, she would complain about how tired she was and how hard it was for her to go pick up Stefanie after school, but Angela would not ask for our assistance. Given her resistance to seeking help from us, we were pretty sure that Angela would not take kindly to us offering help. So we decided to look for someone who could pick up Stefanie from her afterschool program and bring her to Angela's apartment.

I knew a young woman, Jennifer Matos, the daughter of a former boss of mine. I heard from her mom that Jennifer was looking for a part-time job to supplement the hours that she worked as a veterinary assistant. Based on our families getting together a few times, we knew Stefanie got along with Jennifer, so we hired her as the first of our babysitters. Then we told Angela that Jennifer was available and that we'd pay her. Angela voiced no objections, so we moved ahead, and Jennifer became one of the first of many helpers who came along just as we needed her.

That fall Stefanie had noticed the swimming pool at the YMCA and asked if she could take lessons. When Stefanie had waded into Lake Washington the previous summer, we knew she didn't know how to swim, which is why Stan dashed into the lake to rescue her. We learned that Stefanie had never been in a pool and registered her for swimming class. She was not afraid of water and took to her first class called the tadpole class. She swam like a real tadpole. Stefanie was a natural swimmer and always looked forward to her Sunday morning swimming classes. Stan and I realized that Stefanie always had her eye out for new experiences. Parents had begun to give children swimming lessons at a young age, not just for the joy of it, but as a safety precaution so they were comfortable in the water.

While Stefanie was only with us on weekends and holidays, our lives had immeasurably changed since Rosa had asked us to become Stefanie's guardians. Now with Rosa gone, it was not easy negotiating with Angela every step we took with Stefanie. She continued to be very possessive of Stefanie, regularly claiming that she was Stefanie's mother. Guardianship laws give guardians a superior right to raise a child over the person who is designated the custodian, but exercising that superior right was not easy.

Our attorney and friend Ruth had advised us that since we had signed an agreement with Angela that we would honor her custody agreement and share custody of Stefanie, there would have to be a "significant change of circumstances" for us to claim a right to sole custody. It was definitely a gray area as to what would be a significant change of circumstances, but we knew we had to tread carefully in asserting our custody rights. Angela's possessiveness of Stefanie was overt. She constantly referred to Stefanie as "my little baby" or "my girl." In any kind of public situation, as with Stefanie's teachers, Angela introduced herself as Stefanie's mother or stepmother.

Part of us kept hoping that Angela would meet us halfway and show some semblance of becoming more agreeable. We didn't need expressions of gratitude, but it was clear how much we loved Stefanie. Moving Angela and Stefanie to a nice neighborhood in Manhattan had improved their quality of life immeasurably. Angela seemed incapable of acknowledging that we were moving heaven and earth to be good guardians to Stefanie, respect Angela's role, and support her own educational pursuits as much as possible. Stan and I were very aware that we were blessed to be in a financial position to help introduce Stefanie to new experiences and aid with the many transitions she was going through. We were doing far more juggling of work, business trips, and parenting than we were used to. Every afternoon we checked with Angela to make sure that Stefanie had been picked up from her after-school activity at PS 116 and brought back to the apartment. We talked with Stefanie early each evening and then before bed. Usually, she just shared with us what had happened at school that day. She almost never spoke about Angela or what transpired at the apartment.

Every day we felt a certain amount of trepidation about what might happen to Stefanie that day. What would Angela and Stefanie's uncle do that might affect Stefanie or our relationship with her? Would Stefanie be safe with them? We both remembered that Rosa had not wanted her brother to be part of Stefanie's upbringing. Yet we also knew there was no way to introduce this landmine subject that was only hearsay at this point. We were constantly vigilant, keeping our eyes and ears open, trying to make sure that we knew Stefanie was safe. We felt the toll on our psyches and our bodies from being constantly on alert. Mostly, we buried these feelings and didn't talk about them. We were always glad to get through the day without a disagreement with Angela over what was best for Stefanie.

Our love for each other, for Stefanie and the joy she brought into our lives, as well as the growing bond we were forming with her, served as a balancing measure to the tension of this shared custody arrangement.

Given that Stan and I were always expecting another shoe to drop, we were not too surprised when we took Stefanie back to Angela's one Sunday night to find Angela's eighteen-year-old son Barry there. Now that Angela had an apartment in Manhattan, Barry could easily travel via Long Island Railroad from his grandfather's house in Nassau County to Manhattan. What teenager wouldn't like the freedom of travelling into the Big Apple for adventure?

We didn't like the idea of a teenaged boy we didn't know living with Stefanie, but we couldn't forbid him from being there. Barry was one of the three children whom Angela had lost custody of, so it is not as if she had raised him. We tried to be open-minded about him, but it soon became clear that Barry was not a good influence. Our attorney advised us, however, that there was nothing we could do to prevent Barry from coming to Angela's apartment.

We kept a close watch on him whenever we knew he was around. The other disruptive factor with Barry was that Angela gave him Stefanie's room when he was there, and she moved Stefanie into her bedroom. We objected to Stefanie being dispossessed of her own space.

Angela, however, knew no boundaries. We soldiered on, trying to keep good relations with her, being watchful of Stefanie, and holding on to each other. While we had been held to a higher standard of ensuring that Stefanie had her own room, Angela was breaking those guidelines left and right with no repercussions. Our determination not to allow things to get confrontational with her often stretched our nerves to the breaking point.

The fall went by quickly, and it was Christmas again. Stan and I knew it would be bittersweet to celebrate Christmas for the first time without Rosa. We continued with our Christmas tradition of inviting Stefanie and Angela, Jeffrey and David, and our usual group of friends to our home. We included Stefanie's great-grandmother and her cousins, as we had the year before. We wanted Stefanie to have an awareness and connection with her biological family. She always enjoyed being with her cousins, and we tried to give her those opportunities whenever we could.

We shopped for gifts for all of them and arranged for a taxi to bring Stefanie's great-grandmother and her cousins to our house. I cooked a big dinner with turkey and all the trimmings. We all missed Rosa, but we didn't speak about her; we remembered her silently. Stefanie kept her feelings to herself. We were not sure how to navigate these waters, but felt that it was best just to let Stefanie lead the way. Once again, Stan and I fell into the parent role easily.

January 1997: That winter break, the three of us took a mini-vacation to Miami. We had to arrange with Angela to bring Stefanie with us when we traveled over the weekend or on a school break trip. By that time, our close friend, Camila, had a thriving store selling club wear and making clothes of all sorts. We had both purchased apartments in a building close to Lincoln Road, a shopping mall that had seen better days but was slowly emerging from its doldrums. Given that I was doing consulting work for Dade County and was there almost every other week, having a place to stay, rather than at a hotel, made good economic sense.

On that trip, Stefanie's love of the sun and the water emerged. It was Stefanie's first experience with the ocean and its beaches. Stan introduced her to wading in and then dipping under the water, as his Greek grandmother had done with him when his family spent summers on the Rockaway beaches in New York City.

Stefanie also loved walking along the beachfront of South Beach. We would stop for lunch and watch the crowds of people, all ages and ethnicities dressed in all types of different clothing. Usually, in the evenings, we'd go to Lincoln Road and explore the shops. One evening, Stefanie decided she wanted to learn to rollerblade, which was all the rage. We outfitted her with skates, a helmet, and safety pads. She got the rhythm of rollerblading easily and pretty soon we were running alongside her.

In New York, we had gotten Stefanie a bike with training wheels on which she learned. Later, we had the training wheels taken off, and she managed on two wheels. We found a bike rental place in Bill Baggs Cape Florida State Park at the end of Key Biscayne. They had a bicycle her size, so she was set. Stan, however, had never learned to ride a bike because his mother refused to let him try this "dangerous" sport. We rented bikes for Stan, me, and Stefanie, and we tried teaching Stan to ride. We weren't the best teachers, so Stan took a few falls; nevertheless, we all had fun trying to help him learn this sport.

We then discovered the Venetian Pool in Coral Gables. Behind pastel stucco walls and wrought iron gates was the Venetian Pool where Esther Williams and Johnny Weissmuller swam to practice for the Tarzan films. The cascading waterfalls, caves, and Spanish fountain had earned the Venetian Pool a listing on the National Register of Historic Places. The Venetian Pool would become one of our "must-do" stops on our trips to Florida for the next six or seven years. Stefanie had become a pretty good tadpole swimmer and with her swim wings was fearless in the water, where we would spend hours. She never tired of exploring the caves and swimming under the waterfalls.

In early February 1997, we celebrated Stefanie's sixth birthday at our house, this time with a clown. Stefanie had made new friends at kindergarten and was comfortable having them over to our house; she invited six or seven of them to her birthday party. They all enjoyed the birthday celebration. Later that month, it was Rosa's birthday. That year, we began a tradition of lighting a candle at dinner, in memory of Rosa, and saying a short prayer. Stefanie has always been quiet on these birthday remembrances, but we continue to recognize them to this day.

One Friday toward the end of the school year, when we picked Stefanie up from school, she asked me, "Do you know what a jackass is?"

Astounded, I said, "Where did you learn that word?" She explained, saying, "I learned it from Ms. Sanchez. We are studying different animals, and we learned that Jackass penguins only live in South Africa where Uncle Harry lives. Can we visit him and see the penguins?"

That same day, Stefanie received a postcard in the mail from Uncle Harry with Jackass Penguins on the front and an invitation to come visit him and see them. Serendipity at work.

Harry, a dear friend, had retired and been moving to different parts of the world. He was searching for a place to live that he might love as much as Japan, where he had lived since his discharge from the Army in 1948. A few years ago, he had come to the United States and gotten to know Stefanie during the time he spent with us. Harry immediately became "Uncle Harry" to Stefanie, the world-traveling uncle who shared stories of his visits to exotic places.

Then, in 1996, Harry had moved to Knysna, South Africa, just north of the Cape of Good Hope and was eager for us to come visit. So when Stefanie proposed a family trip to South Africa to visit Uncle Harry, we told her we would think about it. Stefanie always saw possibilities, especially if there were animals involved, and she usually didn't want to take "no" for an answer.

We talked with Angela about the possibility of this trip sometime before the school year started. She agreed that Stefanie could come with us. When we told David and Jeffrey about the trip, they both chimed in saying that they would also love to go with us to South Africa. Our friend Camila, from Miami, had also gotten to know Harry during his visits to the US. She had always wanted to go to South Africa, so we invited her to join us. Thus began the plans for this family trip to South Africa.

At her kindergarten graduation, Stefanie was proud to have earned a reading medal for reading the most books and being part of her new school group. When summer arrived, Stefanie wanted to return to the YMCA camp for gymnastics and theater.

We spent most of June and July planning the trip to South Africa, mainly around activities that would appeal to Stefanie. Everyone else would have to come along for the ride. Harry put us in touch with a travel agent, and we worked out an itinerary along the Garden Route, South Africa's southern coast, which is well developed, beautiful, and easy to travel. I had amassed tens of thousands of airline miles from my weekly trips to Miami over the past six years so we could all travel for free. We arranged to rent a minivan with a driver, as none of us was experienced in driving on the left side of the road. I ordered the tickets and booked hotels for ten days in September. We would see elephants, caribou, gazelles, monkeys, lions, giraffes, and, of course, jackass penguins. Stefanie was ecstatic. This would be a real family safari.

In late August, I took Stefanie to the doctor's office for a routine back-to-school physical exam and to update her shots. I mentioned our family safari to the pediatrician and asked if there were any special health precautions we should take. Suddenly, Stefanie blurted out, "I'm not going."

"Why not?" I pressed. "This was your idea, and we've planned for all the things you'd like to do."

"I know," she said timidly, "but Angela says it will be dangerous."

Stefanie's doctor explained that the pediatrician in the next room happened to be South African, and that she would invite him in to see what he had to say. He assured us that our itinerary was very safe. All the restaurants, hotels, and restrooms were extremely clean; the water was safe to drink, and there were plenty of doctors should anyone need them. But Stefanie was steadfast. She was not going. Over the past year, we had traveled to several places with Stefanie, and Angela had approved Stefanie going on this trip with us. Angela had been comfortable with our traveling with Stefanie, and at times relieved to have more than a weekend without being a caregiver. However, when I took Stefanie back to Angela's later that day, Angela admitted that she had told Stefanie she didn't want her to go because it was dangerous.

We decided not to argue with Angela, as we didn't want to create more animosity with her. We knew that we would go ahead with the trip; our sons would have been too disappointed if we had cancelled. We did go, and all of us had a glorious time. We saw all of the wildlife that Stefanie had hoped to see, and it pained us that she was missing out on a trip that she had initiated. We visited a private game reserve where we were able to view elephants up close and slept comfortably wherever we went, including one night at an elephant preserve. Best of all we did not get sick.

We knew Stefanie would have loved the trip. We arrived home and immediately went to Angela's apartment to see Stefanie. We were greeted by a little girl with a bandage on her forehead. She had run into a pole in gym class at school and had cut open her forehead. The gash required five stitches but was deemed not too serious.

More troubling was that Angela's son, Barry, had moved in again and taken Stefanie's room. Stefanie was now sleeping in Angela's bed every night. We voiced our objections about having Stefanie displaced from the refuge of her own room and to having Barry living there. When we came over a couple of days later on Friday evening to pick up Stefanie for the weekend, Barry looked high to me. When Stefanie came to our house that weekend, she told us that Angela and Barry had an argument and that Barry had pushed his mother. Stefanie was standing behind Angela, so they both fell. We were furious. Why did Angela have to expose Stefanie to further trauma? That Sunday, when we took Stefanie back to Angela's, Barry was still there. This time, I noted that he appeared high again. Monday night around 9:00 p.m., after I knew Stefanie would be asleep, I went to Angela's and told her that I was sure Barry was high on ecstasy.

"How do you know?" Angela asked.

"I've been working with drug addicts for twenty-plus years," I responded, "and I know what drug use looks like and what behaviors are related to specific drugs."

While we understood Angela's complicated history and point of view, the importance of having her son with her and her desire for independence, our focus was on protecting Stefanie.

I came home and shared this encounter with Stan. We were both furious, but the evidence of any wrongdoing was circumstantial. Once again, our lawyer advised us that there was nothing we could do. Thus began Stefanie's first grade year with what would prove to be a long string of arguments over what was best for her.

# 9

# Stefanie at PS 116—the Early Years

## Stefanie

I had a wonderful first grade teacher by the name of Ms. Chu, a petite Chinese American young woman, bubbling with enthusiasm. Every morning, Ms. Chu played her guitar and taught us folk and bluegrass tunes written by John Denver and other folk singers. I learned the lyrics to "Country Roads" from Ms. Chu. I remember wailing them louder than any of my other classmates.

I yearned for a place to belong, a place to feel safe and to call home with a mother in it. Those singing sessions with Ms. Chu were comforting and most likely sparked my love for music and musical theater in particular. Music had a certain way of healing that I could not comprehend then, nor to this day.

Later in the first grade, my teachers observed that when a story was read to me and I'd be asked to summarize and retell it, I told a totally different story. I was diagnosed with an auditory processing disorder and was placed in speech classes twice a week. The speech teacher used flash cards, short stories, writing and drawing exercises—all in effort to rewire my brain. It worked (I think) because the following year, in second grade, I was admitted into the Talented and Gifted Program at school. I was a unique student. I had a learning disability, but I excelled in areas like writing and the arts. I mean, look where I am today, writing a book!

## Claire

Stefanie forged a close relationship with Ms. Chu. She loved Ms. Chu's classes and was always eager to go to school in the morning. At the end of the year, Ms. Chu assembled a book of poems written by her first-graders. In Stefanie's copy of the book which was titled *"Mommy Rosa,"* Ms. Chu wrote the following inscription:

> *Stefanie, your spirit has guided so many of us through this year. Words of mine may not describe it well enough . . . but listening to your heart has opened up all of ours. Love, Ms. Chu*

Stefanie loved writing, but as she has related, she had difficulty retelling a story she'd heard or read. I mentioned this to the social worker who had done our home study, Theresa, who explained that her adopted daughter had been diagnosed with an auditory processing problem.

"This sometimes arises from early childhood deprivation," Theresa said, "and perhaps Stefanie has the same condition."

We asked the school to arrange to test Stefanie. We were neophytes at these learning issues. We were ten to fifteen years older than most other parents of first-graders, so we didn't talk about child development issues when we went out with friends our age. The school was very cooperative and arranged for testing and asked me to schedule an interview with the Department of Education assessment group. Since Stan was on the faculty at SUNY Stony Brook, fifty-five miles away on the east end of Long Island, daytime meetings were difficult for him. Therefore, Angela joined me for the school meeting.

Being in a joint interview with Angela was uncomfortable. Telling Stefanie's story was trying, as there was so much that I wasn't comfortable talking about with Angela present. But we got through the interview, and the school assessed Stefanie. When the report arrived, we learned that Stefanie did indeed have an auditory processing problem. The school would give her a Section 504 disability designation and would provide "pull out" speech classes three times a week. This designation would be continued through elementary and middle school, which would give Stefanie needed time to absorb what she read, including written math problems. As new parents, we were learning a great deal through our daughter. We explained what this diagnosis meant to Stefanie, and she said she understood and was ready to accept this extra help.

We continued to plan our own stimulating after-school and weekend activities, as Stefanie was eager to participate in a range of interesting projects. She continued with her gymnastics classes, our Saturday out-ings to the zoo or to a play, and her after-school programs at the YMCA. She became attached to one of her gymnastics teachers, whom I asked, "What do you think would be the best summer camp activity for Stefanie?"

She immediately responded, "Stefanie needs to be outdoors, at a camp or someplace where she can run around and have some freedom. She has a lot of energy and really enjoys being outdoors with the freedom that it offers."

So, we started looking for day camps in the nearby suburbs that in-cluded bus transportation from New York City. We weren't in a circle of young parents who discussed summer camps for seven-year-olds, so we did our own research. I hadn't realized that parents applied for camps in the fall for the upcoming summer. We had already missed the winter "camp fairs" held in New York, but we found a camp called "Candy Mountain" in New Jersey that had a spot for Stefanie.

The next Saturday, we ventured to Candy Mountain with Stefanie, An-gela, and Stefanie's uncle. We met the owners and the staff and learned about the programs and their bus transportation from Manhattan. Stefanie said she liked the camp, so we put down our deposit. I was not sure how well this would work. Stefanie had never been on a school bus before or away all day out of New York. But we knew that being outdoors with other kids her age would be good for her.

At the end of her first-grade year, Stefanie won a reading Olympics medal for reading the most books. Reading was her refuge. She turned to reading whenever she had a few spare minutes and always carried a book with her. Engrossed in a good book, Stefanie would find a reading "nook" and could be lost for hours.

## Florida Interlude

Before camp started, Stan, Stefanie and I went to Miami for a week. I needed to be there for work, consulting for Dade County on homeless is-sues. Stan entertained Stefanie while I was at work. I began to understand why Florida is considered a fantasy place. The sidewalk cafes, the beaches, the sense of endless sunny tomorrows quickly blocked out New York's cold winters, muggy summers, and concrete jungle.

On this trip to Miami, Stan took Stefanie to Sea World on Key Biscayne to see the dolphin show. We knew someone whose son worked there, and we arranged for her to meet him before the show. During the show, the leader of the program asked for volunteers to join the dolphins in the tank. Stefanie raised her hand and was called to come onto the dock. When the leader asked who would like to swim with the dolphins, Stefanie tried a couple of times to jump into the water with the dolphins, before the leader grabbed her to hold her back. This was one of the many times that I wished I had been with her and not working, but I was glad that Stan had been there as her buddy on these adventures.

One day, Stefanie asked if she could go horseback riding. We found a stable where Stefanie would be able to ride in Fort Lauderdale, about twenty miles north of Miami. One hot day, we drove up there. Horses were Stefanie's favorite animals. When on a horse's back, she would bend over to put her face against his head and speak to the horse, knowing that he would hear her.

Stefanie loved our trips to Florida, and her olive skin got darker within a day or two. She loved the freedom of wearing shorts and sandals and just being in the sun. We all relaxed on these trips to Miami Beach. Once, when we returned to New York from Miami, she and Stan were walking ahead of me through the airport. Stefanie was wearing her khaki shorts and Stan his khaki pants; both of them were pulling roller bags. Hers was a small pink one and his a large gray one. I commented that they looked alike. Stefanie simply said, "We rub off on each other."

"Indeed, you do," I responded.

In early July, on the first day of camp, we stood on our corner of Third Avenue and 35th Street, at 8:00 a.m. waiting for the bus. Stefanie knew none of the kids going to the camp and had only been there once, but she still appeared excited. She bounded up the steps of the bus and found a seat right up front. Later that evening, when the bus appeared at our corner on schedule at 5:00 p.m., I breathed a sigh of relief when Stefanie strode down the steps with a big smile plastered on her face. Trusting our child to strangers, even though they had a license to operate a camp, was hard for me. I felt that Stefanie was a precious gem we had to guard. When the camp had family days, we'd drive to New Jersey to see her in a swim meet or a theatrical performance. Her gymnastics teacher was right because being at a camp all summer, out in the fresh air had been great for Stefanie.

## Stefanie

Similar to Ms. Chu in the first grade, I had another amazing teacher, Ms. DiAngelo, in the second grade. At first, Ms. DiAngelo scared me.

She truly lived up to her Italian surname—she was bold in presence and vocally scared the living daylights out of me when she got mad. She had a stern manner and ran a tight ship in her classroom but, unforgettably, she will always be one of those teachers who truly understood me. In one-to-one interactions, she was patient and often asked how I was doing. Since her class was my first year in the Talented and Gifted (TAG) program, there were certain subject areas I'd fallen behind in, but she would make sure to take the time to lean in and help. Ms. DiAngelo was one of those teachers who was not afraid to get in the trenches and really get to know her students. I love that we are now Facebook friends.

## Stan

### The Remedy

There were times when Stefanie was extremely sad or when she seemed to become frozen with fear of being unable to do a particular task or school assignment. Over the years, I had learned that it was often helpful to shift a child's focus to something that engages them in a more positive way. In Stefanie's case, one of the most effective methods I discovered was to make her "a remedy." "What is a remedy?" you might ask. A remedy is a black-and-white ice cream soda, made with vanilla ice cream, chocolate syrup, a bit of milk, and whipped cream. Making a remedy always lifted Stefanie's spirits and, many times, just the suggestion that I would make one would change her mood.

I remember one Saturday morning when Claire was busy with work, and I was home alone with Stefanie. She was sulking on the couch in the living room, and I had to ask her several times what was bothering her. "I have to write a story for school and don't know what to write about," she said.

"Why don't you put this assignment aside," I said, "and we can revisit it later."

In the meantime, I suggested she relax while I went into the kitchen to make her a remedy. When I returned to the living room, I found Stefanie on the couch watching television, clearly in a lighter mood. Beside her I could see she had written something. When I approached her with the remedy, she told me she had written a story and asked if I would read it. Her handwritten story was spread out over twenty pages. To my surprise, it was very coherent. While I do not remember the story's subject or characters, I do remember her saying, "I just started writing and before I knew it, I had finished the assignment. I knew I could do it."

I realized that Stefanie had the ability to write, even if her spelling and grammar needed more work. After all, she was only seven years old at the time.

## Claire

When Stefanie turned eight in February, we began to think about the promise we'd made to Rosa to raise her as a Catholic. I was Catholic and Stan was Jewish; however, neither of us were practicing those religions. We did not have any ties to local Catholic churches. I knew that I did not want to take Stefanie to a traditional Catholic church. I looked around and found a Jesuit church in Chelsea, St. Francis Xavier, which we had heard was very welcoming to people of all faiths and backgrounds, had a charismatic priest, and programs for young children. The three of us ventured there one Sunday and met the young priest who led their Family Faith Program, designed for parents and children to meet weekly and learn more about the Catholic faith.

He invited us back the next Sunday. We arrived at 9:30 before the 11:00 a.m. Mass. Stan was amazing. Going to church had definitely not been on Stan's agenda, but he led the way, always making sure that we left the house on time for the Family Faith Program. We were the oldest parents there, but we met about a dozen other couples and single parents who shared with the group why they attended St. Francis. Most had children Stefanie's age and had felt a pull to come to church as their children were reaching the age for First Communion. This began a five-year association with St. Francis and their Family Faith Program, in which Stan was the "resident Jew" who explained Passover and Chanukah. Stefanie had a good relationship with the other kids, and they began to share common interests. We became friends with several of the families. For the next five years, until after Stefanie's Confirmation, we rarely missed a Sunday.

During the spring of second grade, Stefanie asked if she could go horseback riding. We knew that she had a deep love of horses and wanted to spend time with them. So we found Kensington Stables in Brooklyn, which offered riding lessons for kids in Prospect Park. We made an appointment for a riding lesson one Saturday. While the stable was old and poorly maintained, which was reflected in the dusty stalls and sawdust floors, the owners and instructors had friendly, gentle manners with both the horses and the kids.

Stefanie enjoyed her lesson that day with an eager young riding instructor and asked if we could come the following Saturday. The lessons on Saturdays continued until one day, as we were driving back to Manhattan, I turned around to see Stefanie in the back seat. Her face was red and swollen. It was the first time she'd had an allergic reaction to horse dander. We gave her an antihistamine and within an hour the swelling and redness had abated. This was our first real health scare with Stefanie, but would it mean the end of horseback riding?

Stan called his cousin Jay, who is a horse vet in Colorado, and told him about Stefanie's reaction. "I guess that's the end of horseback riding for Stefanie, but she loves it so," Stan said.

Jay replied calmly, "I would approach this differently. I would give her an antihistamine to control the symptoms before she rides and take her to a clean stable with as little horse dander in the air as possible and limit her exposure. Over time, she's likely to develop a resistance to the horse allergy."

This advice sounded hopeful, but we knew we couldn't go back to Kensington. That barn was old and musty, the outdoor riding space was covered with sawdust that was musty and dander-filled; none of this was in line with Jay's recommendation of a clean barn. We began a search for a better place to take Stefanie riding.

All the while, we continued to have our regular "encounters" with Angela on Sunday nights when we took Stefanie back to her apartment. Sometimes there was a new roommate and sometimes her son Barry was there. It was very common for Angela to complain about how we were raising Stefanie. We swallowed hard when we brought Stefanie back on Sunday afternoons/nights. We just kept trying to help Stefanie have kid experiences on the weekend when she could just be herself and not be "on high alert" for the new situations into which Angela seemed to put Stefanie. Our lawyer and our friend Ruth had made it clear that we shouldn't push for full custody then, as there had been no precipitating event or clear change of circumstances that would warrant this request.

Given this new issue with the horse-dander, we reflected on how, the morning after Rosa's funeral, Stan and I had driven to the Bronx, picked up Angela and Stefanie and driven to Connecticut for an appointment with Dr. Tom Brunoski ("Tom"), which we had made weeks before to have him assess Stefanie's allergies.

Tom had reviewed Stefanie's blood work and determined that she was allergic to almost everything, including dust, pollen, grass, cats, dogs, dairy products, and wheat, among many other triggers. Tom advised that she needed to be on a dairy-free and gluten-free diet and needed to take the drops he prepared for her.

We had then embarked on what became a two-decade program that gradually helped Stefanie to overcome these allergies. By reducing her asthmatic reactions to several triggers, Stefanie's life was opened up immeasurably. For example, she could now be around dogs and cats, have a pet, participate in sports, and she would only have to use a nebulizer occasionally. Over time, she was able to eat almost anything.

### Stefanie

In fourth and fifth grades, Ms. French was my teacher. She was another one of my favorites, mainly because she allowed her students to call her by her first name, Nancy. In my two years with Nancy, I felt I got to know myself better, especially learning about what I wanted to do. That year, I started viola lessons at the Third Street Music School in the East Village, and I played soccer with the Downtown United Soccer League. By the middle of my fifth-grade year, I continued to spend a lot of time with Stan and Claire and would later become estranged from my uncle.

I have many gaps in my memory during fourth and fifth grades, maybe because I wanted to forget some incidents at Angela's. It was also due to my psyche protecting me in some way. The structure of school gave me a regular and predictable schedule, when everything else at Angela's apartment seemed so unpredictable and unknown. Turning in homework assignments gave me a sense of control, and learning gave me a sense of hope. Interacting with my classmates and teachers gave me an escape from the custody battle between Stan and Claire and Angela, which emerged when I was in the fifth grade.

### Claire

Stan and I yearned for some regularity and predictability. During the second through fourth grades, Stefanie continued to live at Angela's apartment. Her uncle lived there as well, along with Angela's son, Barry. To the extent we could, we tried to help Stefanie establish a regular routine. We talked to Stefanie by phone daily and made sure our childcare helper picked Stefanie up every day from school and took Stefanie to her after-school activities. If it was a day for her viola classes or soccer lessons, which usually ended around supper time, we'd take Stefanie to these activities and then have dinner together, before going back to Angela's apartment.

Stefanie was with us on weekends. Given the uncertainty of life at Angela's apartment, with different people coming and going, we never knew what to expect. Stan and I focused on protecting Stefanie and helping her grow up healthy and happy. Even though Stan and I were constantly on alert for what might happen to Stefanie when she was with Angela or her uncle, we tried not to think about what the future would bring. We did not know how long we would be co-parenting Stefanie with Angela and, indirectly, with her uncle. We were committed to Stefanie and so, for now, Angela and her uncle were part of this life.

We felt we were constantly on an emotional roller coaster. We devoted every minute, when Stefanie wasn't in school, to her happiness and well-being. We saw our friends less often, rarely went to social events (except those of Stan's family who were mostly in New York City and where Stefanie was welcome), and dedicated our attention to supporting Stefanie. We accepted the reality of our lives, though it was stressful for both of us. We dealt with this crazy situation in the best possible manner because we loved Stefanie, and we both had a sense that eventually we would gain sole custody. The stress was easily balanced with the joy Stefanie added to our lives and the loving family unit we had built.

We focused on day-to-day matters, such as where would be the best place for Stefanie to ride horses. Our son, Jeff, had been taking riding lessons at a barn called River Run Farm in Brewster, New York, about ninety minutes outside of the city. He thought Stefanie would enjoy it. One weekend that fall, we arranged to meet its riding instructor, Reinhardt.

After watching Stefanie ride for a few minutes Reinhardt decided she was a beginner and introduced us to a young woman riding instructor, Lucy. She was a high school senior and, at seventeen, was only a little taller than Stefanie. Lucy's horse, Playboy, was a spirited Mustang, but was very gentle with Stefanie. Our new routine became driving to River Run on Saturday mornings for Stefanie's lessons.

One day, Stefanie was riding Playboy in the indoor ring. He suddenly took off at a gallop, as he rounded one of the curves in the ring, and Stefanie fell off. She fell into a pile of hay. Her helmet and vest protected her, and she was not hurt. Lucy knew what to do. She asked Stefanie to climb back onto the saddle and showed her how to steer Playboy into a wall, if he ever tried to bolt like that again. Playboy did bolt again; but, this time, Stefanie deftly steered him toward the wall. Before Playboy hit the wall, he stopped. He never tried to run off again while Stefanie was in charge. That was the first of many tense moments I had while watching Stefanie ride. It was clear that Stefanie was taking horseback riding seriously. She followed Lucy's instructions religiously but still had fun.

We bought Stefanie her own riding gear: jodhpurs, boots, vest, helmet, and a saddle of which she took very good care. Mostly, Stefanie and the horse she was riding did groundwork, which meant working with the horse on the basic horse gaits of walking, trotting, cantering, but no jumping. Stefanie loved cantering when she would pick up some speed with the horse. We continued with Jay's approaches to controlling her allergies. We gave Stefanie an antihistamine before we left home, made sure the barn was a clean one, and, as soon as we were home, Stefanie would shower. Stefanie's allergies to horses were abating. We were still following the dairy-free and gluten-free diet for her that Dr. Brunoski had advised, along with giving her his allergy serum drops once a week.

Stefanie began writing more stories about horses. Stan gave her a black hardcover sketch book, which she used as a journal. Stefanie quickly became a cartoonist. She divided each page into a grid with boxes in each of which she would draw a cartoon horse named "Pancho" along with his adventures. Whether she was home, on a car ride, or any place she had free time, she spent hours writing and drawing in her book.

Stan and I continued to adjust our work lives in order to devote more of our attention to Stefanie. School was her refuge, and PS 116 seemed to fit Stefanie perfectly. Much of the education was project-based learning in which multiple subjects were taught through a single project, often on a topic of each student's choosing. Stefanie enjoyed integrating story with art, history, and sometimes with science. I don't remember her ever complaining about school or faking a stomach ache to get out of going to school. Stefanie made friends cautiously, but when she made a friend, it was a good friend.

By the time Christmas came, we were going to the Family Faith Program at St. Francis Xavier regularly. Angela almost never joined us; while she professed to be a Catholic, she didn't want to participate with us in the program.

Stefanie had joined the Children's Choir the previous year, so we attended the Christmas Eve Midnight Mass when her choir performed. Stefanie sang a solo, "The Little Drummer Boy," with her angelic voice. Stan and I were in tears as she sang for the audience of the thousand congregants in St. Francis Xavier Church. I looked up and felt Rosa's presence smiling on us, so proud of her little girl.

On Christmas Day, we hosted our annual large gathering. We invited Stefanie's great-grandmother and cousins again and, of course, Angela and Stefanie's uncle. David and Jeff brought friends; so it was a very diverse crowd. The kids hung out. Later, we all ate Christmas dinner and opened presents together. Somehow, despite the ongoing tension between Angela and the uncle, we were able to put it aside for family gatherings like this.

The summer after she turned eight, Stefanie went to a new day camp and enjoyed it. She made new friends and reported to us that she liked the activities. She came home each night a "good kind of tired," having spent the day outdoors. Angela had agreed that when Stefanie went to summer day camps, she could stay at our house during the week because the camp bus picked her up in the morning and dropped her off in the late afternoon at our house.

Angela had started her bachelor's degree studies when she was in prison through a prison college program with Mercy College and then continued when she lived at Woodycrest. After she graduated, Angela was admitted to Hunter College for a master's degree in social work, identifying herself as Hispanic on the application form. We recognized that this reference to being Hispanic was not true, as both her parents were Italian; but we said nothing, as this was her application. Stan often helped her with some of her more challenging subjects, such as statistics, working with her over the phone at night or sometimes in person when we were at her apartment.

Rosa's brother ("the uncle") had moved into Angela's apartment full-time. That summer, Stefanie's Friday nights and Saturday were spent with Angela and the uncle. Tensions were brewing among us. Angela and the uncle treated Stefanie like a china doll, a fragile object. Angela braided Stefanie's long hair very tightly and dressed her in matching outfits. This clothing usually had a designer label, not at all similar to the casual jeans, shorts, and t-shirts worn by most kids her age.

When we brought Stefanie to Angela's apartment after playing in the playground or climbing around at one of New York's zoos, Stefanie's hair was often mussed and sometimes there was dirt on her clothes. Angela would criticize me for not keeping Stefanie's braids perfectly in order and for letting her play around in dirt. I bit my tongue. Stefanie wasn't comfortable saying that she didn't want her hair braided and that she didn't mind dirt on her clothes. I remember one day Stefanie announced, "I'd like to get my hair cut." Angela's response was, "Do not even think about cutting off that beautiful dark brown hair" and that was the end of that conversation.

Angela and the uncle never took Stefanie anywhere, except to the playground where she would ride her bike. Usually, the three of them hung around the apartment watching TV. The two distinct lives Stefanie lived, at our house and at Angela's apartment, were in stark contrast to each other. Stefanie never talked about what went on in Angela's apartment, and we never probed. We told Stefanie that she could always tell us anything she wanted, but when we would ask about her time with Angela and her uncle, Stefanie would just say that she didn't want to get in trouble. We were very concerned by that remark, but we were cautioned by our attorney that unless we had concrete evidence of abuse, we shouldn't say anything to Angela.

Angela graduated from Hunter with a master's degree in social work, which was a major accomplishment. Angela started to work in discharge planning in a city hospital. At the same time, she started to study to pass the test to get her license in social work. All the while, she continued to permit the uncle to live in her apartment. He was not a good influence on Stefanie. He was often arrested and spent time in the city jail, and he chain-smoked and routinely drank beer in Angela's apartment. He could not read, so he couldn't help Stefanie with her homework. He had no interest in her activities, like soccer and music lessons. Angela would never discuss the uncle or his negative impact on Stefanie with us.

After school ended, we took Stefanie to Miami for a week. I was working every day with the Dade County Homeless Trust, and Stan and Stefanie would explore Miami Beach. One day Stan decided to take Stefanie to the Miami Seaquarium to swim with the dolphins. Earlier Stan had taken her to Sea World to see the dolphins swim for a few minutes, but this was a bigger experience, actually swimming around with dolphins for half an hour or so. Stan called to see if there was availability that day. The staff member said, "Yes, we have one slot left at 11 a.m. How tall is your daughter?"

"About 4'3" tall," Stan replied.

"Well, one has to be 4'6" to swim with the dolphins," was the response.

"Wait a minute, let me measure her," Stan responded. "I haven't measured her height for a while." A minute later, he returned saying, "She has really grown. She is now 4'6'."

"OK, you can book a ticket for the 11 a.m. session," the clerk replied.

Stan did so and dashed off with Stefanie, and they arrived at Seaquarium just in time. Stefanie was given a wet suit and goggles and paired up with a young woman from Holland. They were invited into the pool and given some instructions about how one "swims with dolphins."

After about thirty minutes, the instructor announced the session had ended and the swimmers should exit the pool. Stefanie climbed out and stood on the deck, but as the instructor was telling the crowd more about swimming with the dolphins, Stefanie turned around and dove into the water to swim with the dolphins again. An instructor dove in to retrieve Stefanie from this unsupervised swimming. Stan reported to me that evening that Stefanie was a natural, swimming with ease alongside the dolphins.

## Stan

I made it my business to attend events whenever Stefanie was involved, even if they were held during the week. At this point in my life, I was now part of the Stony Brook administration, requiring me to be at the University five days per week. The drive from Manhattan to Stony Brook was about 1.5 hours if there were no traffic issues on the Long Island Expressway.

Those early years getting to know Stefanie were powerful lessons for me. I became one of Stefanie's loudest cheerleaders at her performances and games. I knew she counted on me being there. One afternoon, Stefanie was performing in a gymnastics program at the Vanderbilt Y. I left Stony Brook University early to make sure I was on time for her event. However, I ran smack into one of the nightmarish days on the Long Island Expressway with traffic congestion and stoppages all the way. It took me over two and a half hours to arrive at the Vanderbilt Y.

I parked my car and ran, hoping I could catch the end of her program; but, as I approached the front door, Stefanie was leaving with Angela. I quickly explained what had happened and apologized to Stefanie for missing her performance. All Stefanie said, over and over again, was *"you were not here."* Those four words felt like a dagger in my heart. My rational explanation meant nothing to her because I had disappointed her and had violated her trust that I would always be there for her. I decided it was time to find a job in New York City because I did not want to risk disappointing her again, nor experiencing the deep sense of failure I felt at that moment.

### The Downtown Soccer League

In the fall of 1999, Stefanie decided she wanted to play soccer. She had played soccer on the school playground, enjoyed running, and had the skill needed to kick the ball. Claire found a local league for girls Stefanie's age, the Downtown United Soccer Club, and Stefanie was assigned to a team coached by Jane Smythe, the only woman coach in the league. Most of the coaches were fathers of one of the team's players. One of Jane's daughters was on Stefanie's team. Jane's philosophy and approach were different from those of the other coaches. Her idea of playing soccer was to have fun, be safe, and enjoy the competition of team sports. There was a large variation in the level of skills playing soccer among the girls on Jane's team. Some, like Stefanie, were physically fit, but had no experience playing soccer or knowledge of the game. Others were more challenged. However, this did not matter to Jane, who gave everyone on the team an opportunity to play different positions. Winning was less important to Jane than sticking to the principles of safety, sportsmanship, and enjoyment. The team was disappointed if they lost, but Jane always encouraged them to do their best and applauded them for their effort at the end of each game.

It quickly became clear to me that Jane's approach was the exception. Other coaches screamed and yelled at their players if they made a mistake or when they lost the game. They were often particularly hard on their own daughters, who sometimes were brought to tears. I can only wonder what impact this had on the self-confidence of those girls. I had never played soccer and did not know the game's rules at all. My job was to help carry equipment, give the players water when they came off the field, and be their cheerleader. It was important for the players to feel good about themselves, because it is too easy to make girls feel that they are less capable than boys. I wholeheartedly agreed with Jane's approach, because Claire and I wanted Stefanie to play soccer to help her feel good about herself. Given all she had been through as a very young child, it was no wonder she believed she could not do anything when we first became involved in raising her. I must admit I did feel excited whenever our team made a great play. Watching the girls gain confidence over the course of the season was wonderful.

On one occasion, Stefanie ran from a larger girl on the opposing team and came over to the edge of the field crying. She was very upset, because the girl scared her, but also Stefanie felt she had let her team down by running away.

"What can I do?" she asked me.

"You can run at that girl and show her you're not afraid of her," I advised. Stefanie went back on the soccer field and in a few minutes was confronted by the same girl. This time Stefanie ran right toward her. The girl was so surprised that she turned and ran in the opposite direction. The look on Stefanie's face was priceless.

At the end of the soccer season, Jane asked the team and the girls' parents if they wanted to play as a team in the softball league that was starting up that summer. Stefanie was enthusiastic about learning a new sport.

### Softball Flashback

The time was 1951 or 1952, and I was a kid, not much older than Stefanie and her teammates. We stayed in New York that summer because my father purchased his first car, a two-door Nash Rambler. As a result, we could not afford to go to Rockaway that summer. So I joined a summer softball league with most of the neighborhood kids I hung out with and played sports with during the year. We were known as the Wildcats. The summer league involved teams from New York City's five boroughs—Manhattan, the Bronx, Brooklyn, Queens, and Staten Island. First, we competed against teams in our home borough of the Bronx. The winner of the borough competition moved on to playing the winners of the other boroughs. The ultimate winner was declared the New York City Softball Champion. We lost in the final round to Brooklyn. You never saw a sadder group of kids.

I played catcher and was very good at the position, mostly because I talked with my pitcher. To my pitcher, I spoke words of encouragement and to the batter, words to rattle his concentration. I was good at my job.

One day, when Stefanie's team was a player short, I volunteered to serve as the catcher. Jane worked the same way in softball, as she had as a soccer coach, and wanted the girls to have fun and experience playing different positions. She chose Sarah, one of the least athletic girls on the team, to be the pitcher. Sarah had no idea what to do, so I did what came naturally to me, and I began talking to her. I would periodically walk out to the mound, like in big league games and movies, to talk with her about relaxing and breathing and how to hold and pitch the ball. Behind the plate, I would praise her whenever she pitched a ball that came even close to home plate. I smiled at her, and I encouraged her. After a while, she settled down and her pitching improved.

By the beginning of the third inning, the game had gotten into a rhythm. We were losing by several runs, but Sarah was throwing the ball over the plate, and our team was doing a reasonable job fielding the other team's hits. Suddenly, out of right field, Stefanie ran to the infield screaming at me.

"You do not love me anymore, and you love Sarah more than me," she cried.

Everyone looked dumbfounded at what was happening. Obviously, Stefanie had interpreted my helping Sarah as an expression of loving her. If I loved Sarah, Stefanie concluded, I could not also love her. The game stopped and all attention was focused on Stefanie. I hugged Stefanie and explained that I loved her and that my talks and encouragement of Sarah were simply part of my job as catcher. I do not think my explanation eliminated Stefanie's fears, but she stopped crying and became calmer. The game continued. This was the only time Stefanie became this upset throughout the rest of the softball season.

After writing this story about Stefanie and the softball game and remembering how unusual it was for Stefanie to have felt threatened, I realized that I had had a similar episode in my own childhood when my Uncle Seymour told me he was going to marry my Aunt Dorothy, and I drew the erroneous conclusion that meant he no longer loved me.

## Claire

Soccer continued to be Stefanie's sport for several years, with Jane as a great coach and mentor for her.

Stefanie also continued gymnastics classes after school at the Sutton Gym. I have vivid memories of either myself alone or with Stan waiting for Stefanie to complete an activity: soccer, gymnastics, viola, or acting classes. Armed with my briefcase, I did most of my work-related writing and thinking in these waiting sessions. This was before laptops, but legal pads worked just as well. Stefanie thrived on these outlets and never complained about being overloaded with activities. They were all different, but they worked like a mosaic for her, helping her to explore different sides of herself.

On Sundays, we continued to go to the St. Francis Xavier Family Faith Program. Parents gathered in a room in the church's school building and talked about raising kids and other topics: coming back to the Church, our endeavors, and our challenges. The kids were in another classroom with the Family Faith Director, a young woman named Leslie. She shared with us that Stefanie was engaged with the program, often volunteering for parts in the Christmas or Easter plays. Leslie brought to this program a multifaith dimension, and Stan became the teacher on all matters of the Jewish faith.

When December came, the kids planned a Chanukah celebration one Sunday, at which Stefanie taught them how to spin a dreidel. That Sunday, I overheard one of the other kids ask Stefanie if she was Jewish. "I'm part Jewish and part Puerto Rican," she responded. Stefanie was adding to her identity in a very matter of fact way. It was interesting that Stefanie's comparison of her two identities was not to Catholicism and Judaism, but rather to the cultural components of being Jewish and Puerto Rican.

Stefanie had always had an interest in music, and we had arranged piano lessons when she was about seven. We had a piano in our house, on which Stefanie would practice. But Angela didn't encourage music lessons or even the suggestion of a portable keyboard in their apartment so Stefanie could continue to practice. After a year, we stopped the piano lessons.

One of Stefanie's friends at the Family Faith Program, a girl her age named Susan, played the violin. Stefanie asked Susan and her mother about violin lessons. Susan's mother suggested Stefanie start viola lessons because the school needed viola players. Stefanie mulled that over and then asked us if she could take viola lessons at the Third Street Music School where Susan took her violin lessons.

"I want to play a portable instrument that I can carry with me between our house and Angela's apartment," Stefanie explained.

She did not comment on Angela's lack of support for playing an instrument or the aborted piano lessons. She just figured out a way to deal with it. We were open to viola lessons and made a date to visit the school and find a teacher. Stefanie was matched up with Laura Warren, a young musician who played both the viola and violin. We purchased a viola for Stefanie and so continued her musical journey. Laura had a great way with Stefanie, gentle but challenging.

In addition to private lessons, Third Street had group lessons on Saturdays, which worked well during the winter months when it was usually too cold to ride horses even indoors, as the indoor rings were rarely heated. We added viola lessons to our activity schedule. I am not sure how we managed all these activities. Stefanie was so eager to explore many avenues, and somehow it worked and didn't seem overwhelming. Bringing another practice into Stefanie's life did, however, create problems with Angela and her uncle. They questioned why Stefanie would want to learn to play the viola and wondered what it would do for her. We said learning to play an instrument would be an activity that she could carry through life and that she would meet new friends who shared her love of music. Thus, even viola lessons became a point of contention between us.

We were never clear on why Angela and Stefanie's uncle put up so much opposition to the positive things to which we exposed Stefanie. There were any number of activities they could have introduced in Stefanie's life, which did not require having a great deal of money. Eventually, it began to feel that they were intent on being at odds with anything we did.

Angela and her uncle questioned Stefanie as to why she needed to practice and "make all that noise." So, nightly practice sessions were difficult for Stefanie. We worked out a plan. We had learned from friends of ours in 12-step programs that sponsors are required to support new members. When the new member faced a challenge, the sponsor would "bookend" them by talking to the member before facing a challenging step, like a job interview, and then arrange a review session afterwards. I suggested we bookend her practice sessions. Stefanie understood the concept and called us before she started practicing and at the end of her half-hour session. To this day, we still use the practice of bookending when Stefanie is taking on a challenging task.

Stefanie continued to live at Angela's apartment during the school week and at home, with us, on the weekends and during parts of the school vacations. She was very engaged in school, in all her extracurricular activities, her homework, and playdates with friends. Managing her schedule by itself was time consuming; but we were also dealing with our emotional turmoil that emanated from our dealings with Angela and her uncle. They continued to object to most things we did with Stefanie and were unfriendly to the point of being hostile.

Some of this was natural, I suppose, as they wanted sole custody of Stefanie. Their reasons were not clear. Angela's health appeared stable, given that she took antiretroviral drugs to suppress her HIV infection, but her energy and stamina were limited. The uncle was unreliable at best. He lived in the apartment but would go out most evenings and not return until the next day. We suspected that, at times, Angela might be out as well when the uncle had promised to watch Stefanie but then didn't come home. We never knew this explicitly, but we had our suspicions. Stefanie needed at least one full-time adult to be with her overnight. We never knew exactly what went on at Angela's apartment, and we didn't want to press Stefanie to tell us.

As relations with Angela were getting more and more tenuous, we decided to engage another attorney, Robert Rubenstein, who had significant experience in the New York City family courts. He repeated the counsel of our friend Ruth, "Don't push for custody until there is a precipitating incident that *changes the circumstances* of Stefanie's living arrangements, or you could lose it all." So, we kept quiet and did not push things with Angela and the uncle. It was difficult for both of us to see some of the negative things to which Stefanie was exposed and say nothing, but we kept our emotions and comments to ourselves. Had we felt she was in any physical danger, that would have changed our approach.

In June 1999, Stan became the dean of the School of Public Affairs at Baruch College. It was on Lexington Avenue, just a few blocks from our house. For Stan, this was a major academic appointment. He was happy about working in the city and being able to be around for Stefanie when she needed him. I was still heading HSI, the not-for-profit housing organization I had founded thirteen years earlier. My workload was heavy, but I could often set my own schedule. Between all that we had going with Stefanie and our jobs, we had little time to think about the predicament we were in as guardians and co-custodians of Stefanie. We also did not always have much time or energy for ourselves or friends. It was tough, but we did our best.

I am not sure how I had the energy to take on something else, but I had a long-standing interest in "natural medicine" and, for years, had wanted to train to become a practitioner. But when Stefanie came into our lives, I dismissed the idea. However, that summer, when Stefanie was at the New Jersey day camp and Stan started his new dean's job, I decided to take a two-week foot reflexology class. To become certified, I had to complete ninety one-hour practice sessions on individuals. Stefanie and Stan loved that. Stefanie began to call my sessions on their feet "professional foot rubs." I realized how much Stefanie yearned for warm human contact, as she asked for foot rubs almost every night that she was with us.

Given the chaos in Angela's apartment with the comings and goings of Angela's girlfriends, Stefanie's uncle, and Angela's son, Barry, it was no surprise that Stefanie had trouble sleeping. We tried to calm her before going to bed by reading stories, playing soft music, and giving her warm soy milk to drink. Sometimes these sleeping aids helped; other times they did not. Often, I slept on an air mattress in her room to comfort her. Life was definitely easier now that Stan was working in the city, only a few blocks from Angela's apartment and our house.

Later in 2000, we decided to tackle something Stefanie had been wanting to do for a while—correct the eye problem she was born with called wandering eyes. While this condition did not interfere with her eyesight, she felt that it did alter her appearance. Stan and I did not push her to have the operation, but her fellow students had been commenting on her eyes. So that year Stefanie asked if she could have the eye operation. We said that we would investigate. Her ophthalmologist referred us to a well-respected eye surgeon, Dr. Wang. We had several visits with him, and he set the surgery date for early December.

We had worked out a plan with Angela and her uncle that would allow Stefanie to stay with us the night before, since we had to report for surgery at 5:00 a.m. at the New York Eye and Ear Hospital. I was terrified but tried to be calm with Stefanie as we got up, dressed, and headed to the hospital. Angela and her uncle met us at the hospital about 6 a.m. When the nurses took Stefanie to surgery, my heart skipped what I think were many beats.

During the hour-long surgery, we waited with Angela and the uncle. Stan took the opportunity to take Stefanie's uncle aside to broach a topic with him that had been simmering for a couple of weeks. One day, when we dropped Stefanie off at Angela's apartment, Stefanie had shown us photos that her uncle had taken of her while she was in the bathtub that she said had made her very uncomfortable. Realizing that confrontation only made things worse, both Stan and I approached most topics very gingerly and separately. Stan usually spoke with the uncle, while I usually spoke with Angela. These were dreaded moments for both of us, as we feared Angela and the uncle would fly into a rage and seek sole custody of Stefanie. So, we raised topics like this one as carefully as possible, so as not to spark a blow up.

When Stan talked to Stefanie's uncle that day, Stan explained that taking such photographs was inappropriate, and that the uncle should never do this again. The uncle promised that he would never again invade Stefanie's privacy. We had spoken with our attorneys who, once again, did not think this incident would meet the legal test of "precipitating event and change of circumstances" for us to make a convincing case for permanent full custody of Stefanie. We were appalled by the way the child welfare system worked against children. But we wanted to make sure that when we did get our day in court, we would have an airtight case to be awarded permanent sole custody of Stefanie.

When her surgery ended, Stefanie was whisked into the recovery room. I heard her crying, and I ran to the entrance and pleaded with the nurses to let me see her. When they finally did, I went to her and began to rub her feet. The reflexology course that I had taken the previous summer helped Stefanie calm down and fall asleep. The nurse in charge came over to me and asked if I would rub the feet of the other children in the recovery room. All of them were wailing, not so much from pain but from not being able to see, since their eyes were bandaged. One by one, I went to each of them and rendered a five-minute mini-reflexology treatment. One by one, they relaxed and dozed off. I began to see the miracle of this simple treatment.

After a few hours of post-op observation, the head nurse said that we could take Stefanie home. Angela had consented to our taking Stefanie to our house. We had taken the day off from work and had stocked the refrigerator with soft foods and cold compresses for her eyes. We knew we could give Stefanie our undivided attention. We set her up on the sofa in the living room to keep her comfortable and calm for the rest of the day.

The surgery was successful. Stefanie continued to wear glasses and was happy now with her appearance, which was becoming important to her. She was doing very well in school and thriving in the Talented and Gifted Program. Not only was the curriculum at a more advanced level than the regular classes, but there were also fewer disruptive students in the classroom. Having a calm learning atmosphere is important for any student, but especially for Stefanie, as she saw school as a refuge from the chaos in her everyday life at Angela's apartment.

One evening, Stefanie said to Stan and me, "Why didn't you arrange for me to get into the Talented and Gifted Program when I was younger? This is where I belong. I feel good in this class." We gave her a brief explanation about the earlier testing and told her that after that I had gone back to the principal who advised us that they had done away with testing but instead invited the student into the TAG classroom to see how he/she performed. This is what Stefanie had done, and she had excelled in this "interview." So she was accepted into the TAG program.

Another day, she surprised us when she showed us the book that they were reading in class, Elie Wiesel's *Dark Night*. We thought it was quite advanced for fourth graders, but Stefanie told us the story, letting us know that she understood the book. One evening, she told us over dinner, "I have written a letter to Mr. Wiesel asking him to come and speak to my class. Would you read it?"

"Of course," we responded. After reading the letter, we said, "Your letter is very clear. You are an excellent writer. We especially appreciate how you complimented his writing and explained how Mr. Wiesel's book affected you." We gave her a thumbs up, helped her find his address, and mailed the letter. Stefanie placed our home as her return address. In about a week, there was an envelope with Wiesel's return address in our mailbox. Stefanie was very excited and shared the letter with us. He declined the invitation, explaining that his schedule was extremely busy, but added, "I like nothing better than to speak to young people, especially those as sensitive as you" (Elie Wiesel, Letter to Stefanie Mercado, March 22, 2002).

In an effort to reach some common understandings, in early 1999, we had suggested to Angela that she, along with Stan and myself, begin therapy with a specialist in child development to better parent Stefanie. A friend recommended Dr. Martha Bartlett, who worked with a major child welfare agency. Stan and I met with her, and she seemed capable. Dr. Bartlett was African American, and we thought having a person of color to work with us would be reassuring for Stefanie. We brought Angela to the next session, and the three of us continued to meet once a week with Dr. Bartlett. Angela was a reluctant participant; but, over time, she opened up, mostly with a great deal of hostility, especially toward me. Looking back, I guess I know why we arranged these sessions, but I'm not sure why we continued.

We were hoping to improve communication with Angela and maybe with Stefanie's uncle. We were worried that Angela and her uncle might escalate our conflict, pressing further for full custody of Stefanie. We wanted to avoid that, as we knew they were not capable of giving Stefanie what she needed to grow into a happy, healthy adult. Importantly, we also knew that their approach to raising a child was not what Rosa had wanted. Rosa asked us to be Stefanie's guardians because she knew what would be best for Stefanie. Angela's custody order was meant as a temporary solution for days when Rosa was too ill to attend to Stefanie, an order that should not have been issued had the authorities done the proper investigation into Angela's past. And while we knew that Rosa had told us she did not want her brother involved in raising Stefanie, we had no evidential proof of that. Even though Dr. Bartlett did not admonish Angela for her outbursts and tirades against me in these sessions, we continued going for over a year.

Stan, age 3 years

Stan at Bar Mitzvah, age 13 years

Claire walking down aisle with father, Joe Haaga

Claire and Stan wedding, family picture (*left to right*: Sascha Altman DuBrul, Joe Haaga, Robert Berman, Serena Silva, Claire Altman, Sarah Altman, Jack Altman, David Altman, Stan Altman, Margaret Haaga, Jeff Altman)

Claire and Stan at their wedding, March 12, 1983

FREEDOM IN EXILE

ཕྱི་ཐབ་དང་ ཁེ་ལར་རྒྱུར་གི་དམ་དྲེག།

གཏུང་དགོའི་སྤྱར་ཁས་སརུས།

Stan and Claire
As a token of close bond and
with my prayers for your longtime
happiness.        H H

Above: 936 Woodycrest Avenue, Bronx,
NY (Photo credit: By Geo. P. Hall—The
Historical Marker Database, public
domain, https://commons.wikimedia.
org/w/index.php?curid=122319880)

Left: Inscription in *Freedom in Exile*
addressed to Stan and Claire Altman
(Photo credit: Courtesy, The Dalai
Lama)

Stefanie and her mother Rosa at the Highbridge-Woodycrest Center (HWC), 1991

Stefanie and Rosa at Second Anniversary of HWC, 1993 (*left to right*: Bronx Borough President Fernando Ferrer, Claire Altman, Chair of HWC Board, Rosa Mercado and her daughter Stefanie, Robert Sims, Ed Phelan, August 1993

Stefanie held by Mayor David Dinkins (*left to right*: New York City Mayor David Dinkins holding Stefanie Mercado, Claire Altman, August 1993

Stefanie as Pocahontas, Gramercy Park
Halloween party, fall 1995

Stefanie, Claire, and Stan, carriage ride, Central Park, New York City, fall 1995

Claire and Stefanie as dog in *Peter and the Wolf*, summer 1996

Stefanie and her kindergarten teacher, PS 116, Manhattan, fall 1996

Stefanie in gymnastics class, Sutton Gym, Manhattan, fall 1996

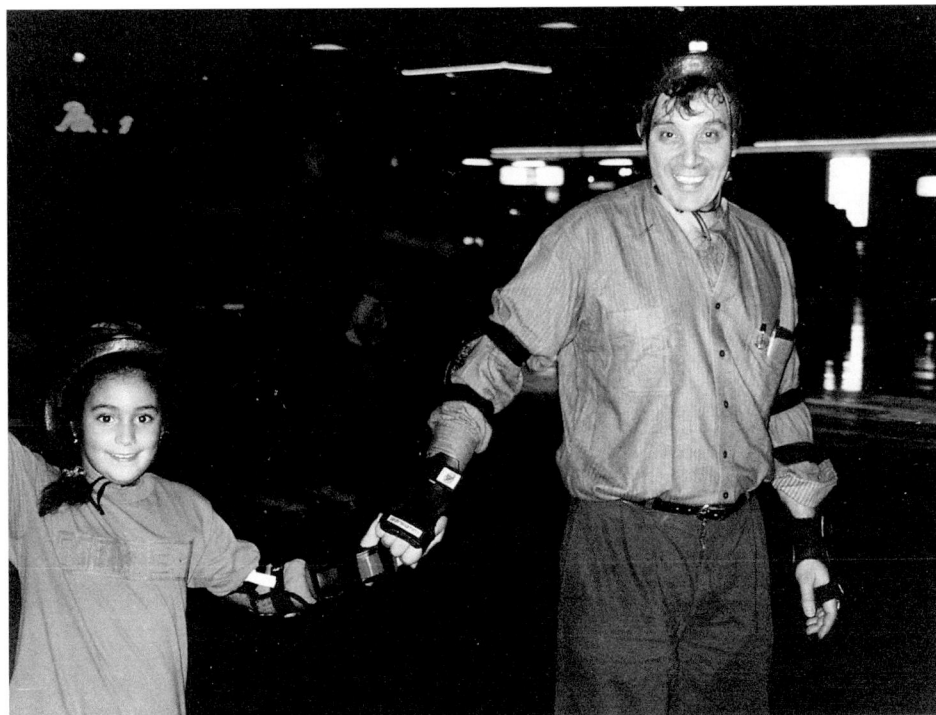

Stan and Stefanie roller-blading, Miami, Florida, winter 1998

Stefanie at River Run Farm with her instructor and horse Mustang, winter 1999

Stefanie swimming with dolphins, SeaWorld, Key Biscayne, Florida, winter 1999

Stefanie playing soccer with Downtown Soccer League, fall 2000

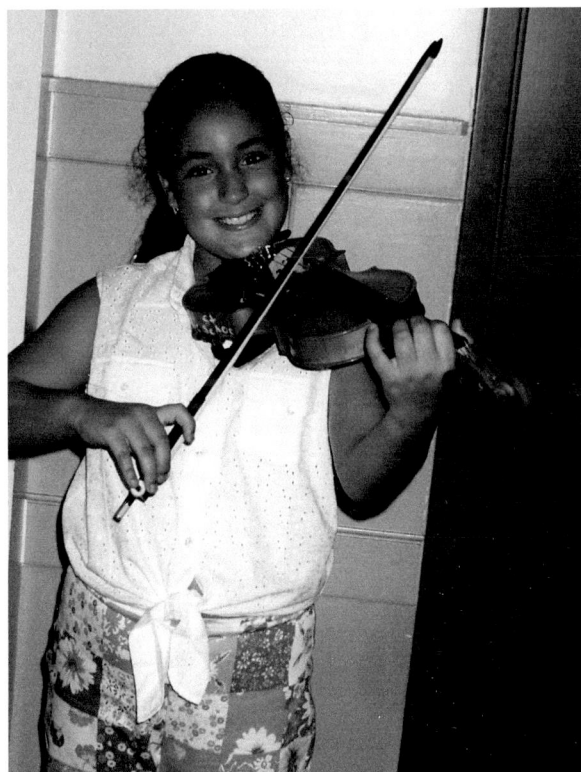

Stefanie playing viola

Stefanie with Grandpa Jack

Stefanie as Sherlock Holmes,
Halloween, fall 1999

Stan, Stefanie, and Claire, Rye Playland, Adoption Day, August 22, 2002

Jeff Altman, Stefanie, and David Altman at David's wedding to Irma, July 2003

Above: Stefanie drumming at Sri Sakthi Amma Peedam in Southern India, December 2003

Left: Stan, Stefanie, and Claire in Southern India, January 2003

Stefanie with Sri Sakthi Amma, January 2003

Stefanie with her horse Dixie Jazz, summer 2006

Stefanie's graduation from Ithaca College, May 2013 (*left to right*: David Altman holding baby Victoria, Irma Altman, Stefanie, Abigail in front, Sara, and Jeff Altman)

Stefanie with Professor Ford Hickson at graduation from London School of Hygiene and Tropical Medicine, March 2017, London

Stefanie with Hugh Jackman at Imperial Theatre, NYC, August, 2005

Altman family photo, September 2024 (*left to right*: Jess Chen, Stefanie, Claire, Stan, Robin, Sara and Jeff Altman, Irma, Victoria, and David Altman)

Stefanie in India, Diwali Festival, November 2023

# 10

■■■

# 2001

## Claire

In the spring of 2001, the not-for-profit I headed, Housing and Services, Inc. (HSI), once again needed more space for its offices. Stan and I had agreed with HSI when we purchased the building on East 35th Street in 1994 that if one party wanted to sell their condominium unit, we would sell the entire building since there was more value to selling the entire building than part of it. We put the building on the market, and Stan and I began looking for another place to live.

We were able to enter into a lease/purchase agreement for a brownstone on East 32nd Street, which had a lovely apartment on the garden level and parlor floor, with three apartments on the upper three floors. We believed that the rental income from the three apartments would be a good way to offset our cost for purchasing the building. We moved there in the spring of 2001. It was a fortuitous move as it put us right across the street from the playground of Stefanie's school where she was now in the fourth grade. When our teenaged helper wasn't available, this location made it easy for us to pick her up and help with her homework or take her to an activity before returning her to Angela's at night. Stefanie liked this arrangement. We saw more of each other, as she came to our house more often where we could work with her on homework whenever she needed help.

Stefanie had never talked much about living at Angela's but now, at age ten, she mentioned that Angela and her uncle didn't help her with her homework and pressed her to finish it quickly each night. They also insisted that she have dinner and take a bath before homework was tackled. Stefanie complained that by that time she was too tired to do her homework. We approached our lawyer again about obtaining full custody of Stefanie, but he urged us not to jump the gun without being able to make a more solid case for a *change of circumstances*. Proving that the situation at the other custodial home had changed sufficiently to be considered a *change of circumstances* was the key to getting a favorable hearing in family court.

Meanwhile, we continued to look for interesting activities for Stefanie after school so that she could explore more of her interests. We had heard about an after-school program called Skyshapers University designed to help young kids build their self-confidence. We described the program to Stefanie, and she was interested, so we enrolled her in the program, which was held in a loft in Manhattan's Tribeca neighborhood near the World Trade Center. The space was outfitted with full height cardboard figures of astronauts and cartoon characters who traveled into space.

They met once a week during which time the founder, Ellen Dunlap, used clever, playful ways to help children with time management, getting organized, and setting goals. We believed this was a good approach to help Stefanie with some of her fundamental self-management skills. Stefanie was up for this. The three of us attended the first session. Parents were allowed to come and sit in the back of the room as long as they stayed silent. Ms. Dunlap introduced a topic and then led the kids in a discussion. She showed them how she managed each issue, such as how to keep a calendar. Then each student would get up and describe how he/she felt they needed to improve in that area. This was a simple concept, but effective, and the kids responded well.

One day an eight-year-old boy stood in front of the class with his backpack in hand, turned it upside down, and dumped the contents on the floor, spilling all of his papers, books, cookies, and toys. He began, "My name is Thomas, and my goal is to become the best pediatrician in the country, but how is that possible unless I get organized? I first have to organize everything in my backpack."

Stefanie always looked forward to going to these classes and seemed to enjoy doing the exercises. One day as I was driving her home Stefanie said, "I have a dilemma."

"What's that?" I asked.

"I need to decide whether to go to your house now and work with Stan on my math problem for the week or go to Angela's, which is what she wants me to do."

"What do you want to do?" I asked.

"Well," Stefanie said, "I have to weigh the pros and cons. By the way, what are 'pros and cons?'"

I suppressed a chuckle. She had undoubtedly picked up the phrase and the process of weighing alternatives in the Skyshapers class but hadn't fully understood what it meant. I was glad that she was eager to learn more about some of these new ideas. We discussed what the "pros and cons" were of her current dilemma. By the time we arrived at our house, Stefanie had decided she'd like to stay there, do her math problem with Stan, have dinner with us, and then we could take her back to Angela's.

I called Angela and told her the plan. She was not happy, but I emphasized this was Stefanie's choice. The lessons Stefanie learned in the eight-week Skyshapers class stayed with her. Stan and I were always having to deal with dilemmas like this, and we tried to give Stefanie a voice in living in this bifurcated arrangement with Angela.

## Stan

### The New Math

In the spring of 2001, Stefanie was in the fourth grade and beginning to do math assignments in the form of word problems. She would get the assignment on Monday and have to turn in her solution on Friday. She was struggling with the assignments and would say to me that she was bad in math. I have seen too many young people conclude they were "bad" in math without realizing that the problem was more a function of not understanding the language of mathematics rather than an inability to think logically.

I suggested to Angela that I work with Stefanie and tutor her in math. She agreed. On Mondays I would pick Stefanie up after school to help her with math. This was easy since we were living at the time on 32nd Street across from where she exited school.

I realized that to start helping her on her assignment by trying to calculate the answer would be a mistake, because she had already concluded she was not good at math. I decided to try a different approach and start by helping her understand what the problem was that she was being asked to solve.

At the start, I explained to Stefanie that it was important to understand what you were being asked to do before we could decide what the problem was and how to approach solving it. We began by setting up the following schedule:

> Monday—we would both read the assignment and discuss what we thought the problem was. No calculations, just focusing on understanding the question.
>
> Tuesday—we would take the results of our discussion on Monday and talk about how we might go about solving the problem—focusing more on the concept of a solution than actually trying to solve it.
>
> Wednesday—we focused on developing a strategy for calculating the solution to the problem—while we might begin to perform some calculations, the focus of our efforts was to prepare for Thursday,
>
> Thursday was the day we took the strategy we developed on Wednesday and performed the calculations and found a solution to the week's problem. Once we had a solution, Stefanie was able to write up her result. The writing part came easily to her as I had learned over the years.

Stefanie's confidence increased as she began to spend more time understanding the problem before plunging into calculating her solution. Over the years, Stefanie has had to use quantitative methods. She had learned to identify the problem and what she needs to do to solve it. When she's not sure how to proceed, she calls me to discuss the problem. My role has been transformed into one of her mathematics coaches.

I learned a lot by working with Stefanie on mathematics and putting myself in "her shoes" rather than adopting the role of teacher and lecturing her. Working with Stefanie and wanting to help her move beyond her fears has forced me to take a deeper look at the assumptions under which I had been approaching teaching and working with young people.

## Claire

In the late spring of 2001, Stefanie announced to us that she'd like to go to sleepaway camp the upcoming summer, especially one with horses. We told her she'd need to check out the possibilities, and she began right away to look into options. Once Stefanie found a dozen camps that she wanted to explore further, she wrote asking for more information. In 2001, the internet was still in its formative stages. Instead, the camps sent videotapes. Once the materials had arrived, Stefanie shared, "I have made a grid of the qualities and programs I want in a camp. I plan to watch all the videos and rate the camps according to a scoring system I have created."

She had picked up some "systems thinking" from Skyshapers and how to do an analytical breakdown from Stan. She felt empowered to make her own choices. We applauded the idea.

After Stefanie watched camp videos for four to five hours, she announced, "I am done. Do you want to see how I graded them?"

"Of course," we responded.

"You see Hidden Valley Camp has the most points," Stefanie proudly announced. "It is in Maine. Do you know where that is? Have you been there?"

"Maine is in New England," we responded. "Yes, we have been there, and it's a beautiful state."

Stefanie explained her rating system to us. The key plus factors for Hidden Valley were that it had a horse program, was in a beautiful part of the country, was co-ed, and offered a wide range of activities, including music, pottery, and drama.

"Can I go there?" Stefanie implored.

"It's OK with us," I said, "but we have to see if there's an open slot. It's already April and we understand that camps fill up quickly."

"Please do that right away, if you will," Stefanie responded.

How could we say no? We would check first to see that there was an opening, then we planned to talk with Angela. We found out that friends of ours had sent their two boys to Hidden Valley when they were about Stefanie's age. Our friends thought the camp owners were a very sensitive and sensible couple who had adopted two children and that the programs were great. Two days later, we called the camp directors, Nancy and Paul. They told us there were a few slots left for the second session, which started in late July. The camp began taking kids at age nine, and Stefanie had just turned ten.

Then we broached the subject of a sleepaway camp with Angela. She did not object. She was becoming increasingly weak from her illnesses and likely welcomed a reprieve from childcaring. We reserved one of the open slots for the second session for Stefanie. She was ecstatic. We were taking a leap of faith that this camp would be good for her. Stefanie had never been away either from us or from Angela for weeks at a time. How would she manage in a completely foreign environment and all new people? We just felt that she had the courage to pursue things that she thought would be enjoyable and helpful to her.

That summer was a whirlwind. In June, we held the grand opening of a project I'd been working on for a couple of years, the Olive Leaf Wholeness Center, which we opened in the retail space in the Kenmore Hotel.

My organization had taken ownership of the Kenmore at the request of the New York City mayor's office after the US Marshals Service had seized the building in 1994 in a drug forfeiture action. The Kenmore Hotel was on East 23rd Street, right across from Baruch College and had, before the seizure, housed some 300 senior citizens, persons with mental illness and drug dealers. My organization acquired the building and had raised $25 million to complete a total renovation. HSI had then evicted the drug dealers and was operating the building as a single room occupancy hotel for very low-income people.

At the end of the renovation of the Kenmore, there was a retail space available for lease. But after two years, we had not found a tenant. The Board of Housing and Services stepped in and suggested that, given my long interest in alternative healing and having built programs utilizing acupuncture and herbs into the treatment regimen at the Highbridge-Woodycrest Center, I should consider opening an alternative health center in the vacant retail space in the Kenmore. My board figured that a wellness center could at least pay below market rent and generate some income for the building. By June of 2001, the wellness center was ready to open with newly renovated space and a core staff hired. The grand opening in early June was attended by a large crowd of well-wishers. We figured we were on our way to having a successful venture.

On the home front, in July my mother collapsed while my sister was taking her to a medical appointment in Memphis, Tennessee. Her doctor diagnosed her as having had a stroke and told my sister to take her directly to a nursing home. Once they arrived, mom collapsed again. She went into a coma shortly thereafter. Stan and I took the first plane to Memphis to be with her. After a few days, Stan flew back to New York to take care of Stefanie. Mom remained in a coma and then slipped into a peaceful passing. My sister and I organized her funeral, along with my sister's husband and my brother and his wife. The funeral was held on a sweltering hot Memphis July day. I was afraid we might have folks fainting at the cemetery, but everyone lasted through the service. I felt very alone without Stan at my side. When the person you love is your support system, it's easy to take their constant presence for granted until a situation like this. He had stayed in New York City because Stefanie's uncle had objected to her flying to Memphis for the funeral. Stan and I had concluded that it was more important that he stay with Stefanie.

After the funeral, I was in a daze. I stopped for an iced coffee at Starbucks, returned my rental car, and boarded the flight back to New York. The feeling of being alone lingered, but I knew Stan was with me in spirit and wondered how Stefanie was doing. I recognized that I had not allowed myself any period to grieve by spending time with my brother and sister processing our loss. But I felt I had to get back to New York to be with Stan and Stefanie, as things had been very intense between us and Angela, as well as with Stefanie's uncle. Despite having no legal standing in our custody agreement, he was threatening not to let her come to our house on the weekends. I didn't want to leave Stan to deal with this battle alone.

## Stan

Shortly after the fourth of July, 2001, Claire and I received the news that her mother's health condition had deteriorated after having a stroke. Claire's sister Kathy had taken her mother to a nursing home, and within hours of being admitted my mother-in-law had lapsed into a coma. Claire and I flew to Memphis to be with the family. After a few days, we decided that I should fly back to New York because we felt one of us needed to be with Stefanie. When I left Memphis on July 8th, her mother was still in a coma. It was my intention to return to Memphis with Stefanie over the weekend.

I called Angela to let her know I was planning to fly with Stefanie to Memphis over the weekend to be with Claire and that we did not expect her mother to live much longer. I explained that I would pick Stefanie up after school on Friday, fly down that night, and return on Sunday evening. Angela did not say a word. She simply handed the phone to Stefanie's uncle who proceeded to scream that he was going to pick Stefanie up on Friday and keep her at their apartment over the weekend.

Stefanie's uncle said he would not let her come with me to Memphis. I told him that our custody agreement was that Stefanie spent weekends, Friday afternoon after school through Sunday night with us. What he was demanding was unacceptable. I pointed out that Claire's mother was dying, and he was threatening me because I wanted Stefanie and me to be with Claire to support her. Her uncle insisted he had the right to keep Stefanie from going to Memphis. There were heated words between us, and, in the end, I did not go to Memphis so I could spend the weekend with Stefanie.

I spoke with Claire after my conversation with Stefanie's uncle. While she agreed with my decision to stay in New York with Stefanie, she was sad that I could not be with her during that difficult time. It broke my heart not to be there with her. In retrospect, this was an example of the lengths Claire and I were willing to go to so we could protect Stefanie.

On Saturday, July 14th Claire's mother passed away. Upon Claire's return to New York, we talked with Stefanie about Claire's mother's passing. Stefanie had come to Memphis with us twice and had met Claire's mother. She had not reached out to Stefanie much, so there was not really a relationship there. Despite that, it was Claire's mother and, as a family unit, we wanted Stefanie to understand this loss. We tried to keep life normal, and that included sharing joyful and sad times.

At the end of July, Stefanie would leave for four weeks at Hidden Valley Camp in Maine. This was the first time she was going to a sleepaway camp. We busied ourselves assembling all she needed to be outfitted for camp. Stefanie was very excited about shopping for camp clothes and gear. She hadn't had much activity in the great outdoors, so we shopped for more horse gear, hiking boots, jeans, and a trunk to hold it all. She enjoyed getting ready for her first trip on her own. About a week before camp began, a camp bus picked up all the campers' trunks at a central location. Stefanie's trunk was on its way.

## Claire

Most campers from New York traveled on the camp bus to Hidden Valley. Stefanie had stayed with us the night before leaving to get her last packing done. The next morning, we picked up Angela and drove to the pickup point at Lincoln Center. The bus arrived, and the driver began to load up the kids and their gear. It was time to say goodbye. Stefanie made sure she got to the front of the line. She hugged us, promised to write, and climbed aboard. There were no tears, no reluctance to go, just a smile, and "see you soon!" Stan and I were excited for her, but Angela was not too happy at letting her "baby" go.

We were thrilled that Stefanie was off to have this adventure, even though we were also nervous about her going off on her own. But we felt that it would be good for her. At 4:00 p.m., we had the answer. Stefanie called to say she had arrived and was settling into her cabin. They would have an all-camp meeting at 5:00 p.m. to begin their orientation.

We were so relieved that she had connected with the owners and some other kids on the bus and seemed comfortable being in a strange place almost four hundred miles away from home with people she'd never met before. Phone calls home were limited to one call a week to wean the campers from being in touch with family all the time. Stefanie called and wrote to us once a week. We never knew if she wrote to Angela. We only spoke to Angela once a week and spoke to her uncle as seldom as possible.

It was a welcome reprieve from the usual arguments and drama with the two of them.

Hidden Valley hosted a parents' weekend about midway through the four-week session. Angela did not want to go. We planned to fly to Portland, Maine, rent a car, and drive to Hidden Valley. We rented a house about half an hour away from the camp so we could spend the first weekend visiting Stefanie and have the rest of the week to relax at the house. We arrived around lunch time. When we entered the dining room and saw Stefanie, we almost didn't recognize her. She was very tanned with her hair in a pony tail. She ran over and hugged us with an air of self-confidence we had not seen for a while. We hugged for a long time realizing how much we missed her. It seemed that we had been away from each other for months, not a few weeks. We participated in the parent weekend activities and joined the campers and counsellors for the early evening meeting. We sat on the ground in the middle of the camp listening to announcements, singing songs, and feeling as if we were part of a community. Stan and I were smiling inside seeing Stefanie so relaxed and happy, just being a little girl.

Stefanie took us to "Nancy's Place," as Nancy's kitchen garden was called and where she helped Nancy work in her garden each morning. Stefanie loved to write stories under a weeping willow tree right beside the garden. She and Nancy had become fast friends. Stefanie had made herself at home. She showed us the zip line that she rode to skim across the treetops and the horses she rode several times a week.

When we retreated to our rented house, neither of us could remember the last time we had been by ourselves, comfortable that Stefanie was well taken care of and that we could relax. I even began to take notes for this book, having some sense that one day I would write about our journey. I believed that Stefanie would be our child one day without the complications of her living in two very different homes. But we didn't know how this would happen, as it seemed there were so many obstacles to our adopting her. Having made the choice not to challenge Angela's custody agreement, we were faced with the constant erosion of our relationship with her, which was exacerbated by the uncle having moved in as well. We just continued on with our love for Stefanie guiding our path and trying not to predict the outcome of this journey.

We returned to New York and took up our work before Stefanie came home from camp. She arrived back in mid-August, tan and fit, tired from four weeks of horseback riding, along with drama classes and workshops in stained glass and pottery. We hugged her at the bus drop-off point and then whisked her to our house. She couldn't stop talking about how much fun she had had at Hidden Valley. It had become a safe place for her. Her only request, besides going back the following summer, was that we help her apply to be in the special horse program called "Brumby," where she would live in a cabin in the middle of the horse fields. She would take care of the horses and teach younger girls to ride.

The rest of the summer flew by while Stefanie was getting ready to enter the fifth grade, assembling her school supplies and reading one of the required books. Stan was prepping for a new semester at Baruch, and I was busy launching our wellness center, the Olive Leaf Wholeness Center. We had hired practitioners of all types, physicians, yoga and massage therapists, acupuncturists, psychiatrists, physical therapists, and our medical director. For me, this was a full-time second job, as I was the chairman of the board, which required that I spend a lot of time launching this new enterprise.

School began September 6, 2001, right after Labor Day. Stefanie's fourth grade teacher, Ms. Russell, was moving with the class from the fourth grade up to the fifth grade. Stefanie was glad to have this continuity in teachers. Neither Stan nor I were experts in elementary-level education, but we had come to realize that the portfolio approach of PS 116 was just what Stefanie needed. She was not a rote learner; she learned by doing and drawing connections between subjects. She was and is an "integrator," a person who can bring subjects together in a way similar to completing a jigsaw puzzle to create a whole picture.

We helped Stefanie assemble her school supplies, read the last summer reading book that had been assigned, and get a few new clothes, always with Angela and Stefanie's uncle in the background objecting to almost everything we did with Stefanie.

Early in the fifth grade, New York City school children apply for their middle school, which begins in the sixth grade. Years before, we had been walking in Greenwich Village and Chelsea, two older residential neighborhoods on Manhattan's lower west side, with tree-lined streets, townhouses, and pocket parks (mini parks accessible to everyone). We had passed by a street fair on West 21st Street in front of an old school building with a sign out front, "Clinton School for Writers and Artists." Stefanie was eight at the time, and she read the sign immediately saying, "That's where I want to go to Middle School."

Stefanie had already made her decision, so we looked into Writers and Artists' admission requirements and helped her prepare whatever was needed.

Angela and Stefanie's uncle did not agree with Stefanie's decision to attend the School for Writers and Artists. Instead, they wanted her to attend her neighborhood school, which was closer to Angela's apartment. Little did we know how this argument would end up later that fall.

Tuesday, September 11th was Stan's birthday and primary election day in New York City. Stan and I planned to wake up early to vote in the primary. The key race was for mayor. Fernando Ferrer, the former borough president of the Bronx, was running against Mark Green, the public advocate for New York City. For some reason, both of us woke up at 4:00 a.m. as if hit by a thunderbolt. By 5:00 a.m., we could not go back to sleep, so we decided to have breakfast at our local all-night diner. We were the first ones at our polling place when it opened at 6:00 a.m., and we cast our votes for Ferrer, whom we had known for years.

Neither of us ever claimed to have any premonition about a sense of foreboding or why we woke up so early with an unusual restlessness. It just happened that way

We went home briefly, and then we each headed to our offices, Stan to Baruch College, and me to Housing and Services. At 8:20 a.m., I decided to go downstairs to grab a cup of coffee as it already felt like midday to me. As I walked onto the street, I saw a crowd gathered at the open windows of the bar next door. The owners were cleaning the bar, and above them they had on two television sets. I heard loud gasps from the small crowd. As I moved closer, the newscasters exclaimed, "The World Trade Center has been hit by a plane!" I didn't know how long before this had happened, but I stood there with everyone else in utter disbelief.

Then a second plane hit the second tower. I ran upstairs to my office and called Stan immediately. Someone had just come into his office yelling, "Turn on the news!" He turned on an old television in his office, which had never worked before that day. We could not believe what we were hearing. But once Stan assured me that he was OK, I went to PS 116 to check on Stefanie. Angela would have taken Stefanie to school at 8:00 a.m.

I literally ran into her school and up the stairs to her classroom where I found Ms. Russell speaking softly to the students. Stefanie was at her desk. I waved to her, and she waved back. Ms. Russell explained that the board of education had issued an order to keep the students in school and parents should pick them up at the usual dismissal time. I called Angela and Stan and told them Stefanie was OK.

I then called Norine, the manager of the Olive Leaf Wholeness Center, who had been my key partner in planning and opening this project.

"Did you hear what happened?" I asked. "Yes," Norine replied. She explained that she had just seen the three police officers who served our neighborhood.

"Our three beat cops were here having tea here when they got the call. They jumped in their car and went down to the World Trade Center," Norine elaborated.

"I guess we should close Olive Leaf since staff won't be able to get in to work," I said to Norine. "I hear they've closed the subways."

"No, Claire, we're a healing center; we have to stay open," Norine replied.

"You're so right. I'll be down in a few minutes," I said and hung up.

When I arrived, Norine was making green tea for neighbors and pass-ers-by streaming into Olive Leaf to have a moment of peace in our Zen Garden.

We heard later that morning that one of our beat cops was unscathed as he fought to rescue people from the crumbling World Trade Center, but his two partners went into the towers and died in the effort. We were overwhelmed with sadness upon hearing this tragic news, but we carried on. It is hard to describe what it was like being such a short distance from the towers, seeing the rising smoke, hearing the constant drone of sirens from firetrucks and ambulances, in utter shock along with everyone else, yet also trying to mobilize efforts to do what we could to help.

We heard from our local 13th Precinct on East 21st Street that police officers and firefighters had already been assigned to work on the "pile," as the rubble of the World Trade Center had been dubbed, searching for any survivors and for the bodies of those who perished. The pile was still burning, and the first responders working on it needed heavy socks and boots to protect their feet, heavy work gloves, hard hats, and face masks. They had no protective gear.

I talked with our manager at the Kenmore Hotel, the building which housed Olive Leaf, and said, "Peter, they need protective gear down at the pile. Will you take this $5,000 check from Olive Leaf and drive out to Queens to the hardware supplier we use and buy as many steel-toed boots, hard hats, heavy socks and gloves, and face masks as you can? Please bring the gear back to the firefighters' union headquarters across the street."

"Sure, I'm on it," Peter replied. He returned within an hour and shared the supplies with the union leaders who were very grateful for our donation.

Norine told me that some of the soot-covered first-responder police and firefighters had returned from the World Trade Center to their precincts and firehouses. They were in shock. They had lost dozens of their fellow officers and firefighters. Some of these first responders came to Olive Leaf for water and a place to rest. In the kitchen, which we used for natural cooking classes, Norine had set up a sandwich production line so we could give those who straggled in from their two-mile walk uptown to Olive Leaf something to eat.

By noon, Angela had picked up Stefanie at school and brought her to Olive Leaf, knowing that I would be there. Stefanie joined the sandwich brigade and was making peanut butter and jelly sandwiches. I hugged her and phoned Stan to let him know we were safe and helping the first responders. He was informing students, faculty, and staff of plans for the college and coordinating the closing of classes and buildings.

By mid-afternoon, Angela said she would take Stefanie to her father's house on Long Island for a few days. I had to agree. Manhattan was not a place for a young child if one had somewhere else to which you could escape. This disaster was incomprehensible. We were all trying to hold it together when all you really wanted to do was sit and cry. In addition to reports of all the lives lost when the towers crumbled, people who lived and worked in nearby offices and schools were stumbling up Third Avenue, the nearest north-south street to Olive Leaf. Covered in white soot, some had lost their shoes and were walking barefoot on a slow march uptown and all were dazed. There was a constant stream of police cars and fire engines blaring their sirens as they raced downtown to the World Trade Center. Jet fighter planes now flew overhead.

There were almost no cars or trucks on the streets, creating an eerie sense of foreboding in a city normally flooded with cars this time of day. The air was increasingly heavy with the smell of smoke. I hugged Stefanie and told her we would see her soon. I was anxious that she would feel abandoned, but I knew this time that Stan and I belonged in Manhattan to help. Stan and I had met Angela's father a few times. He seemed like a nice guy, had graduated from law school and had a small law practice.

When Stan finished his work at Baruch, he walked over to Olive Leaf. We barely had time to embrace and express our shock. The city had ordered most businesses and institutions to close for the rest of the week.

Of course, we canceled our plans to celebrate Stan's birthday that night. I had stayed at Olive Leaf all day doing what I could to help our staff support the first responders and others who found their way into our healing center, and it proved to be that on this horrific day. I greeted Stan and told him that the 13th Precinct was now bursting with officers and commanders because it had become the city's crisis police headquarters.

Without missing a beat, Stan volunteered.

"Why don't I make spaghetti and meatballs for dinner for the police at the 13th Precinct?" Stan offered.

"Great idea! I will buy the ingredients, and you can use the kitchen downstairs," I responded.

By the time I returned with three large bags of groceries, Stan was ready to start cooking. A couple of hours later, Stan and his volunteers had cooked up big pots of spaghetti and meatballs. At 5:00 p.m., Stan and I loaded up carts we had borrowed from the post office next door. We pushed the carts down the three blocks on Third Avenue to the 13th Precinct where the police officers greeted us with open arms. After we were scanned by the metal detectors, the police then put the big pots of spaghetti and meatballs through the metal detector. One could not be too careful.

After we served the officers, we walked wearily back to Olive Leaf feeling that we had done a little bit to relieve the suffering and trauma these men and women had faced. Around 8:00 p.m., the sergeant from the 13th Precinct came to Olive Leaf in a van to return our pots.

"Can you folks cook dinner for my men and women tomorrow night? I can't give them pizza every night, and I know this is going to be a long haul," he asked.

"Sure," Stan said, "see you tomorrow."

Stan and I looked at each other and surely had the same thought of "what do we do now?" Bob Callely immediately came to mind. Bob was our dear friend who had agreed ten years earlier to serve as the vice chair of Highbridge-Woodycrest Center, and he had been invaluable in helping to move that project along. Bob had also volunteered for years at a soup kitchen in midtown and was a pro at making large quantities of food and stretching it to feed hundreds. We were both energized about being able to help in the heat of the moment. But a more sustained effort required a pro, so we called Bob,

"How would you like to become a chef for first responders?" I asked.

"Sure, what do you need?" Bob said. "I'll meet you at Olive Leaf at nine tomorrow morning."

We held a hasty meeting with the Olive Leaf team and planned to assemble in the morning. It had been a long day. It was hard to grasp all that had happened since we woke up early and voted. Stan and I called Angela's father's house where Stefanie was ready to go to bed. We wished her good night and told her we would talk in the morning. Mayor Giuliani, who would emerge as the "Mayor of 9/11," announced that all New York City schools would be closed for the rest of the week.

I do not remember that Stan and I talked much when we got home. What was there to say? We caught up on some of the later news reports, and could feel ourselves crashing, mentally and physically drained. This was the worst disaster through which we had ever lived. No one knew what would follow. We collapsed in bed.

The next morning, we hurried to Olive Leaf to meet with Bob, who was already downstairs in our kitchen making lists of what foods, pots and pans, and volunteers we would need. Susan, Norine's cousin, offered to gather a cadre of volunteers to deliver the food each night to the precinct. Bob easily assumed the role of "chef in charge." Bob made a plan that ran like clockwork. Each morning, neighbors brought food donations as soon as we placed our shopping list on the front door. People started coming in to Olive Leaf to offer to volunteer to help with our work, for which we coined the phrase "Olive ReLeaf."

We sent those interested in helping with the food prep and delivery down to the kitchen to sign up with Bob. By noon, our kitchen had been converted from a macrobiotic teaching kitchen to a full scale "meat and potatoes" assembly line galley. Bob worked his magic with the donated food and by 5:00 p.m. had cooked for over 100 people. That night, Stan and I took the pots of dinner Bob had cooked to the 13th Precinct, where the head count had grown to over 250 first responders. Bob and his team continued to cook meals for 250 men and women for the next forty-five days. Bob brought great cheer to the kitchen staff, and his delicious meals were cooked and delivered flawlessly each evening.

The Olive Leaf crew under Norine's leadership continued to offer relief to first responders and neighbors. By noon on Thursday, Olive Leaf's reception area was mobbed with neighbors asking how they could volunteer to help. I helped staff our front desk by taking names and phone numbers and trying to assign people tasks.

The next few weeks were beyond hectic. Stefanie was back in school, but the after-school programs were closed, so she walked over to Olive Leaf each day after school and did her homework sitting in our reception area or Stan picked her up and brought her to our house on East 32nd Street.

As the country, and especially New York City, dealt with the tragedy we had just experienced, we all tried to return to some kind of normal life. Stan was still pitching in to help with the Olive ReLeaf program, including the meal preparation for first responders.

At the same time, Stan and I were trying to keep our home environment stable to support Stefanie who was still spending most of the week at Angela's apartment. That environment had become more unsettling as Angela and her uncle displayed a great deal of anger toward us. They increasingly pressed to have Stefanie with them all the time. Stan and I did the best we could to keep the time Stefanie spent with us calm and enjoyable. It seemed like a multiple front war. Stan and I were trying to deal civilly with Angela and the uncle who increasingly opposed everything we did with Stefanie. We were also helping Stan's 87-year-old father, Jack, who was suffering with colon cancer. Fortunately, Jack was still able to live alone in his apartment in Co-op City in the Bronx with the help of 24-hour aides.

Stefanie summed up our routines with Olive Re-Leaf one Friday after school when Stan brought her to Olive Leaf to hang out while we finished our workday there. I passed by Stefanie while she was sitting doing her homework in the reception area. At the top of the page where she was working on a math problem, she had written, "I'm trying to do my homework sitting here in a madhouse of healers." That was her very apt definition of Olive Leaf during the long and difficult aftermath of the 9/11 attacks.

Only a week after 9/11, the applications were open for New York City middle schools. Stefanie still held to the same choice that she had told us years before— the School for Writers and Artists. To apply, the school requested a complete portfolio with samples of her work in all her major subjects, including history, art, science, math, and English. I helped Stefanie rummage through her schoolwork that we had filed away in her closet so we could create her portfolio. Meanwhile, Stan was often on the phone with Stefanie's uncle who called several times a day to pick a fight. He would start every conversation with an implied threat saying, "We don't want Stefanie going to that school," or "We don't like her taking music lessons," or "We don't want Stefanie to stay at your house on weekends."

Stan never shared these talks with Stefanie. Privately, Stan would tell me what had transpired, and we would wring our hands and try to think about how to deal with Angela and Stefanie's uncle. As we knew relations with them were reaching a boiling point, we had engaged a new attorney, Robert Rubenstein, a few months earlier (as mentioned earlier) because we realized our relationships with the two of them were unraveling. Robert was a very experienced New York City Family Court attorney who came highly recommended and had a strategy for handling the current assaults on us from Angela and Stefanie's uncle.

In late September, during what was to be our final counseling session with Dr. Martha Bartlett, the social worker we had been seeing with

Angela for the previous eighteen months, Angela walked out of the session and announced she wasn't coming back.

Despite our best efforts, the weekly sessions hadn't accomplished much. They were consumed mostly with Angela screaming at me, saying things like, "Claire, you are trying to take over being the mother. I am Stefanie's mother."

In one earlier session, Angela's accusations were so poisonous that I had to leave the room. Both Stan and I felt that we were on thin ice, as we didn't want to be perceived as precipitating a problem with Angela. She always identified herself as Puerto Rican, although both her parents were Italian. Somehow, she convinced any authorities she came in contact with that she was Puerto Rican. She cast us as the outside "whities." When one of these eruptions occurred, I was devastated. Every nerve in my body was raw.

I was terrified that Angela would snatch Stefanie from us, and she would live the life Rosa never wanted for her. We were trying so hard to help Stefanie live a happy life, respecting her Hispanic heritage, honoring her mother, helping her to grow in self-confidence and self-esteem, and recognizing her unique qualities and strengths. From the time Stefanie came into our lives, we had supported her every interest, loved and cherished her, and did everything in our power to provide her with a happy childhood. This was how we parented this beautiful little girl, while facing the constant unwarranted wrath and opposition of her uncle and Angela at every step. To be called "the outside whities" by an Italian woman pretending she was Puerto Rican almost felt like a breaking point.

Growing up, I had never been comfortable with conflict. I always worked hard to minimize or cover up arguments between my parents. I was mostly quiet and never said anything when they had their weekly fights about money, other family members, or my mother's accusations that my father had failed in business. These encounters with Angela were reminiscent of arguments I witnessed in my family growing up. They ripped at my soul and instead of getting angry, I felt as if all the blood was drained from my body. My muscles had no strength, and I was at the point of collapse. Stan has always been my stalwart companion, and I felt even more dependent on him in these situations when I felt powerless to fight back.

By November, there were repeated arguments with Stefanie's uncle over where Stefanie would attend middle school. He and Angela insisted on her attending the local neighborhood school, while we held firm that she wanted to attend Writers and Artists. Early on the evening of

November 19th, Stan got a call from Stefanie's uncle who immediately started screaming about where Stefanie would attend middle school. Stan made it clear that it was Stefanie's choice and that she wanted to attend Writers and Artists. Little did we know at the time the dramatic events that would shortly unfold and change our lives forever.

# 11

## The Police Raid

### Stefanie

November 19, 2001. I was continuing to split my life between living with Angela and my uncle during the week and with Claire and Stan on the weekends. My uncle had become a type of father figure to me, but not fully. He was incapable emotionally, physically, and financially of being a father. My uncle had a whole host of problems of his own. He was an uninvolved father to the daughter he already had, and I was nine when I finally met her. I didn't know she was a part of his life until the moment when she came to our apartment for dinner one night. My uncle introduced her to Angela and me. I remember it being a pleasant evening. We had rice and beans, *chuletas* (Puerto Rican fried pork chops), and salad. But after she left, I never saw her again.

My uncle worked for a major clothing firm in midtown Manhattan. He told me his job was to help clean, maintain, and set up the showrooms whenever an event was scheduled. Slowly, my wardrobe had changed into the blocky red, white, and blue clothes that famously denoted the designer's label. I had these brand-name shirts, sweaters, and jackets. My uncle claimed he was given these items from the showroom for free in appreciation of his hard work. He began to come home with bags full of adult and children's clothes in various sizes. I understood what an employee discount was, but I was disturbed by the amount of clothes he brought home, though I couldn't figure out what bothered me.

Our closets began looking like store clothing racks, and my uncle continued to come home with more bags of "free clothes" given to him. We started having all sorts of people coming to the apartment to buy the clothes: neighbors, my uncle's friends, people from the building, and Angela's friends. For several months, we had customers arriving every night to buy this designer gear. My uncle seemed elated, as different people filtered in and out of our apartment, and he continued to bring home more bags of apparel to sell.

November 19th was a weekday night. I had just finished dinner and was in my room doing homework, which was due the next day, when I heard the doorbell ring. My uncle answered the door. I went into the hall to see who was there. A man and woman greeted him and said that they had heard about my uncle's collection and wanted to check it out. As any eager salesman would do, my uncle swung the door wide open and ushered them inside. The woman saw me as I peered at her and the man who had walked in with her. She seemed to have a protective energy. Her eye contact gave me that feeling. I felt a bit at ease, just some more strangers come to buy clothes. I turned around to attend to my homework and mind my own business. My uncle led the man and woman into the second bedroom where he kept his supply.

I heard murmurs and exclamations and assumed they were pulling out clothes to admire. I continued to scribble away at my homework, trying to make sense of a science problem, when I suddenly heard an outburst in the next room.

"NYPD! We're undercover."

"No, no, how . . . ?" my uncle said desperately.

Angela dashed into my room from the kitchen. She looked bewildered and confused. The woman soon popped out from the second bedroom, and she held up a metallic badge in a leather holder. "NYPD," she said.

"You are under arrest," she told Angela and asked her to step into the bedroom where my uncle and all the clothes were. Angela looked at me with sorrowful and scared eyes. She looked back at the female police officer and then walked meekly into the other bedroom. I sat there, completely in shock and scared.

"What about me?" I thought. "Was I under arrest?" I got up from my chair and stood paralyzed at the doorway to my room to watch. The female police officer backed Angela onto the bed. Suddenly, a rap of knocks sounded at the front door. One of the officers opened the door, and two more uniformed cops walked in. My stomach fell and twisted onto itself. My entire body buzzed with anxiety.

The female undercover police officer explained to the new officers that they had successfully busted Angela and my uncle. She walked over to where I was standing in the hallway, knelt down on one knee, and asked me if I was okay. I shrugged, wondering how I was supposed to take in what just happened. The female police officer gingerly took my hand and led me to the dining nook off of the living room in our apartment. She sat me down on one chair, and she took a seat by me.

"I am sorry you have to see this, but what your grownups have done is illegal." She described how my uncle had stolen clothes from his employer's showroom and was selling them for his own profit.

"This is bad, but we want to make sure you have somewhere to go. Do you have family or friends you can call who can take you in for tonight?" she asked me.

"*Stan and Claire,*" I thought without hesitation. "Yes, my guardians," I said.

"Why don't you call them to come get you? I'll wait right here as you make that phone call."

I remembered when grownups tell kids to memorize key phone numbers, because this might save you. Sure enough, here I was dialing the familiar number. It rang two or three times before Stan picked up.

"Hello," he said.

"Hi, it's me," I said timidly. This was the first time I was calling and asking for help.

"Hi, Stefanie, what's up?"

"My uncle and Angela are in trouble. Can . . . can you come?"

"I'll see you soon. Leaving now," Stan said.

The phone clicked, and the call ended. I hung up the receiver on the wall and walked back to the female police officer who was waiting.

"Are they coming?" she asked.

"Yes, he should be on his way now."

"Perfect," she said, then sighed. "Why don't you pack some clothes while we deal with them in the other room?"

I nodded my head in agreement and walked to my room. I filled my backpack for the next day, with my half-finished science homework and my notebooks. I threw some underwear, pants, and, regrettably, some designer t-shirts into another duffel bag. About twenty minutes later, Stan showed up.

"Hi, Stan Altman," he said as he reached out to shake hands with the female police officer. "I am Stefanie's guardian and here's my guardianship paper."

"Hi, I am Detective Mendez. She's in her room packing an overnight bag."

Stan appeared in my doorway with concerned-filled eyes. He asked if I was almost ready to go. I nodded and said I was. I packed my toothbrush and hairbrush and zipped up my bag.

"Ready," I said.

Stan nodded with a reassuring smile and led me out of the apartment, with his hand on my shoulder guiding me out protectively. He thanked the female police officer as we stepped out and closed the door behind us. I didn't even look at my uncle and Angela as I passed the door to Angela's bedroom.

"Wait, Smokey. He's still here." I looked up to Stan, "Can we take him?"

I was given the affirmative to harness Smokey up. He was a dog my uncle bought and gifted to me, but then claimed Smokey was his. As always, he had a sleight of hand that was never true. Smokey didn't know who he had to point his loyalty toward, but my uncle coddled him to the point where he favored my uncle a little more than me. I suppose taking Smokey that night was a comfort to me to prove something was mine when so much felt like it wasn't. I thought how callous and stupid this whole thing was. I felt dirty for even wearing anything with blocky red, white, and blue letters as I walked away that night.

The thought occurred to me that maybe Smokey and I would now be able to live with Stan and Claire permanently. Relieved and still a bit shaken, I walked with Stan to his blue Honda hatchback. We drove the short distance to their house on 32nd Street.

The rest of that night was a blur. I went to bed shortly after we got home. Restless and turning, I angrily wondered how Angela and my uncle could do what they'd been doing if they knew it was against the law. I asked myself if it was worth the risk of losing everything to stupidly sell clothes illegally like they did? Did they think it was worth it with a child in the house? All the questions that echoed in my head led to one conclusion: "But you're safe now." The beginning of an end had just begun. I was sure that my life was about to change for the better.

## Stan

It was November 19, 2001, and my relationship with Stefanie's uncle had deteriorated. He increasingly wanted to exercise control over Stefanie and separate her from Claire and me. He had no legal standing, since Claire and I were Stefanie's legal guardians and custody was shared only by Angela, Claire, and me. Earlier that evening, he and I talked on the phone about the middle school Stefanie would attend the following year. She wanted to go to the School for Writers and Artists, a portfolio school in Chelsea. He opposed the idea, saying that he and Angela wanted her to go to the neighborhood school because it would be easier to take Stefanie to school and pick her up. I wondered if he even thought of their rationale: They wanted her to attend the other school for their convenience, discounting Stefanie's gifts and preference.

Claire and I had guests for dinner. Around 7:00 p.m., Stefanie called, and I answered the telephone.

"Can I sleep over tonight?" she asked.

"Did your uncle agree to your sleeping over tonight?" I asked.

She was silent. "Yes, you can sleep over tonight. I will be over in twenty minutes," I said.

"Can you come over right now?" Stefanie asked.

I could hear the desperation in her voice.

"I will be right over," I said.

I called the garage where we parked our car and left our house feeling a deep pit in my stomach. The next five minutes were a blur. I felt like I was in a dark space with no control over what was happening. My car was waiting for me at the garage. My heart was racing as I drove to their apartment building. Fortunately, I found a parking space right in front of the building. I had a sense of foreboding as I entered and took the elevator to their floor. I knocked on the door. When it opened, I was greeted by a six-foot-tall muscular white guy who stepped into the hall.

"Who are you?" I asked.

"Who are you?" he replied.

"I am Stefanie's guardian," I said, as I took my guardianship paper from my wallet and showed him. He silently read the paper, then turned and reentered the apartment and closed the door. Another guy emerged a minute later and asked me the same question. I repeated my prior answer and showed him my guardianship paper. He informed me that he was a police officer.

"The woman and man inside the apartment say they are Stefanie's parents," he said.

"No, the woman was her mother's partner, and the man is Stefanie's uncle," I replied. "Wait here," he said, as though I was going somewhere.

A minute or two later, he returned with Stefanie who wanted to leave immediately. As we approached the elevator, Stefanie asked me if she could take her dog Smokey. I agreed. We went back to the apartment, and a police officer brought Smokey to us.

I was exhausted by the time we arrived home. I realized how much nervous energy I had expended to stay focused from the moment I left for my car, through dealing with the police, and getting Stefanie and Smokey safely home. I don't remember much about what happened next that night. At some point, Claire encouraged Stefanie to get ready for bed. One thing was very clear to us, as we were sure this night's events indicated a very clear change of circumstances in that Stefanie would never be in Angela's care again or around her uncle.

I slept heavily and took Stefanie to school the next day. Since we were living on 32nd Street, we were only a couple of hundred feet from the entrance to her elementary school's playground where students assembled before class. I waited with her for a few minutes. She smiled at me and said she was ready to start another day at school.

I went to my office at Baruch, and Claire went to family court to meet our lawyer and file a motion for sole custody of Stefanie, given the arrests the previous night. The police had used a "sting" operation to catch Stefanie's uncle and Angela, who were arrested for selling stolen clothing. The family court judge granted us temporary sole custody of Stefanie based on these facts.

I felt like I was living in a perpetual state of fear, expecting something terrible to happen at any moment. That evening, Angela called several times demanding that we return Stefanie to her. We refused and explained that the court order had given us sole temporary custody of Stefanie. After being released from jail two days later, on Thanksgiving morning, Stefanie's uncle showed up at our front door at 2:00 a.m. screaming for us to turn Stefanie over to him. I didn't open the door and threatened to call the police. When he refused to stop, I finally called the police, but when they arrived, he was gone.

Over the next few days, he called frequently and left threatening messages on my mobile phone saying, "I know where your office is at Baruch College. I'll come and kill you," and "I'll come and take back my dog and my niece."

He demanded that we return Smokey, insisting it was his dog. Rather than argue, we urged Stefanie to give Smokey back to her uncle as it would give him less to fight about. Stefanie agreed, and we decided to leave Smokey at a friend's workplace where the uncle could go and pick him up. Her uncle continued to call and threaten me, leaving messages laced with abusive language and threatening he would take Stefanie. I was so concerned about his threats that I notified the Baruch College Public Safety Office to look out for him because he could harm me and my family. I finally decided to report him to the police.

I purchased a device from Radio Shack which allowed me to copy voice mail messages from my mobile phone to a micro tape recorder. A few days later, I took a recording of his voice messages to the 17th Precinct at 167 E. 51st Street, and I reported the uncle's threatening messages. After playing the tape of his messages, the officer asked me to leave the tape with him which I did. Fortunately, I had made another copy for our records.

The next afternoon I received a call from a police officer who told me that Stefanie's uncle had been picked up and was in jail.

"Do you really want to send this man to jail?" the officer asked.

"No," I said. "I simply do not want him threatening me and my family and potentially harming us."

The officer asked me to play the tape for him again. After hearing it, he decided to keep her uncle in jail.

There were times I had flashbacks to my childhood and the terror I felt. Growing up in the streets of the South Bronx, I never knew when some kid would try and shake me down or want to fight for no particular reason. I experienced an overwhelming urge to escape the chaos around me, but the desire to protect Stefanie and Claire was stronger. Despite the negative emotions I was experiencing, I kept going. One lesson I learned from this experience was how deeply I had grown to love Stefanie. Little did I know what was ahead once we entered the family court system.

## Claire

I was not at Angela's apartment when the police officers arrested Angela and Stefanie's uncle, but I felt as if I had been. After Stefanie and Stan arrived at our house that fateful Monday night, we had a snack, and Stefanie finished her homework quickly. We told Stefanie that the next day, Stan would take her to school, and I would go to family court to seek an order allowing her to stay with us for now.

"That sounds good," Stefanie said.

We went upstairs and I placed a pair of pajamas on her bed. She had plenty of clothes at our house, so she never needed to bring a bag. She went to take a shower and opened the door a crack and threw the designer clothes she had been wearing into the hallway.

"Can you burn these clothes?" she said through the closed door. "I never want to see them again."

"Sure," I responded. The next day I took the clothes to the corner public trash can and deposited them there.

By the time Stefanie went to bed, it was after 10:00 p.m. Although it was late, I called Robert Rubenstein, our attorney, and relayed what had happened. I told him we wanted to obtain an immediate sole custody order and then file for permanent sole custody. Robert told me to meet him in Manhattan Family Court at 8:00 a.m. the next morning. That morning, we told Stefanie that we were working to prevent her from having to return to Angela's apartment and not to be put at risk ever again. Stefanie nodded in agreement

"That's what I want too," she said.

Stan explained to Stefanie that he would take her to school, and, if she needed us, she should ask her teacher for permission to call us. We would be right by our phones, and we would come to her within minutes. We told her not to leave the school with anyone but one of us. After Stan dropped Stefanie at school, he went to the school office and explained the situation. The staff gave him a form to fill out that forbade Stefanie to leave with anyone we listed who had a history of threatening her well-being. We had no idea the New York City public school system had this form, which they called a "blue card." It was kept in a file box on the school secretary's desk listing the only authorized people who could pick up a child. It was sad that we were not alone in needing a blue card.

With my copies of our guardianship papers, I met Robert in the family court building lobby. He said he would try to have our case placed on the judge's calendar that day so we could argue our motion for temporary sole custody and immediately seek an order of protection against the uncle. About six hours later, we were called into Judge Sally Schwartz's chambers.

Robert made some introductory remarks explaining why we were here. Then Judge Schwartz said, "Mrs. Altman, please state your relationship to the child Stefanie Mercado for the record."

"I, along with my husband, Stan Altman, are Stefanie's legal guardians," I replied.

"I understand there was an incident involving the child last night, Mrs. Altman; please explain what had happened," the judge directed.

When I finished retelling the previous night's saga, she said, "Mrs. Altman, I'm glad you're here—finally! What took you so long to make this motion?"

How could I tell her that in the challenging and confusing family court system I was afraid we'd lose Stefanie if we spoke up too soon? I said something about trying not to disrupt the "household" that Stefanie had lived in with her biological mother's partner. The judge did not waste any time in signing the motion granting us temporary custody of Stefanie and a temporary protection order against Stefanie's uncle.

I went back to our house. Stefanie and Stan were already home.

"Ready for your viola lesson, Stefanie?" I asked.

"Yes, sure. Can we have dinner at Lanza's afterwards?" she asked.

"Of course," Stan assured her. "I'd love some good Italian cooking too."

Stefanie picked up her viola case and led us out the door. On the way downtown, she told us about her day at school.

After her lesson, the three of us walked across First Avenue to Lanza's, a more than century-old restaurant that was a neighborhood haunt. Stefanie ordered her favorite comfort food, spaghetti and meatballs. We fell back into our usual pattern, bantering about the events of the day. We laughed a lot whenever we were together. My cell phone rang, and it was Angela. I stepped outside the restaurant so as not to disturb other diners and to avoid dealing with her in a public place, sure it was going to be acrimonious.

"You can bring Stefanie home now, I'm back at the apartment," Angela said.

"Angela, we're not bringing her back to your apartment. She's staying with us," I insisted.

"You can't do that, she's mine."

"No, she belongs to no one," I explained. "As her guardian, I went to family court today and, given what happened last night, Stan and I have been awarded temporary full custody of Stefanie."

Angela began screaming into the phone.

"I'm hanging up, Angela, we'll talk about this later." She continued to scream at me, and I ended the call.

When I returned to our table, Stefanie asked, "Who were you talking with?"

"Angela," I said. "I told her you would be staying with us. I described how I went to family court today and after the judge heard about what happened last night, she placed you in our sole custody for now. Is that OK with you, Stefanie?"

Stefanie nodded affirmatively and did not ask any questions. Perhaps she was relieved and didn't want to talk about it anymore. We finished dinner and made our way home. Stefanie went to bed early that night. We knew she had barely slept the night before. It was impossible to know how shaken she might have still been from seeing the police raid. Her trusty beagle, Jackson, whom we had gotten for Stefanie when she was nine, slept on the floor by her bed. We were all emotionally spent and knew that tomorrow would be a challenging day as well. We would have to work with our lawyer on a plan for getting a full hearing in the court.

The next morning began early as Stefanie's school started at 8:00 a.m. We had a school day routine: after breakfast, she and I walked Jackson; she would grab her bookbag and one or both of us would walk her across the street to her school. For now, we were skipping Jackson's morning walk together, because we were now looking over our shoulders to make sure Stefanie's uncle was not around. Stan took Stefanie to school, and that day after school we picked her up and took her to her gymnastics class. We did not want her to be out of our sight.

The following day was Thanksgiving. Stan and I had talked about taking dinner to the Bronx to celebrate Thanksgiving with his dad who loved company. We would also be far away from our neighborhood where Angela and Stefanie's uncle knew where to find us. Stefanie's uncle had already come to our house at 2:00 a.m. on Thanksgiving, after he was released from jail, screaming that he wanted us to give Stefanie to him. That was more than enough to convince us to stay out of sight.

We brought a turkey and all the trimmings for dinner up to Stan's father's apartment in the Bronx. Stefanie set the table, and we all ate at his small dining table. He was very fond of Stefanie and was glad to see us and we him.

## Stan

When Claire and I introduced Stefanie to horseback riding we thought of it as just another activity to do with her. But when we were threatened by Stefanie's uncle after the raid and we wanted to help Stefanie take her mind off the disturbing events of the previous week, getting her out of the city to go horseback riding became the one activity that we knew would engage Stefanie. We were concerned about her allergic reaction to horse dander, but on the advice of my cousin Jay, a horse vet, we had continued to give Stefanie an antihistamine before each ride. This helped to suppress her allergy, while her body built immunity to the horse dander. Stefanie took every opportunity she could to ask if she could ride. It became clear that being around horses was important to her.

Stefanie began to work regularly with Lucy. Every Saturday we would drive to River Run for Stefanie to have a riding lesson with Lucy.

## Claire

The next day we took Stefanie horseback riding. Stan made an appointment for her to ride at River Run. Sometimes she worked with Lucy, the young trainer, and other times, Reinhardt, the lead trainer worked with her. We had found that he was pretty good with Stefanie. When we arrived, Reinhardt had a "school horse" that was used for lessons; he was all saddled up and ready to ride. Stefanie had only completed a few lessons with Reinhardt, but she was fearless and focused when she was riding. She had a good ride that day. Afterwards, she dismounted her horse and led him to the wash stall. After the horse was washed and put out to graze, we headed to the local diner for a long lunch, trying to stay away from our house as long as possible.

Stefanie had not heard any of her uncle's threatening voicemail messages left on Stan's mobile phone, but Stan decided to visit the Midtown North Precinct that weekend to leave a copy of the tape from Stefanie's uncle's calls. Stefanie and I stayed home, baked brownies, and watched TV.

Stefanie returned to school on Monday. Our lives were clearly different now, but Stefanie managed to continue her routines— school, after-school activities, home for dinner and homework. She did not ask many questions about the family court process. The three of us just carried on as a family.

A week later, our lawyer, Robert, called to advise us that Angela had filed a petition to return custody of Stefanie to her. Angela's petition stated that while "she was arrested on 11/19/2001, the prior shared custody agreement stated the guardians would take care of the child only if she (Angela) was unable to take care of Stefanie due to her medical condition." Angela said she was incarcerated only for one day, and that the prior order of the family court should be modified to grant her full custody of Stefanie. The return date for this petition was December 6, 2001. We had not contemplated a contested custody hearing.

Robert also advised us that he had set up a meeting with a not-for-profit organization, which provided attorneys for children in family court proceedings. These attorneys were known as "law guardians." They are lawyers appointed by family court to represent children in custody, foster care, and adoption cases. Their conversations with the child, who is their client, are confidential. We had heard how helpful a law guardian can be as a private confidante of the child in a family court case.

After school that day, Stan and I explained this process to Stefanie.

"We talked with our attorney this morning, and Angela has filed papers for her to be given custody of you," I said. "We do not want this to happen, so we are opposing her. But first, the court will assign you an attorney, known as a law guardian. Tomorrow, all three of us will visit the offices of an organization that provides law guardians to children. You will be interviewed by the leading attorney, and then your own lawyer will be assigned to represent you."

Stefanie nodded as if to say she understood. Then, I explained further, "You can speak privately with the attorney and be honest about what you want, any concerns you have, and anything else you want to talk about. We will be right outside the office while you are talking to the attorney. We will not leave you there."

Stefanie nodded again and did not ask questions. We knew that this process was scary to her, as it would be for any child her age. We tried to reassure her that we had to go through this, because we wanted to make sure she would never have to return to Angela's. Stefanie nodded in understanding.

The next afternoon after school, the three of us went to the law guardians' offices in Lower Manhattan, a block from the family court building. When we got off the elevator, the head attorney for the organization greeted us, ushered us into an office, and asked us to wait as she whisked Stefanie into a back office to meet with her. After they met for fifteen minutes, she brought Stefanie back to us and then introduced us to the attorney who would represent Stefanie, Marta Jimenez, a young Hispanic attorney not much taller than Stefanie, with a warm smile.

"Stefanie, I'm going to be your attorney," she said. "That means I will be your representative in court. We'll meet by ourselves so you can tell me what you want, and I'll do my best to make sure you get what you want."

Then she took Stefanie back to her office to chat. When they came out of the office, Stefanie looked visibly more relaxed.

"I'll be working with Stefanie," she said. "She has told me she doesn't want to go back to Angela's apartment. I have explained that the court will most likely require that Stefanie visit Angela at least once a week, but I agree she shouldn't have to spend the night, as Stefanie has shared that she's not comfortable because her uncle lives there with Angela. The court recognizes that there is an order of protection for all three of you against her uncle."

We hugged Stefanie.

"Are you OK if Marta can work this out this way?" I asked. Stefanie nodded her head.

Marta then told us we had a court date in two days. Our attorney, Robert, had been advised by the court officer that given the heavy volume of family court cases, we had two choices (1) we could agree to have our case heard by a hearing officer, which would place us on the docket (court calendar) fairly quickly, or (2) we could wait for a judge to be assigned, which might take six months. Robert told us he had met the proposed hearing officer, Officer Smith, and she seemed reasonable. He advised us to take that option. We agreed, even though we were not sure what this option really meant.

We went back home, had dinner, and talked briefly about what would happen in the next few weeks. We reiterated to Stefanie that we wanted her to live with us permanently, and we wanted to adopt her as our daughter. We asked her how she felt about this.

Stefanie said softly, "That's what I want too."

Stan responded: "OK, Stefanie. We are going to fight to make this happen. Do not worry, we will take care of you."

These were words that were hard to say without tearing up, which both Stan and I did. We all hugged. We wanted Stefanie to know how happy we were with the prospect of adopting her.

The next day, we took Stefanie to school and then headed to family court to meet the hearing officer for the first time. We had met with our lawyer, Robert, the previous day, and he prepped us for what to expect. He had prepared a response to Angela's motion from the previous week and explained that he was also filing a motion for us to be granted sole permanent custody of Stefanie.

We walked with Robert the one block to the Manhattan Family Court, a seven-story black marble building, which was the source of its nickname: the Darth Vader Building. Inside, it lived up to the name. We went through the metal detector, and Stan's small pocketknife set it off. We stepped aside while a court officer logged in the pocket knife for Stan to retrieve when we left the building. We took the elevator to Hearing Officer Smith's courtroom which was just like another office but with different furniture. Officer Smith sat on one side of a long rectangular table, and we, as the plaintiffs, sat at another table. Angela and her attorney were at a third table. There were a few seats for spectators.

Hearing Officer Smith opened the proceedings by asking us to state for the record who we were and our relationship to Stefanie. The first item on the agenda was our testimony about why we wanted sole custody. Stan and I recounted that Stefanie's mother had asked us to become Stefanie's standby guardians, and then when she was unable to care for Stefanie or died, we would go to court to become Stefanie's permanent legal guardians. We explained that Stefanie's mother had died in 1996, five years before this proceeding.

Stan then explained that while we were Stefanie's legal guardians, we had agreed to share custody with Stefanie's mother's informal partner, Angela, in an attempt to work together to raise Stefanie. Over the last five years, ever since Stefanie's uncle had moved into Angela's apartment, our original cooperative relationship with Angela had broken down. Stan went on to say that we did not believe that Angela had Stefanie's best interests in mind, especially when Angela and Stefanie's uncle had been arrested for selling stolen goods in the apartment where Stefanie lived during the week. We knew that it was not "in the best interests of the child" to have her living in the middle of criminal activity and have her custodian Angela arrested and taken to jail in front of her eyes. Fortunately, Stefanie had called us, and Stan had picked her up fifteen minutes later. Now she was living with us in a safe environment. With no comments about what she had just heard, the hearing officer nodded and asked about our proposal for Stefanie's visitations with Angela.

Stefanie's law guardian, Marta Jimenez, spoke up and proposed that visitations with Angela be limited to three to four hours once a week and suggested Sunday afternoons. The hearing officer asked about Stefanie staying overnight at Angela's once a week. Marta insisted that this would not be possible because Stefanie's uncle lived with Angela and would be in the apartment. An order of protection against him had been issued for Stefanie's and our benefit. The hearing officer said she understood why Stefanie could not have overnight visits at Angela's apartment, given that the uncle lived there. It could not be more black-and-white. She then said that she would issue a visitation order for Stefanie to see Angela once a week on Sundays from 1:00 to 5:00 p.m., on the condition that the uncle would not be in or near the apartment and would not attempt to see Stefanie.

While this was an imperfect solution from our point of view, we accepted this plan. The visitation process began the following Sunday after our meeting with the St. Francis Family Faith Program and attending mass at St. Francis. We took Stefanie for a quick lunch at the local coffee shop, and then to Angela's apartment building. I remained in the car, and Stan took Stefanie upstairs. He had always been better at dealing with Angela and the uncle, as I had a hard time talking to both of them. When Stan came back downstairs to the car, we knew we would be back to pick up Stefanie at 5:00 p.m. sharp. That is exactly what we did that Sunday and for the next thirty-two weeks.

We had a quiet Christmas that year with only the three of us, David and Jeffrey. We wanted to keep things quiet when we could. In early January, Stefanie asked if we could go to a beauty shop that could do cornrows in her hair. We had found several beauty shops in Harlem and in the Bronx with hairdressers who knew how to do cornrows. I said "sure."

I had the idea that we could get her hair done in the Bronx and then go to visit her great-grandmother. We had not invited Stefanie's great-grandmother or cousins for Christmas, given that we were now embroiled in a family court battle with Angela, the only party with standing, but indirectly with Stefanie's entire biological family. Somehow, I was deluded into thinking her great-grandmother would still be on our side. She had always supported our taking care of Stefanie, telling us that she knew this is what Rosa wanted. And a couple of years earlier, the great-grandmother had written a letter to me spelling out how she wanted us to take care of Stefanie.

After Stefanie's hair was done, we drove further uptown to her great grandmother's apartment building. I parked on Southern Boulevard, the main thoroughfare which flanked one side of the building, a federally subsidized complex for low-income tenants. It was getting dark. Once we entered, we had to traverse the rubbish-strewn hallways, stench-filled elevators, and then go up to her floor where we had to walk down an outside hallway to her apartment. In our many visits to her over the previous four years, neither Stefanie nor I had commented to each other about this journey. We had done this many times and just wanted to reach Stefanie's great grandmother's apartment.

When her great-grandmother, a 4'8" small Puerto Rican woman with her gray hair tied back in a bun, opened the door, she grabbed Stefanie for a big hug and then gave me a hug. She brought us inside her apartment where Lisa, her twenty-year-old granddaughter, was sitting at the kitchen table holding her two-year-old daughter Mary. Lisa was nursing a nasty black eye with a piece of raw beef liver. I had heard about this natural remedy for black eyes but had never witnessed the treatment before.

I had just said hello to Lisa when the apartment door opened, and Lisa's husband, Juan, burst in. At the great-grandmother's request, I had helped Juan get a maintenance job in one of my not-for-profit's buildings. He was skilled, but within a few weeks, tenants reported that he was stealing from them. We had to fire him. He launched into cursing at me and calling me names. I stood, told Stefanie to find her jacket, and we dashed out of the apartment.

"Walk fast, Stefanie, we need to get out of here," I said.

I hustled Stefanie back across Southern Boulevard and into the car. I had never made such a dramatic and fast getaway as we did that night. I called Stan from my cell phone and told him we would be home soon.

"What happened there?" Stefanie asked.

"Juan is mad at me because I gave him a job at the one of HSI's buildings, but then we had to fire him after the tenants complained about him stealing."

Stefanie just shook her head.

"You saw Lisa's black eye?" I asked her.

"Was that from Juan?" Stefanie responded.

"Yes, I believe so. That is what some people do when they get angry."

Stefanie did not ask any more questions. We just rode downtown in silence. I knew this visit had closed the door to Stefanie wanting to see her biological family again.

Stefanie told us several times after our visit that her cousins had reached out to her on Facebook to try to connect with her, but she blocked them from her page. Stan picked up several messages from them on our home answering machine, but Stefanie said she did not want to talk to them. Her actions made clear the boundaries she was setting. Since the beginning of the guardianship, we had done everything possible to nurture her relationship with Rosa's family. But at ten, Stefanie was aware enough to formulate ideas about whom she wanted and did not want to be around.

We let Stefanie know that we were open to talking about this, but that it was okay if she didn't want to call them. It was becoming clear that Stefanie wanted to close off communication with her biological family. I had seen this all too often in my work. Often, when a child in a dysfunctional family was doing well in school or landed a good job, everyone in the family leaned on him or her for support, money, or to become a problem solver. Sometimes, the child who escaped and was doing well cracked under this pressure. I knew this could become the pattern with Stefanie. She needed time to separate from these family members to allow her to create her own future.

We made it through January. As February approached, we planned a small party at our house for Stefanie's birthday with some of her girlfriends from school for lunch, cake, and ice cream. We were just about to light the candles on her cake when the doorbell rang. When I opened the door, there was a middle-aged Hispanic woman I didn't recognize at first. Then I did.

"Hello, Joanna," I said. "How are you?"

After I recognized Stefanie's grandmother, I could tell she did not look well. It appeared to me that she was high. I had no idea how she knew about this party, but she did. I brought her into our living room where Stefanie was standing at the head of our dining table just about to blow out the candles on her cake. I was not sure if Stefanie knew who she was. I had only met Joanna once at Rosa's funeral, and neither Stefanie nor Angela had ever mentioned her. Stefanie gave Joanna a perfunctory hug and then went back to her friends. I tried to make conversation with Joanna, but there's only so much I could do or say to a person who was in another world. When her friends left, Stefanie did not mention Joanna. We had learned that it was best not to bring up family matters, but to let Stefanie initiate the conversation if she wanted to do so. Joanna didn't ask me or Stefanie how she was doing. She said nothing. After that, we never heard from Joanna. We had no way to contact her, no phone number or address.

# 12

## Family Court

### Claire

In the fall of 2001, we found ourselves facing another challenge—this one on the home front. There had been a construction mishap in the building next to where we were living on East 32nd Street. Workmen had seriously damaged a common wall, which rendered our house potentially unsound. We knew we had to move, as we didn't want to live through major renovation. So we moved back to the townhouse on East 35th Street. We could hardly believe it, but the vagaries of New York City real estate are unpredictable.

In some ways, it seemed it was time to move. We had lived on East 32nd Street across from Stefanie's school long enough for her to finish elementary school there. Since we hadn't exercised the purchase option on the East 32nd Street building and were still leasing it, we notified the owner that we would not exercise our purchase option.

Fortunately, we had not sold the East 35th Street property, so Stan and I bought HSI's share of the building, and we moved back to a familiar and much-loved home. It was also very familiar to Stefanie, as this was where we lived when she first began spending time with us. This move gave us more room. Indeed, Stefanie's suite included the entire fourth floor, a bedroom, sitting room and two baths. We created a bedroom and a bath for ourselves on the third floor, so we'd be close to her. The lower two floors became our living space and a home office for Stan.

Having to move was a minor challenge compared with the curve ball that life was about to throw us. In early 2002, Stan felt some kind of lump in his throat. Not wanting to go to a place of dread, I tried to calmly suggest that he see Tom Brunoski, our family doctor. Stan agreed and made the trip to Connecticut to see Tom. When he returned, he said that Tom wanted him to see an endocrinologist at Mount Sinai Hospital, because he detected lumps in the area of Stan's thyroid. Both of us were frightened about what this could be, but I urged Stan to make an appointment with the endocrinologist Tom had recommended.

Stan went to her office for an exam. The doctor recommended he have a biopsy. Stan said he was not ready to do this yet. Then the doctor became a bit confrontational insisting that he must have this done. Stan got up and walked out of the examination room and hospital.

But, of course, this issue did not go away. It was just put on hold until Stan decided what he wanted to do. This made me very anxious, as I was afraid the lump in Stan's throat might be malignant. I felt it would be better to know this earlier than later, but Stan would not hear of it.

I felt that Stan might be placing his own health on the back burner, because we were about to begin the trial in family court over whether we would obtain permanent sole custody of Stefanie. I knew Stan did not want any obstacles in the way of our case to ensure that we did everything possible to be awarded permanent custody of Stefanie and then adopt her. I'm not sure if Stan was nervous about what a biopsy would reveal, about our ongoing family court engagement, his dad's illness, or if something else was bothering him. But he was definitely anxious.

My father-in-law's condition was worsening. His doctors had determined that his colon cancer was virtually inoperable. Stan's father had 24-hour care, so he was not alone. He could still get around his apartment and the grounds of his building complex unassisted, and he was adamant about continuing to live in his own home. We visited him as often as we could, but on each visit, we could see that he was failing. Life was overwhelming, but we kept our sanity by putting one foot in front of another, relying on the strength of our love, trying to keep life as normal as possible for Stefanie, and holding on to each other as a family.

One piece of good news was that the court had denied Angela's motion to gain sole custody of Stefanie. On November 20, 2001, the day after the raid, we had been awarded full temporary custody of Stefanie, pending the outcome of our petition for sole permanent custody. That order stayed in place. In a parallel family court filing, we petitioned for Stefanie's adoption, which was placed on hold until the resolution of our custody case.

In December 2001, Angela's landlord brought an eviction proceeding against Angela because she had not reported the other occupants living in the apartment, namely Stefanie's uncle and on occasion her son. Worst of all was that Angela and the uncle had been arrested for selling stolen goods from the apartment. She had no defense to either charge. Angela agreed to vacate the apartment by November 6, 2002.

In early February, Stefanie's uncle pled guilty to a Class B misdemeanor involving criminal possession of stolen property. Despite the uncontested facts of the uncle's crime and Angela's upcoming eviction, we still had to schedule a trial in family court to prove that there had been a change of circumstances. Our trial was set to begin in mid-March 2002.

Meanwhile, we focused on Stefanie and giving her our full parenting attention when she was not in school or at one of her after-school activities. The three of us were also eagerly awaiting the letters from the three public middle schools to which Stefanie had applied. Although her first choice was Writers and Artists, Stefanie had also applied to her zoned school in our neighborhood and another specialized middle school. Finally, in early March, Stefanie received the letter for which she had hoped. Writers and Artists admitted her for the fall of 2002. We were all ecstatic. This is where Stefanie wanted to go, and we believed this would be a good fit for her. It was such a relief that we no longer had to factor in Angela's opposition.

Following the arrest of Angela and Stefanie's uncle in November 2001, we had requested an order of protection from him given his threats against us. Stan continued to work with the Manhattan District Attorney's Office to secure a long-term order of protection. Stan spoke with the assistant district attorney (ADA) multiple times to explain why Stefanie's uncle was a threatening influence. Finally, the ADA felt confident enough of our position to argue for a three-year order of protection, and she successfully made the case to the court.

Even though it was only a piece of paper, having the order offered us some solace. If the uncle harassed any of the three of us over the next three years, the order of protection gave us the right to return to court and seek a penalty against him. Stan carefully explained all of this to Stefanie who said she was glad we had the order. I think it brought us all closer. Stefanie saw that we loved her unconditionally as she watched Stan fight so hard for her protection.

Despite an extraordinary amount of trauma and turmoil for anyone, especially for a child, Stefanie's mood was brighter than it had been before she moved in with us full-time. She worked hard at school, spent time with friends at our house or theirs, rode horses on the weekends, and was eager to see plays or participate in other activities. One day, Stefanie asked if she could take musical theater classes. We did some research and found a program, City Lights, which produced several shows a year. We enrolled Stefanie in their classes, which completely engaged her. She loved singing, dancing, memorizing her lines, and the camaraderie of working alongside kids her age.

We still had a helper pick up Stefanie and bring her home after school. Stan or I would meet Stefanie at home and take her to whatever after-school activity was scheduled. Back at home, Stefanie would do her homework. We had dinner and shared what our days had been like. One evening over supper, Stefanie seemed particularly happy and lighthearted and said, "It's so great just to be a kid."

Stan and I smiled. It was a life-affirming moment. We had striven from day one to make it possible for her to just be a kid, and Stefanie had affirmed that what we were doing was working.

The first court date in the family court proceeding was March 19, 2002. We did not know what to expect. We told Stefanie that we were going to court to secure an order giving us permanent custody. She told us that she was glad we were doing this.

After we took her to school that morning, we headed downtown to the family court building. We were now familiar with the routine, the metal detector, sometimes a pat-down, and the long wait for an elevator with the throngs of other supplicants and their lawyers. Stan and I had spent many hours at our attorney's office over the last two and a half months preparing for this trial. These buildings and courtrooms are a somber environment. One is surrounded by people who are so obviously in the throes of tense and stressful exchanges. It is a place where lives are changed, for the worse and better, and entire futures altered.

We understood that to prevail, we first had to show there had been a *change of circumstances*. We thought, as did our lawyer, Robert, that this would be straightforward, given the events of the previous several months. Angela and Stefanie's uncle had been arrested for selling stolen goods from Angela's apartment. Indeed, we learned they had even involved Stefanie in this crime by insisting that she bag the clothes for the purchasers. We had repeatedly asked them not to sell clothes when Stefanie was there as she was exposed to both criminal activity and all sorts of people coming and going in and out of the apartment.

Angela told us to mind our own business. We thought we'd have to prove whether it would be in the best interests of the child for us to have full-time permanent custody of Stefanie, but the hearing officer did not want to hear about the best interests of the child until we had proved that there had been a change of circumstances.

We had followed Robert's advice and accepted having a hearing officer, rather than a judge, hear our case to begin the trial sooner. On March 19, 2002, we entered Hearing Officer Smith's courtroom, and she began reviewing a number of procedural items with Robert, Angela's attorney, and Stefanie's law guardian. Angela's attorney had not responded to items our attorney had requested, so there was a discussion about delivery, addresses, and phone numbers. The first hour of the trial was consumed by Angela's attorney arguing these procedural matters in the case by raising irrelevant issues.

As soon as the trial began, Angela's attorney made a motion to limit the production of evidence to the period after May 1995 when the family court had consented to a custody order to Angela. While our attorney opposed this motion, arguing that it was recognized in family court proceedings that it was important to have all relevant evidence admitted. The hearing officer, however, granted his motion. This was a key decision that went against our case, and we could not help but feel that things were going against us from the very start of the proceedings. The reason Rosa had agreed to give a custody order to Angela was so that Angela would have legal authorization to take Stefanie to the doctor or to meet with her teacher since Rosa was often too sick to handle these parental meetings.

We had learned long ago, after we entered into a shared custody arrangement with Angela, that there was a serious flaw in the process. In an unusual move, the court that issued the custody order in 1995 had not done a criminal background check of Angela as part of awarding the custody order. Yet the law required a criminal background check on anyone applying to be the guardian or custodian of a child.

It is possible that Angela would have been precluded from being awarded custody of Stefanie, given that Angela's record included one violent felony conviction and multiple misdemeanor convictions.

Back in 1995, New York State law did not require background checks of prospective guardians and custodians through the State's Child Abuse Registry. Today, clearance through the Child Abuse Registry is a requirement in custody, guardianship, and adoption cases. If there had been such a registry check of Angela, which became mandatory a few months after she got her custody order, it would most likely have shown that Angela had three children for whom her parental rights had been terminated.

Before our trial began, our attorney had issued a subpoena for both a child abuse registry background check and for the production of criminal records of Angela in New York City and state. These records, which had been produced in January of 2002, showed her prior convictions. However, given Hearing Officer Smith's ruling prohibiting the admission of evidence prior to March 1995, these records were not admitted in our case, which we believed prevented a full and fair hearing.

After the hearing officer decided these procedural matters, I was called to the witness stand and sworn in. Robert explained that Stan and I had brought this case for permanent custody of Stefanie because we believed that there had been a *change of circumstances* on the date of and leading up to the recent arrests. The hearing officer allowed opposing counsel to object to almost every question that Robert asked.

During cross examination, Angela's attorney then spent considerable time probing my background as a person and a parent. He asked many questions about the fact that Stan and I didn't have biological children of our own, that Stan's sons had been teenagers when we were married, and that they had not lived with us for long before they entered college. He also made a point that my siblings did not have children and asked how much time I'd spent with my young cousins. Smith permitted this information into the record, overruling Robert's objections to this line of questioning, arguing that it was irrelevant. Robert tried to limit Angela's attorney's questions, but to no avail.

I was on the stand for an exhausting eight hours over two days. This lengthy and assaultive line of questioning made me doubt my own worth as a parent. I do not think I have ever been so directly attacked by anyone. I was afraid to defend myself for fear of angering Smith. I was afraid that Smith would return Stefanie to Angela and that this child, whom we loved so deeply, would be thrown back into the chaos and danger from which she had just escaped.

Every time Robert spoke, he emphasized that our having custody of Stefanie was *in the best interests of the child*. But Angela's lawyer kept insisting that Angela's original custody order, issued in March 1995 while Rosa was still alive and before Stan and I had been designated as Stefanie's guardians, should prevail. Robert explained that Stan and I had been appointed Stefanie's guardians by her mother and that when we learned of Angela's custody order, we agreed to share custody with Angela until she was "no longer physically able to take care for Stefanie or if she passed away." Angela's lawyer tried to minimize the impact on Stefanie of the arrests of Angela and Stefanie's uncle, even though Stefanie had witnessed the entire event of their arrests.

It seemed obvious to us that the environment in which stolen goods were being sold, with unknown people coming and going from the apartment was *a change of circumstances* and detrimental to Stefanie. However, Robert explained to us again that until the issue of *change of circumstances* had been decided, the hearing officer would not even consider the issue of the *best interests of the child.*

Angela's attorney asked me, in great detail, about where Stefanie was living before and after her mother died and what happened in her life during this period. He also asked why we were seeking sole custody of Stefanie and about the agreement we reached with Angela after Rosa had died. Finally, he asked what had transpired between us and Angela.

I testified that our relationship with Angela had broken down almost completely in June of 2001 when Angela declared that she was Stefanie's sole parent, that she had the power to make all decisions regarding Stefanie, and that we could only step in if she asked us to do so. I also mentioned that Angela had told us that her Hepatitis C was worse, which could affect her capacity to take care of Stefanie. Then on Mother's Day of 2001, Angela refused to let Stefanie come to our house, which was a clear violation of our custody agreement with her. I further stated that Angela had accused me of "stealing" Stefanie because I didn't have children of my own.

Each day felt like a new battle, which if we lost, would harm Stefanie. We were emotionally drained but tried to keep our composure in the courtroom. Once we left, we were frozen with the fear of losing Stefanie and equally baffled by the family court system.

At another point in my testimony, I pointed out that Stefanie's living arrangements at Angela's apartment kept changing when Angela's girlfriends and then her son had moved in, and when Stefanie's uncle had come to live with Angela in 1999. Stefanie had told us that all of these events were unsettling and upsetting to her. I testified that in mid-2001, Stan and I noticed shelving in Angela's bedroom that was stocked with designer clothing. I told the court that Stefanie had complained to us that her uncle and Angela were selling these clothes in the evenings, making it hard for her to do her homework. Stefanie objected to being asked to help bag up clothes for customers. She had also told us that she wanted to talk with her therapist about how to deal with this, and we had encouraged her to do so.

I explained that Stan and I had raised our objections with Angela to the sale of this clothing in the apartment when Stefanie was present, as we felt that this also created an unsafe home life for Stefanie. No one knew who these customers were. Angela's response was that this was none of our business.

Hearing Officer Smith seemed to barely take note of my testimony about how disruptive and harmful these living conditions were for Stefanie. On cross examination, I also testified that:

1. Angela said she was not able to stand up to the uncle when he wanted to discipline or control Stefanie.
2. Angela admitted that she did not have the parenting skills needed to raise Stefanie.
3. Angela told us she "wanted Stefanie to stay a little girl" and that she liked to see Stefanie fat and fed her a high carbohydrate diet.
4. Angela said that she couldn't stop herself from yelling and screaming at Stefanie.

All of this evidence seemed to have no impact on the hearing officer. Stefanie's law guardian, Marta Jimenez, pursued some issues during her cross examination of me, in which I had the opportunity to testify about how Stefanie's health, particularly her asthma, was negatively affected by Angela's smoking, the constant pressure on Stefanie, and the stress that Angela and her uncle created in the household.

Smith asked Marta Jimenez to summarize the testimony that had not been heard. Marta focused on the facts that made this an unusual custody case. She stressed that, in order to inform the hearing officer as to what would be *in the best interests of the child,* and because none of the parties were related to Stefanie, it was important to analyze the relationship between Stefanie, Stan and Claire, and Rosa. Smith seemed to not listen to Marta.

## Stan

After Claire testified, it was my turn. I described my background, stressing my being a college professor and recounted the events following the arrests of Angela and Stefanie's uncle for selling stolen goods. When asked if I noticed any difference in Stefanie after the arrest, one of the things I presented was my analysis of Stefanie's mathematics grades. It showed a drop in her scores after the November 19, 2001, arrests. I thought this would show how disruptive the experience had been for her.

Angela's lawyer objected on the grounds I was simply manipulating numbers, and the differences did not mean anything. The hearing officer ruled in his favor. I felt defeated, as though I had failed Stefanie. With everything the officer had heard, it made me wonder how she could continue to rule in opposing counsel's favor.

Smith indicated I should leave the stand, as there were no further questions. As I was about to leave, I had a flash. I mentioned that Stefanie had showed us photographs that Stefanie's uncle had taken of her naked in the bathtub when she was a young child and a more recent photograph he had taken of her naked in the shower. I explained to Smith that when I learned of these photographs, I spoke to Stefanie's uncle and told him why taking photographs of her naked was inappropriate and he promised not to do it again.

At the end of the session, Smith indicated that she had considered granting Angela's lawyer's request for summary judgment; however, based on what she'd just heard she was now inclined to continue the hearings. The moment of fear I experienced when she began her comments evaporated when she decided not to grant summary judgment in Angela's favor.

When Claire and I left the family court, we felt drained and emotionally spent from the drama and apparent favor Smith showed to Angela and her lawyer. The emotional roller coaster we were on was taking its toll on us.

## Claire

In addition to the stress of these legal proceedings, Stan's father was hospitalized in mid-May 2002. Our sons David and Jeffrey were very attentive to their grandfather, visiting him often. We also visited Stan's father whenever we could in between family court dates. We went to the hospital to spend time with Jack on May 16, 2002, the day before our next court date. Stan and I knew that Jack didn't have long to live. He was eighty-seven and beloved by his nieces, nephews, and his many friends, who were devoted to him. Since we were due to pick up Stefanie from her after-school activity that day, Jeff came to stay with his grandfather overnight. We took Stefanie to a local restaurant for dinner.

When we returned home that night, we helped Stefanie with her homework and were in bed by 9:30 p.m. Around two in the morning, Jeff called to say that his grandfather had passed away. Stan thanked him for staying with his grandfather and told Jeff we'd see him later that day since we had a family court date at 9:00 a.m.

I urged Stan to have Robert ask for an adjournment, but Stan wouldn't hear of it. He did not want to give Angela any opportunity to gain an advantage with the hearing officer. So that morning, we told Stefanie that Grandpa Jack had passed away. The funeral would be the following day, but this morning we'd be at family court and would pick her up after school. We hugged as we always did before we parted in the morning. Stan and I were dazed when we entered Hearing Officer Smith's courtroom. We told our attorney about Stan's dad and requested that he ask Smith not to schedule any further hearings that week while we sat Shiva (a Jewish tradition of a seven-day period of formalized mourning by the family of the deceased).

The hearing scheduled for that day, May 17th, began with Stefanie's therapist, Diana George, who was called to testify. Stefanie had been seeing Diana for five years. She related well to Diana and shared many feelings with her. Diana testified that Stefanie was afraid to go back to Angela's apartment after the raid because Stefanie feared what would be going on there. Stefanie said that she was afraid that "things would be toppled over and the apartment cluttered." The therapist noted that children often blame themselves for traumatic events and that Stefanie was exhibiting this trait.

Next, Stan testified again. He was asked if Angela had ever asserted that she was the "primary decision maker" in matters involving Stefanie. Stan said, "Yes, that was the case." Stan further noted that it was obvious to us that Angela's health was deteriorating, and that she wanted the uncle to step into Angela's role when she died. Stan further testified that Stefanie was caught in the middle of this conflict between us and Angela and Stefanie's uncle. He said that, in his view, while we were looking out for *"the best interests of the child,"* Angela and her uncle were seeking "'possession of the child' much like a chattel."

The hearing officer then adjourned our case until June 3, 2002. Every time there was a lengthy adjournment between court dates, Stan, Stefanie, and I were thrown into limbo again. Stan and I felt that we were constantly at risk of losing Stefanie, whom we had come to love more than we could express. We believed that the three of us were in this together for life, and we couldn't conceive of having Stefanie removed from our family.

We talked with Robert about how Smith seemed to be favoring Angela. We were concerned that Smith had been unwilling to let Robert admit evidence that would shed light on the dangerous life Stefanie was experiencing when she was with Angela and her uncle.

Since our motion to call Angela as our witness had been denied, Robert made a motion to reopen our case, during which we would request that Angela be called as a hostile witness.

Before the June 3, 2002, court date, Angela's attorney filed another motion seeking summary judgment in her favor. If the hearing officer granted this motion, Angela would be awarded permanent custody of Stefanie, and our case would end. This was a frightening proposition for us. We engaged another lawyer to assist Robert in preparing a brief to fight this motion.

Our trial resumed on June 3, 2002. Stan and I were grieving his father's death. The last thing we wanted to do was go to family court, but Stan was particularly steadfast that we shouldn't ask for any adjournments. He said his father would have wanted us to continue our fight to become Stefanie's parents. Angela and her attorney were an hour late that day, and the hearing on their second motion for summary judgment didn't start until they arrived.

Robert called Dr. Malcolm Wilson to provide expert medical testimony on the state of Angela's health, based on his review of her medical records, which we had subpoenaed. He testified that Angela had advanced HIV and Hepatitis C, both of which had dramatically progressed in the last six months. She had been unable to continue the medications for both HIV and Hepatitis C due to the toxic side effects she experienced. Dr. Wilson further testified that Angela's records showed depression, anxiety, and difficulty sleeping, all indications that she was not capable of taking care of Stefanie.

Marta told the court that she believed that the Altmans had "met their burden in showing both *change of circumstances* and what is *in the best interests of the child*. Marta identified three principal factors that should be considered: (1) criminal incident in which Angela was arrested in front of the child, causing trauma; (2) testimony that there "was a dramatic decline in Angela's health from January 2001 to January 2002"; and (3) "serious deterioration in the communication and co-parenting arrangement that the Altmans and Angela had for many years." Marta then stated, "[A]ll of these elements have had an injurious impact on both the child's academic endeavors and on her mental health." She then asked that Angela's attorney's motion for summary judgment be dismissed.

Smith said she didn't believe Angela's health interfered with her taking care of Stefanie, and she didn't believe we had shown a *change of circumstances*.

"However," the hearing officer said, "I am concerned about two other things, and that is the testimony with regard to the incident and the arrest in November 2001, which occurred in the presence of the child and that she had to be removed at night." She paused. "I'm also concerned about the testimony of Mr. Altman, elicited on cross by Angela's attorney, that the uncle had walked in on the child in the bathroom when she was nude and took pictures of the child in the shower. . . . . Because of these factors, I'm not going to grant respondent's motion to dismiss."

Robert Rosenberg, our attorney, argued that the hearing officer should "reconsider her ruling" that "Petitioners (the Altmans) have not shown a change in circumstances." Angela's attorney said at the next court date, he would call Angela to testify. The hearing officer then said, "I would see no reason to have witnesses testify to the mother's ability to care for this child." Stefanie's attorney countered by saying that this is not a case about "unfitness." But Stan and I, along with our attorney and Stefanie's, were puzzled by the hearing officer's referral to Angela as "the mother." Did she actually believe that Angela was Stefanie's mother after all of the testimony that she had heard about Stefanie's mother having died in 1996 and that Stan and I had been appointed as Stefanie's guardians?

Marta then objected to a portion of the hearing officer's ruling, saying said that we had not needed to prove Angela's "unfitness," but our point had been to show a major *change in circumstances.*

Marta told the court, "There is case law in which change of circumstances has been found from less than what's actually already been entered into evidence." She continued, "The court's ruling did not address the deterioration of communication between the parties."

Smith responded that she didn't think deterioration of communication "rises to a *change of circumstance.*" Smith then adjourned the trial to June 5, 2002, and requested that the parties submit briefs on the matter of Stefanie's uncle taking photographs of Stefanie naked in the bathroom.

At that time, Robert requested in his motion that the hearing officer reopen our case given that certain case law had found that "[I]t was an error to deny a motion to re-open because in the family court, the court needs a complete record and all the available information."

Our motion also stated that "it is noteworthy that no investigation or clearance of the prospective custodian of the child, as is currently mandated, was required at that time (referring to the 1995 when Angela was originally granted custody of Stefanie)."

Robert explained that there was an exhibit attached to his motion, which included a stipulation between Angela's landlord and Angela requiring Angela to vacate the apartment where she and Stefanie had been living by November 6, 2002. Marta voiced her support for Robert's motion by distinguishing between case law in criminal court and family court, "in which (the Family Court) has 'parens patriae' (the state in the role of the parent) responsibility to look at the totality of the circumstances in any case involving the welfare and well-being of the child."

Marta stated that key issues in this case, criminal activity and housing, are two issues that are directly relevant to the welfare and *the best interests of the child*. For the next hour, Angela's attorney, Robert, and Smith had a lengthy discussion about Robert's motion to re-open our case, given his belief that in order to introduce all the necessary evidence into the record, he would need to reach back for information about Angela before 1995, and he would also need to call additional witnesses. Angela's attorney strenuously objected. Smith ordered both sides to submit briefs on Robert's motion to re-open by June 14th and said she would rule on it by the next court date, June 26th.

Robert's brief cited those factors that should be considered by a court in determining whether and how to modify custody provisions between parties, which include:

> the quality of the home environment and the parental guidance that the custodial parent provides for the child, the ability of each parent to provide for the children's emotional and intellectual development, with particular weight given to the parent more sensitive to the child's emotional needs and more likely to support a continuing relationship between the child and the non-custodial parent, especially if the child is already vulnerable in some way; the financial status and ability of each parent to provide for the child; the relative fitness of the respective parents, as well as the length of time the present custody arrangement has continued. Finally, the Court should ascertain the wishes of the child, especially where the child is mature enough to articulate to the Court his/her needs and preferences. (Notice of Motion, Stanley and Claire Altman, Petitioners, Index No. V-11983/01, p. 5–6, submitted June 14, 2002.)

On June 26th, Smith denied Robert's motion to re-open our case and call Angela as a "hostile witness" given that he had previously presented all the facts and arguments for the Altman case. Smith said she based her ruling on, "safeguarding the rights of Angela, the court's duty to determine *the best interests of the child*, and the need of the child for continuity, stability and closure." Smith further said there would be an opportunity to question witnesses in cross-examination during Angela's case and during cross-examination of Angela by Stefanie's attorney, Marta Jimenez. The trial was adjourned until July 9, 2002.

Each time the court adjourned, Stan and I would try to pick up things where we had left off before the last court appearance and try to help Stefanie cope with the massive uncertainty in her life, while simultaneously suppressing our own anxiety. It was no surprise that Stefanie's sleeping problems had been exacerbated since the raid with the ongoing uncertainty that followed. We all felt we were in a legal limbo, and that our lives were hanging in the balance of the vagaries of the family court process, which so far continued to ignore Angela's full history, discount the trauma of the police raid on Stefanie, and had further questions as to the seriousness of a man taking nude photos of his niece.

There were some moments when we felt that despite all that Stefanie was going through and her sleep issues, she was emerging from these experiences with a stronger sense of who she was and what she wanted from life. In early April 2002, Stefanie had shared with us a journal entry she had made that morning.

> I have changed so much over six months. I have been opening up to people and they have been reaching in for me. I feel as if I were in a box and couldn't get out. But when I was at my fullest, I broke through! I would never think that I would make friends with my classmates Julia and Sasha. They're both great people and I like them very much. I also would not have thought I would start to like a boy the way I do now!! LOL. I am really fascinated by how much I have broken out of my shell! Yes, I have done it! I am free now.

This eleven-year-old child had expressed her keen awareness of her own emotional and social growth, and written it as well as a high school student. It gave us both a sense of satisfaction that despite all the opposition we had faced from Angela and the uncle over these past few years, the safe nurturing environment we had provided for Stefanie was evidenced in her maturity and growing self-esteem. Against all those odds, our little family was solid, and Stefanie sharing her journal entry with us was another sign of that. This ongoing struggle to maintain and advance our family unit was worth the fight.

Seven months had passed since Stan and I were awarded temporary full-time custody of Stefanie, but the case was far from resolved. Stefanie's elementary school career, at PS 116, ended that June. Stefanie was now eleven, an age when most kids are pretty settled in school and their family lives. Sadly, that was not the case for her. While Stefanie was settled and enjoyed school, especially after the second grade when she entered the Talented and Gifted Program, her family life with Angela was chaotic.

She had difficulties getting to sleep at night. We worked with Stefanie on ways to help her get to sleep. I remember one vividly. Given her love of Broadway musicals, Stefanie had memorized the lyrics to many of the songs in the musicals she had seen. Some nights I would take her upstairs to her bedroom, and she would sing the lyrics to these songs until we both fell asleep, she in her bed and me sitting on the floor beside her bed. Her voice was clear and strong, and I can still hear her singing.

The trial continued on July 9th and July 11th when Angela's attorney called Angela to the stand. Over those two days, Angela testified about the great relationship she and Stefanie's uncle had with Stefanie. Angela's attorney asked if Smith would approve a visitation/overnight of Stefanie with Stefanie's uncle for the upcoming weekend. Even though the criminal court had issued a very clear, three-year order of protection prohibiting any contact between Stefanie and Stefanie's uncle, Smith entertained this request. Finally, after further questioning of Angela by her attorney, the hearing officer denied this request.

At the end of the hearing, Robert raised the fact that on July 12th, Stan and I were planning to travel to Memphis, Tennessee, my hometown, where my family was having a gathering to commemorate the one-year anniversary of my mother's passing. We planned to take Stefanie with us, as she was part of our family. Smith then set the next court date for September 6, 2002.

We called Robert to explain our concern that Angela would miss her regular scheduled Sunday visitation with Stefanie. He advised us to go to Memphis, as we planned and that, given the circumstances, our plan was reasonable.

## Stan

I called Angela and informed her that we planned to take Stefanie with us to Memphis the upcoming weekend to commemorate the one-year anniversary of Claire's mother passing. We would be returning to the city Sunday night and stressed a willingness to have Stefanie spend a lot of time with Angela the week upon our return, given that Stefanie would be leaving for camp at the end of that week.

Angela was furious, and she screamed at me saying if Stefanie did not visit with her Sunday, she did not want to see her at all. I was surprised at her "all or nothing" position. In retrospect, I should not have been surprised. While I was concerned about the repercussions of our plan, I was committed to go to Memphis. especially since the year before I had stayed in New York City while Claire attended her mother's funeral alone.

## Claire

The three of us flew to Memphis and were glad to see my sister and her husband, my brother and his wife, along with many cousins and our two aunts and their husbands. Saturday was a family fun day with a barbeque and swimming at my cousin's pool. Stefanie met many of my cousins, aunts, and uncles, and spent most of the afternoon in the swimming pool with my cousins' children, who were close to her age. Soon, everyone was playing pool games, at which Stefanie excelled. By then, she was an excellent swimmer. My whole family welcomed Stefanie warmly, and everyone accepted her as our daughter.

We flew back to New York Sunday evening, and the next week we helped Stefanie pack for camp and shop for last-minute essentials. The issue of visiting Angela did not come up. Although we invited Angela to join us at the camp bus pickup site, she declined. So, the following Saturday, Stan and I took Stefanie and her gear to the bus pickup point, and with lots of hugs bid her goodbye for her four-week camp session.

When their bus arrived at camp later that afternoon, Stefanie called us and said she was ready for a fun time. We were relieved that she had arrived safely.

Three days later, I was in my regular therapy session at 9:00 a.m. Therapy had been a helpful outlet for me during this stressful time. Midway through my session, my cell phone rang. I took the call, as it was from Stefanie's sixteen-year-old cousin, Julie. She told me that Angela had gone into the hospital over the past weekend and had passed away the day before. I was speechless.

"What happened," I asked?

Julie said Angela had contracted pneumonia and died. "I'll let you know the details of the funeral," she added.

I left my therapy session, called Stan to share this news and raced home. We then called Stefanie's therapist Diana, who had testified in our trial. Diana advised us that we should call Stefanie at camp to tell her this news, but to make sure that we notified one of the camp owners first, so he or she would be with Stefanie during the call. Diana also suggested that we let Stefanie decide for herself whether to come back for the funeral.

We phoned the camp and Nancy, one of the owners, answered. We told Nancy that Angela had died, and we needed to talk with Stefanie. Nancy knew about our family court situation and told us she'd send someone to find Stefanie and bring her to the office. Nancy told us to call back in fifteen minutes.

When Stefanie arrived in the office, Nancy said, "Claire and Stan are on the phone and want to talk with you."

Stefanie picked up the phone and asked, "Hi, why are you calling?"

"Stefanie, we wanted to let you know as soon as we learned that Angela passed away yesterday," Stan said.

"We are so sorry, Stefanie," I chimed in. Stefanie was very quiet. Then her first words were, "Do I have to come back to New York for the funeral?"

"Not if you don't want to," I said.

"I don't want to go to the funeral," she said in a low voice.

"Would you like for us to come up to the camp so we could spend some time together?" Stan offered.

"Yes, I'd like that," Stefanie replied.

It was in moments like this that Stefanie expressed what she wanted and didn't want; however, we rarely saw that behavior when she was around her uncle and Angela. She told us that she didn't want them to get mad at her.

We told her we'd catch the first plane to Portland, Maine, rent a car and would be there by mid-afternoon. We boarded the noon flight and arrived at camp around 3:00 p.m. that day. A staff person told us that Stefanie was swimming. We found the path down to the lake. Stefanie came out of the lake when she saw us. We all hugged for a long time. As we made our way back to her cabin for some dry clothes, she asked, "Does this mean that the family court stuff is over?"

"Yes," Stan and I replied in unison.

That was the last time Stefanie ever mentioned Angela's death during our visit. We stayed a few days. Each evening, we would pick her up and take her into Belfast, the local town, for dinner. Stefanie did not ask what would happen next. Following her lead, neither did we. It was as if the Angela chapter was closed, and we could all move on with our lives as a family.

Upon our return, we informed Robert about Angela's death and asked how we could move the adoption proceedings forward. Robert affirmed that the family court custody case was now over since Angela had been the only other party. He instructed us to go to the city's Department of Health to obtain a copy of her death certificate as soon as possible. He would then file it with Judge Mary Brandt, who was assigned to our adoption case. The next day, I went to the Department of Health and requested Angela's death certificate in person. To retrieve a death certificate for a non-relative is a complicated process, but I obtained the correct form and provided an explanation of my relationship to the deceased.

When I presented the form to the clerk, she asked me to explain what I had written and said, "This is very complicated."

"I agree," I said. "Thank you for being so understanding."

"You can come back tomorrow, and I'll have a copy of the death certificate," the clerk said.

I called Stefanie's cousin and found out the funeral would be the next day. We planned to attend out of respect for Angela. We sent flowers to the funeral home where there would be a wake that evening. Early the next morning, when I went out to walk our dog, I found that the flowers we had sent to the funeral home, a spray of lavender roses, had been tossed over the gate into our courtyard. I sank to my knees to pick up the flowers and then went inside to share this eerie news with Stan. We called HSI's security director Philip, a retired New York police department former detective, to relay this event to him.

"If you were planning to go to the funeral, don't," Philip said calmly. "I do not know what they would do. And I suggest you not try to contact the family. I'll go to the funeral mass and let you know if I find out anything."

Philip called us late that afternoon to say that the funeral was uneventful. He had no further information to share. Stan and I tried to take in all this. Even our empathetic gesture made as a peace offering had been rebuffed. Our attorney encouraged us to move ahead with the adoption. After that, we would have no further contact with Stefanie's family.

I returned to the health department, retrieved a copy of Angela's death certificate, and delivered it to our attorney to file with Judge Brandt's law secretary. The next day, Judge Brandt's law secretary called us.

"Do you still want to adopt Stefanie?" he asked. "Of course, we do," I responded.

"Well, the three of you should be in the Judge's conference room on the third floor at 10:00 a.m. Thursday morning, August 22nd," he said. "Bring your identification."

"Of course. Thank you." I said and ended the phone call.

I immediately called Stan at his office and shared this amazing news. I was crying.

Could this really be happening? After six years of living in limbo, not knowing what would happen next, and being tormented, the three of us were finally going to officially be a family. Angela's sudden death, which brought an end to the contentious custody hearings, was a shock and certainly not something we could have anticipated. Even at the end, our effort to respect her role in Stefanie's life was rebuffed by her family. We were ready to turn the page on this stress-filled chapter in our lives and could now look to the future.

# 13

**ııı**

# Adoption

### Claire

Stefanie knew what she wanted in her life. I felt that she could hear Rosa's voice, urging her to pay attention and do her best in school, learn how to live a spiritual life, not let anyone abuse her, and pursue her interests in sports, music, and writing to help her be a better person. Stefanie's image of sitting beside her mother as she painted is powerfully etched in my mind. Rosa wanted Stefanie to pursue what she wanted and to speak up for herself, which she had done so masterfully on the night of November 19, 2001, when the police executed their sting operation in Angela's apartment.

Stefanie had shown extraordinary courage and presence of mind that night when she called us to come pick her up and then calmly packed her backpack and overnight bag and walked out of the apartment with Stan, without looking back. These actions spoke volumes about her ability to choose how she wanted to live her life. She wanted to escape a life where she was exposed to drug users, crime, yelling and screaming, and abuse. She was choosing us to be her parents, and we had demonstrated that we were shaping our lives around hers, so she could access opportunities for the life she yearned to live. Our unconditional love for Stefanie carried us through these rocky times.

After the eight months of battle we had just fought in family court, Stan and I were emotionally drained. Stefanie was as well. It had been a wrenching experience since the previous November when we first went to court to gain permanent custody of Stefanie. The actual trial process itself matched the summer weather here in New York City, as it was intensely hot and unrelenting. As I reread the ten volumes of court transcripts preparing to write this book, I was reminded of how often we had stated to the hearing officer our declarations of love for Stefanie and our commitment to raising her. It seemed that every day we appeared in court, the hearing officer would ask whichever one of us was on the witness stand that day, "Why did you want to become Stefanie's guardian?" There were many variations, but they always touched on the same themes.

"Because we love Stefanie, and we promised her mother we would raise her the way she wanted—giving her unconditional love, a safe, nurturing environment in which to grow up, and the opportunities to blossom as a young girl, find herself, and become the person she wants to be" was our standard answer.

We recognized that family court proceedings are influenced by the social norms of the day. In the early days of family courts (around 1910), white males were favored, then the pendulum swung in the direction of women, then in favor of birth families, and on and on. In the United States, family courts are traditionally underfunded, and family court judges and lawyers are typically not trained to see their own biases and prejudices. We were caught in the middle of the family court's systemic problems. At that moment, we were just relieved that we had made it through the last eight months and were now going to be able to adopt Stefanie.

It was a sweltering August morning as Stefanie, Stan, and I, accompanied by Bob, our dear friend and Stefanie's "adopted" godfather, made our way to the family court building. Stan and I were trepidatious about how this process would go.

Stefanie's lawyer Marta Jimenez, who had been an invaluable advocate for Stefanie during the trial, and Rachel Morrison, the associate working with our lawyer, were already at there, outside of the judge's courtroom where the adoption proceeding would be held.

Shortly after we entered the courtroom, Judge Brandt walked in with her Birkenstock sandals sticking out from beneath her robes. The Birkenstocks gave us a good feeling that she was a down-to-earth person. Our experiences to date in family court had shown us that the process was unpredictable and very stressful.

Hopefully, Judge Brandt had Stefanie's best interest in mind as she proceeded with the adoption.

The clerk read the petition. The judge asked Stan and me if we still wanted to adopt Stefanie. We said "yes." Then the judge turned to Stefanie. At age eleven, Stefanie was old enough for the judge to ask her what she wanted.

"Do you want to be adopted by Claire and Stan Altman?" she asked Stephanie. "Yes, I do," Stefanie replied softly.

Stefanie had told us she wanted to take the name Rosa as her middle name and Altman as her last name, so her name would now be Stefanie Rosa Mercado Altman.

After the three of us affirmed our desire to proceed with the adoption, the judge simply declared, "Stefanie Rosa Mercado Altman is hereby adopted by Claire and Stan Altman as her parents. The birth certificate will be changed to reflect this. Congratulations to you all." She banged her gavel.

The judge rose and walked out of the room. Stan, Stefanie, and I always think of this as our shared adoption. We adopted her and she adopted us. I remember we hugged Stefanie and Bob and then sat there stunned for a few minutes before we could stand up.

As we left the courtroom, as unbelievable as it seems now, we ran into Hearing Officer Smith in the hallway. She greeted us by saying, "I'll see you in my courtroom in September." We were shocked, as we knew that she was aware that Angela had died three weeks earlier, effectively ending our custody case. Stan responded to Smith saying, "We won't be there, since we have just adopted Stefanie. The case is over." Smith turned on her heels and walked down the hallway.

As we exited the building, Stefanie said, "What shall we do today? I think we should go to Rye Playland and ride the rides."

"What a great idea!" Stan chimed in.

## STAN

We could not think of a better way to celebrate becoming a family than to have fun, to all be kids for a day. Bob joined us for breakfast at a local diner but declined the trip to Rye Playland. We retrieved our car from the garage and headed north.

Rye Playland was built in 1928 and had a full array of carnival rides. We spent the day trying out most of them with Stefanie squealing with delight as we climbed aboard each one. Then we came to the log roll, which involved climbing to the top of a two- to three-story-high ride, piling into a hollowed-out log, and hurtling down a steep incline with water splashing over us. Stefanie begged, "Can we do this one?"

My first thought when Stefanie asked to ride the log roll was, "This is not safe. How can we know that this would be the way to start a celebration of her adoption?" The solution was that I decided to take the ride with her. Stefanie had a great time loving being splashed as the ride came to an end. I, on the other hand, did not find getting wet to be fun.

"What am I doing at the age of sixty-one being the playmate of an eleven-year-old?" I thought.

I remember getting wet when we were in Seattle and Stefanie had walked into Lake Washington. But the big smile that day at Rye Playland on Stefanie's face and the sparkle in her eyes made the whole log-roll experience worthwhile. Our age difference disappeared as Stefanie brought out the child in me.

"That was fun," Stefanie exclaimed. Those three words said it all to us, what our guardianship had been about was letting her be a child and enjoy all that comes with riding the rides that one encounters.

As we left Rye Playland, we knew the road ahead would not be easy, but we also knew in our hearts that we had laid the foundation for Stefanie to grow up safe and with the opportunities to live a fulfilling life. And we knew that we would be stronger and happier for being in this family with Stefanie. I felt Rosa smiling down on us as we drove back to Manhattan.

We were glad that Stefanie had taken her mother's first name as her middle name. It was fitting to acknowledge her birth mother, who had gone to great lengths to make sure that her daughter would have good parents to bring her up for the next phase of her life.

We arrived back at our house just in time to prepare for our special dinner with Stefanie, our son David, his new fiancée Irma, and our son Jeffrey. This was indeed a momentous evening to celebrate both Stefanie and Irma joining our family. Over glasses of sparkling cider, David offered a toast to two Latina princesses joining our family, Stefanie, Puerto Rican, and Irma, Peruvian.

It was as if the struggles of the past six years were now distant memories. Stefanie had been the daughter of our hearts for years, but she was finally our daughter legally, and we did not have to look back. Within the year, Irma and David would be married, and Stefanie would be in the wedding party. The ground beneath our feet had become more solid. We could now move forward to help Stefanie grow into the next phase of her life without the specter of uncertainty and negativity looming over us as to whether she would become part of our family.

# 14

## The Middle School Years

### Claire

With the beginning of the fall, Stefanie entered the School for Writers and Artists. We continued our routine that we had begun the previous fall of taking Stefanie to ride every Saturday at River Run, the stable in Brewster, New York.

Going to the School for Writers and Artists had been a dream of Stefanie's since we passed this school one day while she was in the second or third grade. Stefanie's writings have helped her heal from the trauma of her early years, especially losing her mother when she was five. One of her first poems, "Mommy Rosa," demonstrated how she used her writing to deal with her grief over her mother's death.

*I miss the fun we had together and when you gave me a kiss on the cheek*
*And that kiss is like when two clouds come together.*
*Our love is the biggest thing in the whole world.*
*Our love is a powerful thing.*

Stefanie's love of writing became evident to us when she was in kindergarten and wrote in what we called "hieroglyphics," her phonetic spelling, which we couldn't decipher. But when Stefanie read her pieces to us, they made perfectly good sense. Many of Stefanie's early stories involved a horse and a girl and how they bonded and communicated with each other. Others focused on dogs.

In the third grade, she wrote "Frisky and Fantasia," a story about a Labrador and a Golden Retriever, that managed to take a trip to Las Vegas by hiding out in two pet carriers in the bowels of a plane. Stan, Stefanie, and I had just taken a vacation to Las Vegas as part of a family vacation where she reveled in the bright lights, watched Cirque du Soleil shows, and held a baby lion at the MGM Pictures Hotel. Stefanie wove her experiences into a tale narrated by two dogs.

In the fourth and fifth grades, Stefanie began spending hours developing what we would call today a graphic novel. She took an artist's sketchbook that Stan had given her, drew a grid across each page, and in each block of the grid drew a picture and wrote what was happening in that scene. Stefanie would take the book with her wherever she went and slowly began to fill up its several hundred pages.

In the sixth grade, she wrote another piece about her mother, which she titled "Racing Heart," which was published in the *American Anthology of Poetry for Young Americans–2004 Edition*. Writing was also a way that Stefanie shared personal stories and expressed how she felt. Somewhere in middle school, Stefanie wrote a piece titled "An Outcast in Kindergarten" in which she described her first days in kindergarten as "feeling different, not fitting in with the kids in my class, afraid of not making friends—feeling jittery, like little ants running inside of me." Stefanie described how she took out her anger at one kid who called her stupid, tugged at her braids, and pulled her off her seat in the lunchroom:

> *I noticed it was the kid who called me "stupid." Anger rose in me, and I grabbed his forearm and bit into it. Hard. With all my might. He wailed and screamed. He clutched his wrist in agony. I sat there in victory.*
>
> *The day before I had bitten the boy's arm, tension rose and fell within me. I was like a dragon, ready to blow fire at anyone who passed by. I stood, leaning against the brick wall of the playground where a mural was painted. It showed a bunch of kids having fun. Big smiles crossed their faces while mine had no expression. I felt excluded, left out. An outcast, I was alone and needed a friend.*

Stefanie was struggling with how to deal with her feelings of being left out; writing about them was one way that worked for her.

While the three of us were becoming a real family and Stefanie was getting adjusted to middle school, we faced another big challenge. In the spring of 2003, nine months after we adopted Stefanie, Stan finally had cancer surgery to remove his thyroid and what had turned out to be malignant nodules in his throat area. This was a scary period for all of us, although Stan and I tried to keep our feelings to ourselves so as not to frighten Stefanie. During Stan's recovery, Stefanie, although only eleven, helped Stan by bringing him lunch or snacks, keeping him company watching some of their favorite television shows together, or filling him in on her day at school.

The surgery was mostly successful, but the doctor was not able to remove all the malignant lymph nodes since some were too close to Stan's carotid artery. I thought Stan needed a post-surgery doctor, since he would still be living with cancer in his body, and he needed ways to handle this. Stan's cousin Norine, who was managing Olive Leaf, our wellness center, introduced us to Dr. Mitch Gaynor, an integrative oncologist.

At first, Stan resisted seeing another doctor, but he finally agreed. Dr. Gaynor had a reputation as a true healer who employed both classic medicine and alternative techniques, such as sound healing, which I believed might be helpful. Dr. Gaynor greeted us with a warm "hello, how are you today?" As soon as we sat down in Dr. Gaynor's office, both of us, but particularly Stan, were struck by Dr. Gaynor's welcoming manner. On the wall behind his desk was a picture of an Indian guru. Stan asked who this was, and Dr. Gaynor explained that this was Sri Sakthi Amma, his spiritual teacher who lived in India. Dr. Gaynor's reassuring manner convinced Stan to work with him.

The first step was weekly visits with Dr. Gaynor for sound healing, a technique using a small cushion in which speakers are embedded. The patient, lying on a massage table, wears headphones to hear healing music, while the therapist gently massages the patient's back and front with the cushion. The sound goes directly into the body, providing healing vibrations to the patient. After the sound treatment, Stan would have a consultation with Dr. Gaynor. Stan began to have more energy, and his outlook was more positive. He was clearly benefiting from this post-op care that was helping him live with cancer.

One day during Stan's visits with Dr. Gaynor, he invited Stan to the monthly Hindu prayer ceremonies, called pujas, that he led at his home every month on the evening of the full moon. Stan usually went by himself, as we weren't yet comfortable leaving Stefanie with a babysitter. In September, Dr. Gaynor told Stan that Amma would be staying at his home later in the month, performing puja and giving teachings for several days and evenings. We took turns attending Amma's sessions so one of us could be with Stefanie all the time she wasn't in school.

We were both taken with Amma, her gentleness, kindness, and talking about attaining joy in one's life. One Sunday evening, Stefanie asked if she could join us in Amma's session and bring her friend Susan along. Stefanie had met Susan at the St. Francis Family Faith Program, and Susan had introduced Stefanie to the Third Street Music School.

"Of course," I said, "but are you ready to sit on the floor for a couple of hours to listen to Amma's teachings and witness the puja?"

The girls both agreed, and so we went to Dr. Gaynor's apartment on Central Park West.

They both sat quietly and were very still during the two-hour service.

### Travel to India

In early October, Stan came home from his weekly appointment with Dr. Gaynor and asked Stefanie and me if we wanted to go to India around Christmas time. I was surprised. Stan and I had had many opportunities to travel with our earlier spiritual teacher, Ellen Resch, to India and even to meet with the Dalai Lama, which we declined. Now, with Stefanie in our lives, we were entertaining this possibility. I had no hesitancy. I had felt a connection with Amma from the moment we met, and I was sure Stan and Stefanie had in ways I could not describe.

Stefanie's only question about the trip was, "Doesn't Amma live in South India?"

"Yes, why do you ask?" I responded.

"Well, if that's the case, I guess we won't be eating hamburgers."

"Is that a problem?" I asked her.

"No, it's just that I wanted to know," she said.

Stan and I discussed how we would manage a trip like this. We had our passports. We would need to get Indian visas, and we had to figure out all the clothes and supplies we would need.

We quickly obtained our visas, and we made trips to Jackson Heights in Queens to shop for Indian clothes. Amma asked all who stayed in the spiritual village in India to wear Indian garb. Since we were not familiar with how to wear saris, we bought mostly Kalwar pant suits for Stefanie and me that women and girls often wear in India. We booked our plane tickets and made arrangements with the guesthouse in Amma's spiritual village for accommodations. We would be in India for two weeks, leaving after school ended for the fall term and returning before school would reopen. We were all a bit anxious, but we were looking forward to this adventure.

Stefanie had shown us she was a good traveler from an early age, so we were not concerned about our 24-hour journey with the flight from

New York City, a layover in Frankfurt, followed by the leg to Chennai on India's east coast, and finally a three-hour car ride to the spiritual village. We arrived about 4:00 a.m. Indian time and drowsily tried to wake up enough to explore the guesthouse and orient ourselves. Stefanie sat up in the back seat and opened her eyes as Stan paid the driver. Leaving the guesthouse on their way to an early morning puja were three tall blond Australian young men in their twenties. Stefanie was twelve at the time and had begun to notice boys. She was already sitting up.

"Well, this trip might not be so bad. Those guys are cute," she said.

The next morning at breakfast, we met the Aussies, all of whom were friendly young men who offered to show Stefanie around and help her get acclimated. We attended a morning puja, took a tour of the Peedam, as Amma's spiritual village is called, and then went to the evening puja in the Temple. Amma had been identified by the local villagers as the rebirth of a Hindu goddess called Narayani who, when he was sixteen years old and from that point on, was referred to as she/her.

By the time Amma was twenty-six, she had begun to build an entire spiritual village with temples, schools, farming projects, and orphanages. The plans included building a 200-bed hospital then under construction, additional schools, and a spiritual park on what was just scrubland. Amma's message was that one attains joy through service to others. We soon learned what Amma truly meant.

The routine at the Peedam began with morning pujas, service work ("seva") in the afternoon, and then the evening puja. In between, the young Aussies and other young devotees took Stefanie under their wings and explored the grounds, sometimes took a rickshaw into town to buy fruits and vegetables, shop for necessities, and generally take in the sights. Often, they went to the roof of the guesthouse where several of the young men and women played various instruments and sang. Stefanie adapted to the South Indian vegetarian diet easily, despite the fact that she was used to the meat and potatoes diet that Angela had fed her, while with us we had always alternated meat with fish and vegetarian meals. She blended in well with local Indians with her long dark brown hair and olive skin, which grew darker the more she was in the sun. She quickly learned how to wrap her own sari, with help from the cleaning ladies at the guesthouse, and went barefoot much of the time. We both found Stefanie's ability to adapt to a new culture and markedly different environment incredible.

I found myself being very comfortable allowing Stefanie to hang out with her new friends both around the Peedam and while going into town, which was about seven kilometers away, even though we wouldn't let Stefanie ride the subway by herself to school in New York City. It was as if we knew that Amma was protecting all "her children."

On the third day we were there, the manager of the guesthouse told us that all the guests would be visiting a local girls' orphanage in a town about thirty minutes away by car. At first, Stefanie said she didn't want to go, saying that she didn't feel comfortable going to an orphanage. We sensed that it was too close to how she might have lived had Rosa not settled on us as her guardians and had we not picked her up to come live with us after the "raid," as she called it, in November 2001. Stan and I had not considered Stefanie's fear of living in an orphanage. We talked about how she felt and told her she had didn't have to come on this outing if she didn't want to. After a few minutes, Stefanie came over to us and said, "I'll come along."

We boarded the bus and traveled to the orphanage, a bare concrete building with dormitories for the girls, and a single classroom with wooden benches and a simple teacher's desk. There were no toys and no closets for clothes since the girls had only one sari apiece. But the smiles on the girls' faces when we disembarked from our bus melted our hearts, as they were clearly so happy to have visitors. Stefanie was the only female child with our group, so when the girls saw her, they were immediately drawn to her. She was the center of their attention. I am sure partially because she looked like them.

The girls, who ranged in age from seven to fifteen, proudly showed us around their home. Without this simple orphanage, many of these girls would be living on the streets of a bustling, dirty, dangerous town. Some of the Aussies asked the head of the orphanage if they could play music and sing for the girls. An informal concert sprang into action. Stefanie did not have her viola with her, so she sat down on a nearby concrete wall. Some of the girls around Stefanie's age came over and asked her to sit with them. Stefanie was soon part of their group. Music is always a salve for people with problems, wounds, and other injuries—be they physical or emotional. Stefanie participated as an audience member in the concert and enjoyed the camaraderie of the girls.

When it came time to return to the Peedam, we shared gifts of pencils, pens, paper, and other school supplies with the girls. Stefanie was hugged by her new friends. The joy in the girls' faces and in ours was visible. It was a quiet trip back to the Peedam. When we returned to our room at the guesthouse, Stefanie said, "I am glad I went. Next time I will bring my viola."

Stefanie's courage on that first trip to India, traveling to a foreign place, told us that she was willing to trust both us and Amma, knowing that we would protect her and that giving of herself was something she could do to help others.

We returned to India for six more Christmases. On each trip, we visited the girls at the orphanage. Stefanie and the girls remembered each other and always bonded immediately. The girls surrounded us and gave us hugs as we got off the bus. Stefanie always brought her viola and joined in the now traditional annual concert for the girls. It was heartwarming to watch Stefanie and the girls grow up together for a few years and how the differences between their two worlds evaporated when they saw each other again.

These trips had a powerful impact on Stefanie, which she summed up in a piece she wrote around the time of her college graduation.

*The obstacles I have encountered and the opportunities and gifts that I have received were put in perspective when our spiritual leader from India, Sri Sakthi Amma, explained to me that the course that life takes is like a stream, and the obstacles we encounter are like the rock bed that interrupts that stream's flow. Like water, we have to be flexible and find a way to move around the obstacles we encounter in life. The first few years of my life were like a jagged rock bed.*

We returned to New York from that first trip to India renewed and refreshed and feeling that now all three of us had a shared spiritual connection in Amma, whom we could turn to for protection and guidance. Amma was closer in age to Stefanie than to Stan and me, and Stefanie developed a particularly close connection with her. Amma talked with her about her issues of the day, like how to deal with bullying from fellow middle-school girls.

Stefanie continued to thrive with her writing, which was the way she expressed her thoughts about the challenges and joys she faced.

In an eighth-grade essay, Stefanie wrote about the negative impacts of body image on teenaged girls. Stefanie describes how she was teased and called names, but then she realized that what really changed things for her was changing how she looked at events in her life.

*I won't say I am the perfect person, but I have changed my way of thinking. Unfortunately, that is what some girls don't realize. All it takes is changing your pattern of thinking. Think, I am beautiful, I am free. I am unlimited. I am a gem. Wake up and smell the coffee. Your true beauty lies within.*

Stefanie's descriptions of the bond between girls and horses were the most consistent theme in her writing. One piece, "Cara Blanca's Beach," was selected to be read at a Barnes and Noble store in December 2004. A short excerpt from this is included here:

> Atop Cara Blanca's back, the aquamarine water reflects the sun's light strongly—making it seem as if millions of diamonds dance upon the surface of the water. It practically blinds me. . . . Something about this moment. Being in the water on horseback feels elusive. All of time and reality is lost. My world is replaced with wonder, fantasy, freedom. I am free to be myself. Free to be. . . . . Out here feels wide. Endless. Out here I feel special. Everything from clouds in the sky to the fishes in the sea. Telling me the outside world is my home.
>
> I think of how strong we are. Together. The energy of being close to one another. Strong. Unbreakable. I also think of the amount of love that is being shared between us. We are a pair. We have an ability to be inseparable. We have a bond so strong that even the forces of nature could not break it. Cara Blanca is my companion. My destiny. Future. My love of caring and being there for someone else. . . . Then I had the most settled feeling. The wind embraces me. Holding my horse and me in its invisible strong arms.

That same year, Stefanie also wrote an essay she called "The Circle of Trust," about her relationship with her horse, which she ends with this paragraph:

> Personally, the world of horseback riding has taught me so much in so many ways. Horseback riding has always been a personal sport. My past was always a struggling part of my life, fortunately, I found horseback riding to be my outlet. During my eight years of riding, I have learned it takes a lot of trust and strength to ride a horse, and in a way, I have developed that over the years. It has made me a stronger person. Above all, I have been given the freedom to do whatever I want in my life.

Stefanie's growth as a person and as a writer was evidenced by her language arts teacher's high school letter of recommendation for her to include in her college application in which he said, "In my seven years as a teacher, I have not met a student with greater character than Stefanie. She is self-motivated, hardworking, insightful, caring and responsible. She is a wonderful addition to our classroom community and her overall potential is excellent."

## Stan

Through middle school, Stefanie continued her riding lessons and worked with different school horses. She might ride one for three or four lessons and then find herself riding a different horse. She was never able to develop a relationship with the horses she rode. The lack of consistency, I believe, hampered her progress as a rider.

One particular horse show made this point very clear. Stefanie had practiced for an upcoming show on the same horse each week for a month or so. We expected that she would ride the same horse during the show, but, to our surprise, Stefanie was given a horse to ride that she had never ridden before. The result was a disaster, as she was so nervous and unsure of the horse that she barely finished the routine she was assigned to do. When she dismounted, the experience had obviously scared her and shaken her confidence in her riding ability.

I was reminded of my early experience with Stefanie when she was frightened to try anything new. Claire and I were committed to not let her feeling of failure persist. As a result of this experience, Claire and I begin to discuss that Stefanie needed to have her own horse because the unpredictability of knowing which horse she would ride worked against her gaining confidence.

Helping Stefanie build her self-confidence was a paramount goal of ours. Whether it was the loss of her mother, her previous unsettling living situation with Angela, or her fears of abandonment that caused her to be so uncertain of herself, we didn't know. What we did know was that when Stefanie was riding a horse, she was in a different zone. Her bond with a horse was palpable. The world consisted just of her and the animal. We were willing to spend money on her lessons and take the time to help her pursue horseback riding because it seemed to be what helped her most to feel good about herself.

In the fall 2004, Stefanie entered the eighth grade, her last year in middle school. Her attention now turned to applying for admission to a high school for the following fall. After much research and many school visits, her choices came down to two private high schools and The Beacon School, one of New York City's most competitive public high schools. While purchasing Stefanie her own horse was on my mind, this would only be possible if she attended Beacon, as the tuition at the private schools was quite high, making the cost of also having a horse prohibitive.

Beginning in January 2005, we anxiously awaited the decisions from the high schools to which Stefanie had applied. In March, we heard the news.

Stefanie had been rejected by the private schools but was admitted to The Beacon School. We were thrilled for her because Beacon had a great reputation as a portfolio school where students worked on multidisciplinary projects rather than following the prevailing standardized curriculum. I was so excited that she would be attending a public high school that I blurted out at dinner that night, without discussing with Claire, that we would now be able to buy Stefanie her own horse.

"Are you serious?" Stefanie exclaimed. "You're really going to buy me a horse?" she repeated.

"Yes, we are, Stefanie." I replied. "We know how much horses mean to you, and hopefully we can find a horse you'll really connect with."

We came to realize that for Stefanie, almost more than all our other expressions of love and commitment, this meant that Claire and I were keenly aware of what made her tick and were here for her always. That moment was significant for Stefanie in ways we did not understand at first. But from then on, she began to refer to us as Mom and Dad. The first time she said those words, I cried inside, and Claire later told me how deeply it moved her.

## Stefanie

In the spring of my eighth-grade year, my dad and I spent many Saturdays horse shopping with a trainer at a stable in New Jersey, which proved fruitless. We decided to look for a horse elsewhere. A friend of the family at the time offered to introduce us to Loretta and Rosie, a mother-daughter duo in upstate New York, who owned and managed a barn that trained racehorses and show horses. Feeling pretty defeated at this point, with little confidence that we would find the right horse, my parents and I figured it was worth seeing what Loretta might have to offer. We hopped in the car on a muggy June day and traveled an hour and half north of the city. Nestled at the foot of the Shawangunk Mountains was a sprawling farm with a large barn, paddocks, rings, and a dirt racetrack in the back, alongside a medium family-sized home where Loretta and Rosie lived.

We were given the heads-up that Loretta had received a retired but young chestnut thoroughbred off the track a few days earlier. She informed us that she would need a few days to see where this horse's head was at and whether he was a good horse for me. Was he suitable to be a hunter jumper horse given his age and projected life of being a racehorse? The next morning, dad received a call from Loretta in which she said, "Listen, you have to come up tomorrow morning and look at this horse. I really don't think he is going to last long if we put him up for sale."

On that phone call, we learned this horse was different from other thoroughbred racehorses like him, as he was really laid back, chilled out, and supposedly had the right disposition to become a jumping horse.

The next day we pulled up to Ontrack, Loretta's farm that she had owned for years. I recall getting out of the car and my body riddled with buzzing. Something about the prospect of this horse felt different, something in my bones knew we would have many shows together, trail rides, gallops, tears, laughter, all of it. Loretta and Rosie met my parents and me at the entrance to the barn. They led us back to where Dixie was all tacked up (bridle, saddle, and all) and hooked up to the cross ties ready for the long-awaited trial ride. Dixie was the sweetest horse I had ever seen right from the onset. Usually, most horses would back up and proceed with caution before allowing you to touch them, but Dixie was sweet. His doe-eyed gaze welcomed an initial touch to his velvety nose, face, and neck. After a couple of minutes of measuring his "on the ground" manners, we took Dixie to the ring for a ride.

We started off with a walking warm-up. Loretta stood in the center of the ring encouraging me to just feel him out, get a sense for how much tension to keep on the reins, and the feel of his gait atop his back. So far, so good, as we made one round around the ring. Two. Three. It was almost beginning to feel natural and easy the way we matched, saddle to seat. Loretta asked me to go into a trot. I signaled Dixie with a slight squeeze of my leg to pick up his gait. His walk brightened into a lilting trot. We cut across the ring diagonally, made circles, stopped and halted, all to get a feel for his ability to listen and be responsive. Dixie proved to us he could do that and more. Of all the horses I had ridden, I felt the most taken care of by him. I sensed he just wasn't going through the motions of the ride, but he was cognizant that each married effort was a partnership and dual task.

After a couple of drills and passes in the ring, Loretta instructed me to dismount and walk Dixie back to the barn. Hopping off, I gave him a solid and heavy-handed pat to his neck and whispered, "That was good, thank you," as I simultaneously rolled up my stirrups. Dixie seemed like an old soul, and I could almost feel him say back to me, "You're welcome. It takes two to trot." Following my returning Dixie to the barn, Loretta and my parents agreed that we would circle back with her in a couple weeks when I returned from a two-week class trip to Sardinia. We needed a chance, as a family, to discuss Dixie and make a decision on whether to buy him.

I believe over dinner that night it was pretty clear to me that Dixie was the horse for me. I expressed to my parents how easy it felt to ride him, how surprisingly in sync we were, even on the first ride, and how I had never felt that with any of the other horses we had looked at over the last couple of months. It seemed to be a deeper knowing. From the first glance, Dixie felt like a sleeved glove, and he just fit. He seemingly had all the right traits to become a novice hunter jumper horse, and the spark I felt when meeting him signaled that he was really was the one.

Dixie had come from a lineage of racehorses. His sire, Dixie Brass, was an American thoroughbred racehorse who was a leading middle-distance runner in the 1990s and early 2000s. Dixie Jazz, his full name, was born in 2000 in New York State's Hudson Valley.

## Stan

Having decided to buy Stefanie a horse we spent months working with a local New Jersey trainer trying to find the right horse for her. After being disappointed at the quality of the seven horses we were shown, we finally decided to seek the help of a different trainer.

Our friend's introduction to a horse trainer named Loretta proved fruitful. She owned a horse farm and stable called On Track in New Paltz, New York, that she ran with her daughter, Rosie. Loretta told me about Dixie Jazz, a five-year-old thoroughbred gelding that had been taken off the racetrack circuit six months earlier.

At Loretta's urging, we drove up to her stable to see if the horse might be a good fit. Stefanie got up on his back, and Loretta began to work with her and the horse. We could immediately see a change in Stefanie's riding. Loretta kept the session focused on the basics of riding posture and basic gaits, walk, trot, and canter. By the end of the session, our daughter's eyes were glowing. It was so evident that she liked this horse. We arranged to return in two days to see how the two of them got along.

While Stefanie was a careful rider and had learned a lot, she was still in the early stages of her development. Loretta described her as a beginner/intermediate. All the horses we had looked at were in the nine- to twelve-year-old range, which was more mature than five-year-old Dixie. Older horses have been around long enough so they are schooled in what is expected of them.

My cousin explained that five-year-old thoroughbreds were still young, adolescent horses who can be playful and less disciplined than older horses. He also said that thoroughbreds are highly intelligent, but also temperamental, which might make Dixie a questionable choice for Stefanie. According to him, the odds were one in fifty that a thoroughbred horse this young would be suitable for Stefanie. "Proceed with caution" was his advice.

Yet contrary to statistics and the general rule of thumb, Stefanie and Dixie had begun to bond. Stefanie had a big smile on her face after riding Dixie a second time. She looked at me and said, "I really like this horse." It would appear that she and Dixie might be the one out of fifty.

Meanwhile, Stefanie was getting ready to leave for her two-week trip to Sardinia, an Italian island in the Mediterranean, with her classmates. Loretta clearly understood our dilemma.

"Why don't we see how he works out?" she said. "He will learn a lot in two weeks. Call me when your daughter returns. I will not show him to anyone else until then."

Stefanie's two weeks in Sardinia went by quickly. We heard from her that she was having a great time in Italy. She asked if we had heard anything about Dixie. We went to meet Stefanie on her return, with family members of other students who had gone on the trip. Shortly after midnight, they emerged from customs. We hugged Stefanie, and the first thing she said, "What's happening with the horse?" That cleared up any questions we might have had as to how she felt about him.

The next day, we drove back to On Track to see how Dixie's schooling had progressed. The love affair between horse and girl continued. She seemed to have found her horse. Dixie continued to be well behaved, and they worked well together. They were not perfect, but under the expert guidance of Loretta, they had a productive session. We agreed to come back midweek to watch the vet complete the pre-purchase examination, which Dixie passed.

After discussing the results of the vet's evaluation of Dixie's health with my cousin Jay and Stefanie's growing bond with him, we decided to purchase Dixie. We continued to board him at On Track to have continuity with both his and Stefanie's schooling. It was a personal challenge for me to take Stefanie to On Track every Saturday for a lesson and again during the week when we stayed overnight in a bed and breakfast to permit Stefanie to work with Dixie two days in a row.

I would periodically send my cousin Jay videos of Stefanie during her lessons riding Dixie. After several weeks, he wrote back and said that Stefanie appears to be a different rider working with Loretta, more confident and comfortable with Dixie; it surprised him how well behaved Dixie was.

Claire worked during the week, so I was the chauffeur for the August trips during the week to On Track for Stefanie to train with Dixie. During this time, I was experiencing prostate problems and was very uncomfortable. However, in spite of the physical stress during this period, I can truly say that the time with Stefanie was wonderful. I enjoyed our conversations as we drove up to the stable, and I learned a great deal about riding and horse care that summer.

By the end of August 2005, we decided to move Dixie to a farm in Bedford, New York, about forty-five minutes closer to New York City. Loretta and her daughter Rosie would handle the move. Loretta planned to end the summer by entering Stefanie and Dixie in a schooling horse show to gain some experience competing.

## Stefanie

Dixie's and my first summer together flew by. Days and days of training and getting to know one another commenced and continued with many drills in walking, trotting, and cross rails. After several weeks, Loretta decided that Dixie and I were ready to participate in our first horse show together at the end of the summer. She signed us up to show in a regional horse show at Crystal Waters Farm, a small hunter jumper barn in Orange County, New York.

Before my class started (a class being a round of competitions a hunter jumper rider completes), I stood in front of Dixie. He was tacked to the cross ties of the trailer, and my hand followed the broad white blaze on his face. Nerves were coursing through my body. A couple of months of preparation, a couple of falls, endless circles in the ring brought us up to this moment. Petting him regulated the buzz of nerves I felt in my body.

"Hey boy," I started talking to him. "Today's a big day for us. We have had a crazy summer, and you've joined our family. We have trained and prepped for today. Whatever happens today, since it really is a first go around for both of us, I love you no matter what. If we do great and win, then let's kick some ass. If we don't, we will still kick ass." I petted his big strong neck. Dixie seemed to have taken in every word with care and caution. He acknowledged me with a small snort and head rub to my shoulder as if to indicate, "That's right, we got this."

I prepped Dixie—brushed his mane, picked out his feet, and tacked him up. Following this routine, I got myself ready for the show. Horseshow clothes are very official. I slipped into my dress shirt, jacket, and riding boots, tied up my hair into a low bun and put on my helmet. Loretta and I touched base before I mounted Dixie. We went over the plan for the flat class and the cross rails jumping class.

"Remember, you are going to circle before and after you jump. If things get crowded in the ring for you with the other riders in the flat class, circle then too. It is important for you to have space."

Loretta gave me a strong pat on the back. "Don't worry, you will be great. Just focus on you and Dixie, and you will be fine."

I mounted Dixie. Loretta walked us to the top of the ring, where the other riders were getting ready to go in as well. There were six other riders in this class. The first of three classes was the flat class, where riders were judged on their technicality and form in the walking, trotting, and canter gaits. Dixie and I flawlessly transitioned between each gait. Riding atop him felt like I had a trusty co-pilot with me in the cockpit, and our motions came as easily as with the press of a button, but for us it was the pressure of my leg to his side. We went through a walk, trot, and canter in each direction.

When the flat class was over, riders were asked to move to the middle of the ring so their numbers could be called for the ribbon placements. Dixie and I placed first in the beginner flat class. To say the least, I was stunned. I gave my boy the biggest pat I could on his massive neck and felt a smile spread across my face from ear to ear. As we walked out of the ring to meet Loretta and my dad, I whispered, "We did it, thank you!" But then I looked at the smiling and elated faces of my dad and Loretta, who had to be cheering the loudest from the sides of the ring! When I got to the top of the ring, I was met with the jubilant exclamations of "class well done" expressed by Loretta and my dad.

"Ok, we must keep this momentum. Great first class!" Loretta said excitedly. "You ready for the jumping over cross bars class?"

I nodded my head, still a bit dazed that we'd won first place. Different round this time, and Dixie and I would be in the ring by ourselves, being judged for our jumping technicalities. The last two classes would involve us doing the jumps first in one direction, then the next class in the other direction.

When the jumping class commenced, Dixie and I weren't the first team to go. A couple of riders went before us. As we waited, I hyped myself up, letting myself know that this is what it felt like to sing on stage or act. I had done this before, but obviously not within this context. It was very different, as now I had 1,000 pounds of power beneath me to carry me through. "We can do it again," I telepathically said to Dixie. I didn't want to look crazy talking to my horse. At that moment, Dixie bobbed his head as if he agreed, and we entered the ring to begin our jumping class.

Dixie and I opened with a circle at the top of the cross-rail jumps. This was a defining moment to get in the right head space and hyper focus on our canter and measure the distance to each jump. Dixie's cantering was smooth throughout the whole course. The rest of the horses and people fell by the wayside as we methodically charged through the jumps. We went around twice, completing a total of eight cross rail jumps, and closed with a circle. I transitioned Dixie down to a trot, then walk, then came out of the ring.

"Very good, very good," Loretta said as we walked out. "That was awesome. Now we just wait for your number to be called."

Dixie and I decompressed as a couple of more riders after us took their turns around the cross rails. When they had completed their rides, the judges read out their numbers. In the lineup, Dixie and I placed second in the jumping class. We returned to the ring to complete the third and last class. We placed third, and the total points Dixie and I earned for the three classes were the highest point total of the day. A voice announced, "Grand champions of this beginner hunter jumper division go to Stefanie Mercado Altman riding Dixie Jazz."

I could not believe what I was hearing. The steward of the show came over to us and presented Dixie and me with a big beautiful ribbon.

Elated and over the moon, Loretta asked if I thought I could compete in a more advanced division just within the first flat class.

"You've done amazing so far! You're the champ, and I think you could bring that to the next class. What do you think?"

Nervously, I nodded and said, "Let's do it."

The following division started off with the flat class. Dixie and I entered the ring. As I awaited the judges' call for the first trot, I filled the silence with a couple of exhales. I let the tension go from my shoulders and shook it out of my body. We walked at a brisk pace until we were about half way around and the judge called for a trot. Squeezing Dixie's side with both legs, we elevated our gait into the trot. We circled, passed riders and horses who were either shorter, smaller, or a tad slower than us. Dixie always had a graceful gait, and we seemed to cover the ring a couple of times around before the judge asked for a canter. I signaled for Dixie to come down from a trot to canter by a simple and soft pull on the reins. As smooth as a finely tuned car on automatic drive, Dixie seamlessly then went into a canter.

It had rained that morning, and the dirt in the ring was moist, with puddles spotting the outside track where horses and riders made their way around the ring. As we were coming around the top half of the ring, I felt a jolt from under Dixie. My heart skipped a beat. It wouldn't have been like him to jump and start bucking me off all of a sudden. That just wasn't in his character. As Dixie restabilized and formulated his canter, I took a quick glance behind me and saw a puddle. Dixie had lost his footing. *Is this slipup going to cost us a couple of points?* I thought. I hoped not. I gained my composure and decided to focus on finishing the rest of the flat class. Following whatever little slipup we had, Dixie and I were fine. We completed all the drills as called by the judge and then were called into the middle of the ring.

The silence felt heavy as Dixie, the other riders, and I awaited our rankings. After what felt like an eternity, Dixie and I placed second. Surprisingly content with our placement, I gave Dixie a pat on the neck and walked him up to one of the show hands to retrieve our second place yellow ribbon. "Good boy," I told him. "If it weren't for that slip, we might have placed first, but that's not your fault." Walking out of the ring, I always looked to the side for Loretta and my dad. Both were clapping. "Job well done," Loretta said. "You guys did okay, and second place is great."

Getting that reassurance from Loretta was consoling for my overly analytical mind.

"Let's call it a day," Loretta said.

I dismounted Dixie and walked him to the trailer that was parked a few yards away. Everyone was tired, but happy. I untacked Dixie, took off my saddle, the blanket, and his bridle. He had a saddle-shaped sweat mark on his back, my boy had worked hard. I gave him a quick dry-off, some sweet treats, and had him drink some water. I stood there, holding the lead as he bowed over the water bucket he was guzzling water from. I couldn't believe I did it. That *we* did it.

At the beginning of that year, the idea of buying a horse was just being tossed around. Now it was August, and here I was next to the best four-legged companion I could ask for, who carried us through our first horse show with flying and winning colors—blue, red, and yellow never looked so good. I just had to let the feeling sink in and *feel* it. *Appreciate* it.

We put Dixie in the trailer to go back to On Track and said our goodbyes to Loretta. My dad and I got back in our car to drive back to the city. As soon as we hit the road, I was out like a light. It was as if someone had put a pause to my life force. But I did have some semblance of comprehension when I could hear my dad on the phone with my mom, who was in Rome attending a conference.

"If this means we spent twenty grand for her to feel this way, it would have all been worth it," he said to mom. "She's floating five feet above the car."

## Stan

Claire was at a retreat in Italy when the horse show took place. Loretta and Rosie would bring Dixie to the show at Crystal Waters Farm in Warwick, New York. We were up early and on the road by 7:06 a.m. The sky was overcast, and it was raining, but we made great time in getting to Crystal Waters.

The start of the first competition was delayed because of Loretta's late arrival with Dixie. The competition began with Stefanie and Dixie completing the three classes. At the conclusion of the competition, all seven riders and their horses moved to the center of the ring for the award ceremony. Dixie stood perfectly still as if he had done this thousands of times before, even though it was his first time in a competition. Two minutes later, Stefanie and Dixie were awarded a first-place blue ribbon, a second-place red ribbon and a third-place yellow ribbon. Based on their point total, Stefanie and Dixie were declared the overall champion. Wow! To place first, second and third and then be declared the division champion was incredible.

Stefanie was beaming, and looking with pride at her championship horse. Loretta was excited and pleased with their performances. I was the proud father and slightly shocked at the outcome, because I never imagined they would do so well. Rosie and other riders were screaming their support and good cheer. Loretta was so pleased with Stefanie's work that she suggested Stefanie and Dixie do the flat class in the next division that was starting shortly.

This involved walking, trotting, and cantering. Again, Loretta worked with Stefanie and Dixie before the event began. Twelve horses moved first counterclockwise around the ring. Stefanie and Dixie placed second! At the conclusion of the horse show, we said our summer goodbyes with exchanges of hugs and kisses. We expected to see each other again, but the moment spoke of the bonds that had developed between Stefanie and Dixie, with Loretta's expert and patient guidance.

Stefanie fell sleep in the car as we drove home. Claire called from Rome while I was driving and wanted to know how Stefanie did. After describing Stefanie's and Dixie's performance, I said to her, "Stefanie is floating twenty feet above the car. What she accomplished and experienced today was worth every dollar we spent purchasing Dixie."

That night, we hung her ribbons proudly over Stefanie's bed. The effect of the day's events and the entire experience of acquiring Dixie, watching her and Dixie develop under the guidance of Loretta and then being champions in their first competition together was not lost on me. Stefanie beamed, reflecting her growing self-confidence not only as a rider, but also as a person. She had grown up a great deal that summer.

Claire's and my lives would never be the same.

# 15

###

# High School, College, and Beyond

## Claire

Stefanie began high school on a high note with having a horse of her own, whom she lovingly called by his given name, Dixie Jazz. She made an easy transition academically to high school, as The Beacon School was a portfolio school, just like her middle school. The curriculum didn't focus on standardized testing and routinized learning but instead taught their students through multidisciplinary projects. Stefanie took to this approach with excitement.

She learned to love a subject through multiple lenses. One of her first projects, in which she integrated art, history, writing, religion, and much more, was to construct a model of a house of worship (not your own religion) in a country not your own and write a story about it. Stefanie decided to construct a synagogue in Argentina and capture the story of an innovative rabbi who found ways to grow the congregation. To help her with her project, we trekked with Stefanie to the Jewish Museum for background, to stores in downtown Canal Street for art supplies and model building materials, and to the public library for historical information.

Stefanie carried this approach with her throughout high school. She enjoyed doing research and exploring new fields. In addition to taking some musical theater classes, her primary extracurricular activity was spending weekends riding Dixie. In her first year of high school, we boarded Dixie at a barn in Bedford, New York, about half an hour away from Manhattan.

That turned out not to be a good fit. The barn staff focused mostly on training riders for high-end national competitions, rather than supporting riders in getting to know their horses and caring for them.

By that spring, we had decided Dixie and Stefanie would be happier if they could be back at On Track upstate. We decided to look for a house to rent in the nearby town of New Paltz so that we could go there on the weekends for Stefanie to ride. I made an appointment with a real estate broker who warned me that New Paltz, being a college town, mostly had rentals for college students. When we arrived that Sunday morning to meet him, he said he'd lined up houses for sale for us to see. There were no rentals that he thought would be appropriate.

He took us to see three houses, but they were either too small, since our sons might join us on some weekends, or too much like cookie-cutter houses. If we were going to be "in the country," we wanted a house that felt like it was in the country.

The fourth house was on the edge of New Paltz on the side of a mountain, part of the Shawangunk Ridge popular for rock climbing. It was over fifty years old, but had been recently refurbished, and had four bedrooms, plenty of living space, and a great kitchen. Importantly, it was only about fifteen minutes from On Track, the barn at which we would board Dixie.

We told the broker we were interested. On the drive home, we decided to make an offer, which we did that night. It was readily accepted. We made a plan to sell our condominium in Miami, which we hadn't been to in two years because of Stefanie's weekend riding schedule, in order to be able to afford this house.

Within two months, we had purchased the house, moved Dixie back to On Track, and begun a regular schedule of driving up to New Paltz on Fridays for Stefanie to ride Saturdays and Sundays. Then we returned to Manhattan for Monday morning school and work. The three of us quickly adapted to this new routine, which left little time for activities other than Stefanie's riding, but it seemed worth it. Stefanie took her riding seriously and had fun doing it. She and Dixie bonded very quickly and pretty soon he was following her out of the barn without a lead line (the line that is used to walk a horse).

Stefanie quickly made friends with her mates at the barn, and one of her instructors informed us the second weekend we were there that she understood we had bought a house in her mom's neighborhood. Indeed, her mother lived down the street from our new house. That summer, Stan stayed up at our country house with Stefanie so she could ride every day, and I commuted by bus to my job in New York. If Stan had to be at the college, I'd stay upstate with Stefanie, and he would commute. By the end of that first summer with Dixie, Stefanie was entering many local horse shows and winning ribbons in almost every competition. She and Dixie were a great team.

So it went throughout high school with busy work and school weeks and then busy weekends at the barn. We became part of the barn family, especially with Loretta and her daughter Rosie, who took Stefanie under their wings to encourage her in her riding.

Stefanie's relationship with Dixie was a key emotional support for her in what are often difficult high school years, especially for young girls. One day, the plan was for me to drive up to Stefanie's school to pick her up at the end of the school day and then we'd continue uptown to pick up Stan and head up to New Paltz. I stopped in front of Stefanie's school. She opened the back door of the car and threw her backpack in the back seat.

"Take me to my horse," she said. "I'm tired of being pressured about boys, parties, and things I'm not interested in."

"Gladly," I said, grateful that Dixie was there for her.

The year we bought Dixie, our daughter-in-law Irma gave birth to our first grandchild, Abigail. So now she, David, and Abigail would come up and visit us upstate. The house became a getaway for them from the city, as it would for our oldest son Jeffrey, his wife, Sara, and their son in the years to come.

The following two summers, Stefanie worked at a local day camp, often training campers to ride. Then, after camp was over for the day, Stan and she would go to On Track for an early evening ride.

Stan and I still had our jobs. After a six-year stint as the dean of the School of Public Affairs at Baruch College in New York City, Stan had returned to the faculty where he taught and led many projects. I had moved on from Housing and Services to head up another not-for-profit, and I was still the chair of the Olive Leaf Wholeness Center, the wellness center we opened in 2001. Other than these responsibilities, we were oblivious to the rest of the world. Our world was wrapped up with Stefanie, supporting her in her school work and with her riding.

## Costa Rica

In early 2008, when Stefanie was sixteen, we were at Peedam again in India. By now, Stan and I were very comfortable with Stefanie going out and about with our various friends whom we had come to know well on our annual trips. One day, Stefanie came back to the guesthouse at lunchtime with Cathy and John, a Canadian couple with whom we had become good friends. Cathy greeted us cheerfully and announced that Stefanie had agreed to travel with them to Costa Rica in March. It was a clear example of our daughter being on the verge of adulthood that she felt comfortable making that decision without first seeking our permission.

"We're going on a mission to speak with women who have been the victims of crimes against women, especially femicide," Cathy explained.

"What's femicide?" I asked.

Cathy told me that it was common in Costa Rica for husbands to come to the states for work, while leaving their wives and children in Costa Rica to take care of their houses and property. In many cases, drug dealers showed up, kidnapped the wives and children, often killed the wives, and illegally took possession of the property. Nongovernmental organizations, such as the one Cathy and John worked with, had been researching this type of crime and were trying to gather more information by meeting with women who had been victimized.

We asked Stefanie if she understood what they were doing and if she still wanted to go. She was very firm about how she could help document these horrible events so that the Costa Rican government could take action to stop these crimes. We told her we understood. We trusted Cathy and John, but we did not want her to go without us. We spoke with Cathy and John and decided to let Stefanie go if we could come along. While we respected Stefanie's passion about working on this human rights issue, the concerned parents in us weren't comfortable with her being so far away from us in a place with which we weren't familiar. Stan and I had no idea what we were getting into, but we obtained our visas, worked out our travel arrangements, and met Cathy and John in Costa Rica in March.

Our first day, we met with several women who told us stories of loss and suffering. We returned to our hotel and decided to take a walk in the center of San Juan, the capital city of Costa Rica. I asked the hotel concierge for directions to the nearby shopping district. He showed me on a map where we could walk, but said, "First, the city is not safe for gringos like you. Come with me to the hotel office and we'll make photo copies of your passports. You take the copies, and I'll place your originals in the hotel safe. When you're on the street, speak to each other only in Spanish and be back here before dark."

I shared these instructions with Cathy, John, Stefanie, and Stan. We followed them explicitly, but they had a chilling effect on us. For the next two days, we met with women's groups from morning until evening and tried to digest the horrific stories they told us. We flew home at the end of the week, humbled by these women and thinking about ways we could help them. Our trips to India and working with the orphanage, and now this experience in Costa Rica, grounded each of us with a different perspective on the many inequities in the world. While much of my career had been centered on providing affordable housing to those in need, Costa Rica was jolting. We came home, each of us grateful for the many blessings in our lives and with a new commitment not to take them for granted.

Back in New York City, we returned to work and school. Stefanie began her prep courses for college entrance exams. A tutor met with her three afternoons a week, and she also attended a group class on Saturday mornings. We had breakfast together on Saturday mornings at our corner diner and then headed up to the class site. The next Saturday the headline of a front-page story in the *New York Times* shouted, "Abuse Trails Central American Girls into Gangs" (April 11, 2008, p. 1). Stefanie asked to see the paper and when she finished reading the story she said, "I'm going to write a letter to the editor of the *New York Times* about our trip to Costa Rica. What do you think?"

I said it was a good idea, but that it was difficult to have letters published in the *New York Times*. This did not deter Stefanie. That night, she wrote a letter, which she e-mailed to the *New York Times*. Within a few days, Stefanie received a response saying that the *Times* would like to publish her piece. After a few questions regarding her authorship, they told Stefanie they would try to publish it soon. On April 18th, when we opened the *New York Times*, there was Stefanie's letter in print.

Letter to the Editor

*Central American Gangs: A Window into a Violent World*

To the Editor:

"Abuse Trails Central American Girls into Gangs" (*NYTimes*, April 11, 2008, p. 1) sheds light on the rising problem of femicide in Central America.

Last month, I traveled to Costa Rica with a delegation from Horizons, a Canadian nongovernmental organization, to meet with leaders of Cefemina, a group that is documenting the extent and causes of femicide in Central America, advocating for stricter law enforcement, training girls and women to report these crimes and teaching them ways to protect themselves.

Gangs in Central America are just the tip of the iceberg; women of all ages are being killed as pawns in drug wars and other criminal activities.

I am a 17-year-old born in the South Bronx, who was exposed to violence at an early age. Now I attend one of New York City's great public high schools, the Beacon School, and hope that the world will begin to pay attention to these outrageous crimes so that young girls everywhere can live to have the opportunities that I do.

Stephanie Mercado Altman, New York, April 13, 2008
(published in the *New York Times*, April 18, 2008)

Our trip to Costa Rica had inspired public advocacy in Stefanie. She connected her personal experiences to larger world issues, which had prompted her to write her letter to the editor. We were beyond proud.

## Ithaca College

In the fall of 2009, Stefanie entered Ithaca College, in the city of the same name, a little over four hours outside of New York City. Neither Stan nor I were surprised at how easily she adapted to college life. Ithaca had been her first choice of colleges. Once again, she had created a rating scale that included a liberal arts curriculum, a small campus outside of New York City and, importantly, a good stable nearby at which to board her horse, Dixie Jazz. Early on in the college application process, Stefanie had asked if she could bring Dixie to college with her. Stan and I approved because Dixie was her best friend and supporter, and she was his. We did not know what bringing her horse to college would entail. But as we started visiting colleges, it was important to Stefanie that we find a barn near the college, at which we could board Dixie and had turn-out fields that were large enough so that Dixie could run around. As it turned out, Ithaca was a great choice not just for Stefanie but also for Dixie.

## Stefanie

Dixie was an escape and steady anchor for me in the college chaos. In my freshman year at Ithaca, I joined the equestrian team, which was based out of a small barn about twenty-five minutes north of Ithaca. Dixie became a part of the team, as much as I was. We schooled (aka took lessons) with the rest of the team on Tuesday and Thursday nights for the next four years.

When we went to competitions, you had to ride a horse from the host school, but I offered him to be a lesson horse for the other girls when all of us trained at home. As a competitor within the collegiate division at the D3 level, riders don't ride their own horses. Riders from all college teams draw a number, which corresponds to their horse for that day, and that is their horse for the competition.

No one has any idea of what the disposition of the horse is like or what their feel is like when you are out in the ring. All you can hope is that you do well and at least stay on. On any given show day, there could be an upwards of ten to fifteen horses that are up for draw. I had my fair share of interesting rides on my show rotation throughout the year at different schools but home, for me, was always on Dixie's back.

Outside the show ring, Dixie continued to be a best friend, aside from my good human friends at school. He was stress relief. Dixie was an excuse to not go out and party hard, as many of my other college friends did. Sunday mornings, when they were all recovering from the night before, I'd be getting up at 7:30/8:00 a.m. and heading to the barn for a couple of hours.

He was my refuge from the academic and social pressures and a shield from the pressure of exams. He regulated me when I felt my emotions out of kilter and calmed me when I was down or upset. Dixie, whether on the ground or on his back, was what made my college experience great. He taught me the value of routine, dedication, and discipline, and that served me so well in school. Long before the valid use and often misuse of the designation of "emotional support animals," Dixie was that for me in every real sense. I was forever grateful that my parents had bought Dixie for me and the lengths they went to in supporting my riding interests. They knew how important he was to me.

## Claire

One story exemplifies how Stefanie and Dixie were connected. The summer before college we were at a horse show when Stefanie sensed that there was something wrong with Dixie as she felt his walk was different. She expressed her concern to her horse trainers who insisted, after a quick inspection, that he was fine. Their assurance did not convince Stefanie that he was okay. Instead, she dismounted Dixie and "scratched from the show" saying, "Something's wrong with Dixie's leg. We need to have a veterinarian see him tomorrow."

Within twenty-four hours, Dixie's leg became swollen. His regular vet saw him but was unable to identify the source of the swelling. We were concerned about Dixie moving to Ithaca while we were trying to address his condition and all but decided that Stefanie would move to Ithaca without him. Stan called his cousin Jay, Dixie's personal vet, who suggested we let her take Dixie to Ithaca, arguing that he would heal better if Stefanie could be around.

Jay also reminded us that Dixie was likely to receive more advanced attention at Cornell's veterinary college, one of the best in the nation, which was in Ithaca. A few weeks into the first semester, the barn where we stabled Dixie called in a vet from Cornell, as Dixie's leg was still swollen and tender. The vet diagnosed the problem in one visit as an abscess in his foot. He figured out a way to treat his foot and within a couple of weeks Dixie was fit to ride.

The bond between Stefanie and Dixie was palpable. As long as Dixie was nearby, Stefanie could face the challenges of college. She did well, explored new subjects and became increasingly interested in issues of equality and diversity. In her junior year, she and a friend formed an "intersectionality" (a term she had learned in anthropology classes) group that met once a week discussing issues of race, ethnicity, and gender. Stefanie had decided in her freshman year to major in anthropology, instead of writing—her intended major. The world of anthropology opened many doors for Stefanie, from volunteering at a farm that had been purchased by two of her professors and returned to the Native Americans who had been the original inhabitants, to volunteering at a local health clinic.

## Junior Year Abroad

In early December of her junior year, Stefanie called me asking, "Do you know anything about palliative care?"

"Yes, I do. Why do you ask?" I responded. I was working at the Health-Care Chaplaincy in New York City where we trained chaplains and placed them to provide chaplaincy services in various health care institutions. One of the special services the chaplains provided was palliative care.

Stefanie had enrolled in a junior year abroad community health course in South Africa for the spring semester of her junior year. She continued, "At the end of our term in South Africa, we have to do a month-long independent study research project on a topic of our choice. I want to learn more about pediatric palliative care for children in South Africa."

"You do know, don't you, Stefanie," I told her, "it means working with terminally ill and dying children?"

"Of course, I do," she responded. "That's what I want to do."

"Great! How can I help?" I asked.

"Do you know anyone who could connect me to people working in palliative care with children in Durban where I'll be?" Stefanie responded.

"The one person I can call," I said, "is Dr. Kathleen Foley, the founder of the palliative care movement in the United States, who has been leading the advocacy efforts to have palliative care recognized as a medical specialty in the United States. I know that Dr. Foley has done some work in South Africa. I will give her a call."

"That is great, Mom. Thanks," Stefanie said.

I had gotten to know Dr. Foley when she was a board member of the HealthCare Chaplaincy. She is one of the most knowledgeable and caring people I have ever met. Dr. Foley had become an advocate of palliative care when it was still a very unpopular concept in medicine. I called her and explained what Stefanie needed. Immediately, she offered to introduce Stefanie to a South African nongovernmental organization (NGO) whose staff worked in pediatric palliative care in Durban. Stefanie contacted the Bigshoes Foundation and asked if she could work with them in the spring and document what she observed. They readily agreed. Stefanie was definitely not afraid to step into new roles. She submitted her research project to the program she was entering, which approved it. In January, Stefanie flew to South Africa to join this community health program for four months, followed by a final month in Durban working with the Bigshoes Foundation in their palliative care program.

Stan and I were anxious about Stefanie being so far away for four months even if we were entrusting her to a program endorsed by her college, but it was a program that we didn't know that much about. But mostly we were in awe of the person she was becoming, a young woman committed to tackling tough social issues. Stefanie made it clear she didn't want to go to an easy place like London or Paris. She wanted to explore more underdeveloped countries. We agreed to stay in touch through WhatsApp and email and planned to talk on Sundays. Stefanie began to write a blog of her trip and work as soon as she left.

Stefanie enjoyed the group of students in her program, found ways to explore the culture, and had fun. One week in March, Stefanie emailed to tell us she had a surprise for us when we spoke the following Sunday. We couldn't image what it was. Then on WhatsApp, she appeared with three of her friends who had shaved their heads to donate their hair to "Locks of

Love" which makes wigs for people with cancer. Another time she sent us a photo of her and several friends galloping on horses on a beach along the Indian Ocean. They lived with families and at youth hostels. Stefanie managed to make friends with the families she stayed with and incorporated these new experiences into her life.

In April, she settled in a hostel in Durban by herself with a contact from her study abroad program a phone call away. She would be working in the main hospital where the Bigshoes staff had their office and rotating with the Bigshoes doctors and social workers among three hospitals in Durban with pediatric palliative care wings. When we visited her at the end of the semester, I asked how she traveled from hospital to hospital.

"I hitchhiked," she responded.

I was glad we had learned this at the end of the program. Whenever we spoke with Stefanie, she was eager to share her experiences working in the hospital settings with the Bigshoes staff. Stefanie wrote a blog detailing her experiences of this semester abroad "*Uthando: Being and Experiencing in Kwa-Zulu Natal.*" The following blog entry indicates her willingness to extend herself to others, about how she had developed the ability to connect with people across oceans, cultures, and racial and ethnic groups.

## Excerpt from stefanie's blog

*April 21, 2012, Durban, South Africa: Whether it was the beating of one's heart or the beat of my footsteps down the intensive care ward or the beat to house music blaring in minibus taxis, swerving to the rhythm of the city, or the beat of the two hearts coming together in the union of a hug—today was the dance of life.*

*At age 21, I was spending a semester abroad in Durban, South Africa, studying community health. My last month was spent shadowing and doing observational research with the pediatric palliative care team of the Bigshoes Foundation. Today was my last day at Bigshoes. I knew it would be emotional as I had moved past my fears of being around very sick and dying children and had become attached to them, their families, and the Bigshoes staff. One of my first experiences with the Bigshoes team was when I joined them in going to a hospice in Veralum, a section of Durban, where Dr. Ambler saw a couple of pediatric patients. All of these children were infected with HIV and were experiencing various symptoms, including ear infections and breathing and heart problems.*

*The spirit and service of love at this particular hospice is what is so needed in the wards of the hospitals I had visited. If there is anything that I have noticed, it is the need for more empathy and compassion in these very sad places. I sat in on a counseling session today with the parents of a pediatric patient who suffered from brain damage and cardiac abnormalities. The Bigshoes team had to inform the parents that he was likely to die very soon as he was suffering from multiple strokes, and his brain damage was extensive. They talked with the parents for a while about the importance of letting their son go, so that he would not suffer more.*

*As my final day on this project was coming to a close, and knowing my time with Bigshoes was ending, Melody, a 13-year-old-girl whom I'd befriended in the high care unit, went into septic shock. When I heard the news, my heart sank. Two days before, our team had visited Melody. The doctor and nurse were called away to deal with another patient.*

*It was lunch time, and Dr. Ambler said, "Stef, will you stay here and feed Melody? We have to go to the ICU."*

*As I fed Melody mouthfuls of broth, she confided in me. At 13, she had been through multiple operations and had been living in this hospital for several months. After lunch, I held her hand, and Melody told me she was ready to go, she did not want to suffer any more. Life in the hospital, transferring from ward to ward, eating, sleeping, and being in pain was, she said, like "the life of a stray dog." Melody saw no purpose in going on. We talked as if we were sisters, Melody, a 13-year-old from the Zulu tribe dying in a South African hospital, and me, a Latina American college student whose mother had died of HIV/AIDS when I was five.*

*The 5,000 miles between our homes collapsed into inches. I shared Melody's pain and knew she was ready. She was the most peaceful person I'd ever seen.*

*To admit she was dying was a tremendous feat. Personally, I would be scared to admit death was upon me, but she saw peace in death and death in peace. The beat of her life song was slowly dying out, and she was ready to go into a song of silence. One day, I was talking to and feeding Melody. Two days later, she was barely clinging to life. My time with Bigshoes had opened my eyes to the sanctity of life and especially that of a child's life. There is no doubt that all of us are going to die one day, but for a child, what is that like? It takes people like Melody to encourage me to reevaluate my life and to count every moment I have to dance through life. Yes, there may be those moments when you fall and stumble and don't quite find your footing. But you try and try again.*

*This three-month song I have been singing joyously in South Africa is about to come to an end as well. I have been feeling melancholy about ending my semester in South Africa, but am able to recognize the excitement of returning home. Our group is due to go St. Lucia's, which I hear is a beautiful place, three hours up the coast. We will have the opportunity to decompress and come down from the stresses of these independent research projects and to prepare for our departures home—that transitory period between songs.*

*Holding Melody's hand that warm April day in Durban brought back a flood of memories of how my mother, Rosa, held my hand as a toddler when I walked through the halls of Highbridge-Woodycrest, the residence for families (mostly mothers) and children where I spent the first few years of my life.*

## Claire

Stefanie's blog reminded us that from an early age, Stefanie showed empathy for others through her actions in standing up for her friends who were bullied by their classmates. Whether the bullies were threatening her young friend who had just recovered from cancer or a small girl who the bullies were trying to push around, Stefanie announced clearly that they would have to deal with her to get to her friends. The bullies backed off.

Stefanie's empathy also extended to people she did not even know. One Sunday, when Stefanie was about ten, we were at mass at St. Francis Xavier Church when a very large unkempt woman came up from the back of the Church toward the altar screaming that she was angry about the way society was treating her. Several men in the congregation moved toward her, gently took her arms, and led her to a seat in the front of the church, near us. She quieted down but was still agitated, twitching her head and looking around. Stefanie stood up and walked over to her, bent down and said,

"Don't worry, you are protected by angels. You will be safe."

The woman reached up to Stefanie, hugged her, and thanked her. The congregation was silent. Everyone appeared awestruck by Stefanie's courage in reaching out and extending compassion to this woman. The mass proceeded without further outbreaks. After the service, Stan and I commended Stefanie for comforting this woman.

"I felt bad for her," Stefanie said. "She seemed so frightened and alone."

Her South African experience was a major formative one for Stefanie. Her worldview was definitely being shaped as she increasingly became a global citizen. It had been no surprise when Stefanie had declared her college major as anthropology, with a special focus on medical anthropology. She used her problem-solving techniques that she had learned from Stan's math "classes" during her undergraduate days at Ithaca College and during her studies for her Master of Science in Public Health degree at the London School of Hygiene and Tropical Medicine.

In 2013, Stefanie graduated *cum laude* from Ithaca College. We rented a house on Cayuga Lake for the occasion, and our sons David and Jeffrey and their families, joined us in celebrating Stefanie's graduation. It had been a whirlwind four years, beginning with Stan being asked to serve as president of Baruch College for a year the same weekend we took Stefanie to begin her journey at Ithaca. That year was followed by Stan traveling around the world with visiting scholars in a State Department–funded program on climate change. I continued my work at the Chaplaincy developing a palliative care residence.

After graduation, Stefanie knew she wanted to go to graduate school, most likely in public health. The South Africa experience and her own background had made her acutely aware of the need for better public health services. During her first year home, Stefanie had various jobs as she decompressed from a very good, but intense, four years in college. Then she was offered an AmeriCorps post working in a community health clinic in New York City. Midway through that year, she decided she wanted to apply to a university to earn a degree in public health, and she applied to six schools. One in the Midwest offered her a handsome scholarship.

The following May, following her college graduation, we took a family vacation to London, both for Stan to give a speech on his work integrating the arts into the curricula at Baruch College and to see our friend Angela Lansbury starring in *Blithe Spirit*. We had met Angela in 2009 when our friend Bob Callely, then her manager, introduced us. Stefanie was at college, but we had several dinners with Angela when she was in New York City. When Stefanie returned from college, she met Angela, who was very warm and supportive of Stefanie.

In London, we met up with one of Stan's former students, who was studying at the London School of Hygiene and Tropical Medicine. Mohammed took us on a brief tour of the school and suggested Stefanie meet him the next day for a more fulsome tour, which she did. She was very taken with the school and its hundred-plus-year history, its work in developing countries, and its overall mission. She reported to us that she wanted to apply there.

That evening we saw *Blithe Spirit* and went backstage after to see Dame Lansbury. Angela was warm, as always. On the way back to our hotels in her limo, Angela talked with Stefanie about her options.

"London is where you belong, Stefanie," Angela said. "Don't give it a second thought, just come here."

Angela confirmed what Stefanie was already thinking. She felt she would be most "at home" at the London School. Fortunately, a year later she was accepted, and the fall of 2015 saw the three of us on a plane to London. We helped Stefanie get settled, and she was on her way. She came home that Christmas, and then we saw her again when we traveled back to London in February for Stan to give another talk about the arts programs he had created.

Stefanie discussed with us her tutor's recommendation that she apply to do her thesis while working in the Harris County Texas Health Department in Houston. They were looking for someone to propose ways to prevent or reduce the impact of arboviruses, such as the Zika virus, carried by mosquitoes. Stefanie applied and was awarded a paid internship. She came home in June, just as Stan had to have emergency surgery for a serious stomach problem. I needed to stay with Stan, so I canceled my plan to go with her to get settled in Houston. Thankfully, Stan made a full recovery after five weeks in the hospital and a week in rehab for physical therapy.

Stefanie had wanted to stay in New York City and make sure Stan was recovering, but I told her that her dad wanted her to do what she needed to do. So, she did what she always does. She made herself at home in Houston and spent the summer visiting communities and meeting with public health officials. Her thesis recommendation was that to be effective a plan needed to involve community residents from the beginning. Stefanie was beginning to see that health was a grassroots issue.

That September, Stefanie came back to New York, found an apartment in Harlem, and a job with a local hospital's school health program. Since then, she has had three other jobs—each one building on the other as a learning experience in how to improve community health. Our little girl has become a compassionate and accomplished young woman.

## Stan's and Claire's Reflections

### Stan's Reflections

Watching Stefanie graduate from the London School of Hygiene and Tropical Medicine with her Master of Science in Public Health in 2017 brought tears to my eyes. I was so proud of her. I flashed back on my early experience with Stefanie when she was a frightened and withdrawn four-year-old, a child who believed she would fail at whatever she was asked to do.

I thought about my reaction in the fall of 1995 when Claire raised the proposal of our becoming Stefanie's standby guardians and my negative reaction to the idea. How different my life and partnership with Claire would have been had we not become Stefanie's guardians and adopted her. I would never have experienced the joy of watching her grow up. What I saw that day in London at her graduation was that our daughter had become a warm, loving young woman who was passionate about helping others, and willing to take risks like the one she took in doing her semester abroad in South Africa or her public health internship in Houston, Texas. She now exhibited a quiet strength in searching for meaning in her life. Parenting Stefanie has made my relationship with Claire grow stronger. It has given meaning to our commitment to each other that "we are in it together."

In the summer of 2016, I was rushed to the emergency room because my hernia had ruptured, and I had developed peritonitis. My surgery was complicated, and the doctors were not always sure I would make it. Two days later, I had a second surgery and was in the hospital for a month. At one point, Stefanie expressed concern about me. The look on her face made me think she was worried that I was going to die. Then I reminded her, "I made you a promise that I would give you away at your wedding. I am not going anywhere." I could see the relief on her face.

As I write this, I realize how Stefanie has brought joy back into my life and, in her own quiet way, she has helped take down the walls that I had built to bury my feelings so long ago.

Friends and others who hear the story of adopting our daughter say how fortunate she was to be adopted by us. Claire and I always respond that we are the fortunate ones to have Stefanie in our lives. Our love for her has been returned manyfold and strengthened our love for each other.

Stefanie continues to grow and thrive in many ways, and we continue to support her however we can. Love is what carries us through, all those years ago and now.

## Claire's Reflections

Our journey with Stefanie has taught us how rich life can be when love carries us through and that we can overcome many obstacles that seem insurmountable when we approach them with love in our hearts. When Stefanie's mother asked us to help her find a guardian for Stefanie, we asked a number of people until we realized that becoming Stefanie's guardians was something we were meant to do. Accepting that challenge with love for Stefanie and her mom made the path manageable. At times, we wondered if we could survive the repeated challenges we faced, but we found the strength and carried on. Stan and I knew how Stefanie had shown extraordinary courage in dealing with her mother's passing, living in two worlds between her mother's former partner and living with us, dealing with self-esteem issues, and all the while finding and following her own bliss.

Sometimes, we found extra reserves just hearing her say, "It's great to be a kid," or showing us how much horses provided her emotional support in ways that we couldn't. Stan and I learned to listen to cues from Stefanie about what she needed from us. We knew that probably the most important thing we could give her was showing her how much we loved each other and loved her. Our main goal in life became giving her a sense of stability. Providing her with the things that brought her joy, watching her face light up and embracing us as her parents became our joy.

One of the most poignant examples of this was about three years ago, when Stefanie was dealing with dating and exploring what kind of mate she wanted. Stan said to her, "What are you looking for in a partner?"

Stefanie responded, without missing a beat, "I want what the two of you have."

That was the greatest compliment that a child could give her parents. Stan and I feel so grateful to have been blessed with the opportunity to become Stefanie's parents, helping to prepare her for her life and to live that life to the fullest.

Stefanie continues to grow and thrive in many ways, and we continue to support her however we can. Love is what carries us through.

# The Art of the Heart

## Stefanie

There is something that sits differently on your heart when you know you have been chosen as a child into a family. Since the beginning, my mom and dad have told me that I am their love child. When people say "blood is thicker than water," I have always wanted to say "love is thicker than blood." Before becoming an Altman, I never had a strong relationship with my birth family, except with my mom. I stopped talking to them around the time Angela passed. My uncle faded away when the order of protection was issued against him, and my mom and dad's custody took full effect before our official adoption.

Some people glamorize adoption. They imagine a scenario of a child hugging his or her newly found parents for the first time, jumping on a new bed in a crisp white room, knowing new opportunities abound, smiles shared at the dinner table amidst a feast, a collective joy shared where troubles and trauma don't hang in the air. Society tends to wrap adoption up in a bow and present it as a gift to both parents and child, without consideration of the journey that came before. Yes, adoption is a labor of love, but it's not as glamorous as one might think. Nancy Verrier, a clinical psychologist, and author of several books on adoption said, "There is a great deal more to preparing for an adopted child than fixing up a nursery or having money in the bank for a college education. There is a real need for emotional stability, honesty, and the willingness to become truly informed about what

this process means for the adopting parents and for their child" (https://
www.yourtango.com/experts/suzanne-jones/21-best-inspiring-quotes-for
-parents-raising-kids-via-adoption, accessed November 19, 2024).

Adoption is about getting to know each side's love language, allowing for
openness, and allowing mistakes to happen so the new family can learn,
grow, and love. Establishing a loving and accepting place took effort on all
sides from the three of us and gave us the opportunity to grow and become
closer. I did not enter into that arrangement easily. I was still scarred by
trust issues from my past with Angela and my uncle, but slowly, as time
passed, I gained trust and opened up.

There is power in story. Stories are meant to connect us, bind us, and help
us find our common humanity. Through the ages and a multitude of cultures,
stories are a way to impart wisdom to those who still wonder and seek the
truth. Every story is going to affect each one of us differently, and some people
may or may not relate. I found a connection to my adoption through the arts.

And now, at age thirty-three, I am co-writing a book with my parents.
I hope to provide inspiration for people who are looking to adopt, and to
those children who have been adopted, to see their experiences reflected
in the larger world. Even though I have loved to write since I was a child, if
you had asked me, even as a writing minor in college, whether I saw myself
a decade later writing a book, I would have scoffed at you. Ironically, and
much to my surprise, I am, and it has been a true labor of love.

In particular, I wish to include the following story to illustrate how my
experience is reflected in the larger world of theater. It resonated with me.

In 2003, I was in my last year as an eighth grader at Writers and Artists in New York City's Chelsea neighborhood. My brother, David and his
fiancée, Irma, were due to be married that summer in Glen Cove, Long
Island. Three years before when my brother was dating Irma, they took
me to see *X-Men* in Miami on a family vacation. The brooding, scruffy,
smart-ass character of Wolverine caught my pre-teen eye, but more so, the
actor who was playing him.

One day, some of my middle school friends and I were discussing
celebrities whom we thought were cute. Each of us went around the
lunch table and cited our respective crushes. Names like Orlando
Bloom and Daniel Radcliffe were offered. I said Hugh Jackman. Nods
and expressions of "oh" were expressed. They seemed indifferent and
shrugged, and we continued on with our lunchtime banter. A couple
of weeks later, as our graduation culmination project, Clinton School
eighth graders were assigned to complete a graduation project. The
project was to take the form of a personal written and/or performance

presentation. I decided to create a tap dance routine, along with a narration, about Judy Garland.

Ms. Harris was the drama teacher. If you were to combine Whoopi Goldberg and Patti LuPone, you got Ms. Harris. She was no joke, and she directed great student productions as a result. Even with only a year of tap dance lessons, I was still determined. I knew I had a lot to measure up to, especially under Ms. Harris's keen eye. My presentation of Judy Garland had been inspired when I saw her, played by the amazing Isabel Keating, in *The Boy from Oz*. Making his Broadway debut in this musical biography of Peter Allen was none other than Hugh Jackman. Yes, the same Hugh Jackman who was a steel claw wielding, slicing and dicing machine in *X Men* was doing high kicks onstage, playing the piano, singing, and tap dancing. Peter Allen, married to Liza Minnelli before he came out as gay, had been discovered by Judy Garland at a night club where he was performing.

Captivated by the person Judy Garland was, I knew I wanted to base my eighth-grade graduation project on her life. Through four weeks of pen to paper and tap shoes to a wooden board, I compiled a multi-genre piece about her. I traced her career from her beginning as a teenaged star in the MGM studios of the 1930s to her becoming a Hollywood starlet, her career-defining role as Dorothy in *The Wizard of Oz*, and developing her heart-breaking addiction to drugs later in life. I suppose I connected with Judy Garland on a number of levels from growing up in a broken home. Both of her parents were vaudeville stars and were very controlling of her career. She experienced continuous unhappiness unless she found it outside of herself, whether it be through the external approval of strangers or the temporary relief of the "uppers" she took.

Performing was a way to escape and heal. She used her addiction as a way to cope. I had a pretty hard time in middle school, with selective eating disorders and using laxatives as a way to purge. My connection with Judy Garland was perhaps even deeper than I realized back then. I connected to the story of Peter Allen, who died of AIDS in 1992, just four years before my own mother's passing in 1996. Coincidentally, Peter Allen and I share the same birthday. In addition, I identified with Hugh Jackman, who adopted two biracial children with his wife, Deborra-Lee Furness, and whose outlook on adoption has always resonated with me. In an interview with Caroline Bologna, Jackman explained how he and his wife viewed adoption, saying that as soon as they started the adoption process, their anxiety evaporated, and they began to think of their children as their own children. In this interview, Hugh said:

Now, as we go through life together, sure there are challenges, but everyone's in the right place with the right people. It sounds airy-fairy, but it's something we feel very deeply. . . . A while back, there was a lot of shame attached to it and parents wouldn't tell their kids they were adopted. What's great is that the focus is now shifting to the care of the child. We were very fortunate and open. . . . Adoption is a wonderful thing to do. (Caroline Bologna, "Lovely Quotes about Parenthood from Hugh Jackman," *Huffington Post*, October 12, 2019)

My friends and family know that I am still enamored of Hugh Jackman, and none of us sees that wavering anytime soon. *The Boy from Oz* first opened on Broadway in the fall of 2003, and I saw it three times in its year-long run on Broadway.

This is the perfect opportunity to bring in my godfather. Enter from stage left, Bob C., an ex–Vietnam era vet, who loved attending the theater, and eventually worked his way into executive leadership positions in different theater organizations in New York. My "Uncle Bob" was on the board of directors when the Highbridge-Woodycrest Center was founded, so he had known me from infancy. He and my father are especially close and best friends. Bob has joined us on several family trips to India, and he has been there for me when I have performed in recitals and musicals. He also joined us at my adoption. Uncle Bob is caring and lovable, playful and a bit sassy, all while hiding underneath a permeable "rough Irish brogue" façade.

While I was still in middle school and completing my multimedia Judy Garland project, I saw *The Boy from Oz* a second time in May 2004. It was a way to research, understand, and capture Judy's spirit. I studied the very talented Isabel Keating, who originated the role of Judy Garland in the show, to see how she conveyed Judy's joys and pain. I remember closing my eyes to focus on just listening to her. She sounded just like Judy Garland, brassy and full mezzo-alto, a vibrato that shook the house when she let a note rip. Bob got us comp tickets and took me to this performance.

Shortly after my project was due in early June, Bob was at our house one night for dinner. Everyone was kidding me for wanting to go to *The Boy from Oz* a third time, rolling their eyes as if to say, "This girl just can't get enough." That was true; wasn't three times always the charm? They were trying to reason with me that since Hugh Jackman had won a TONY award for his performance in *The Boy from Oz*, getting tickets was especially difficult.

As a serious suggestion to my yearning to see it for a third time, Uncle Bob proposed that I send Isabel Keating a copy of my Judy Garland project and ask if we could meet backstage. I typed a letter, included a bound copy of my project and the CD cover to the cast recording of *The Boy from Oz*, and sent it to Ms. Keating at the Imperial Theater. I was hoping that in some way Ms. Keating could get Hugh to sign it. A couple of weeks later, a manila envelope came in the mail with Isabel Keating's return address at the Imperial Theater. She had handwritten a letter to me stating how impressed she was with my project and that she would love to invite me backstage when I returned to see the show. Also, to my surprise, behind her handwritten note was the signed CD cover with Hugh's penmanship, "Best wishes, Stefanie." Needless to say, I was on cloud nine, and it is still a cherished memento.

We replied to Ms. Keating to confirm the date when we would attend the show, as my dad had managed, with some help from Uncle Bob, to get two tickets to see it in the last couple of weeks of its run in August. My dad and I attended a sold-out Sunday matinee on a blisteringly hot August day. The energy surrounding the show was electric. When Hugh sang the final song "I Go to Rio," a celebration of life and love with brassy Brazilian rhythms and the cast dressed in white, the standing ovation was monumental. Isabel Keating, Stephanie J. Block (who played Liza Minnelli), and Hugh Jackman looked joyful, grateful, and exhausted as they bowed to thunderous applause. The show had two more weeks before the year-long run ended.

There was something melancholy and magical about this moment, the end of an unexpected Broadway hit, and the end of summer.

As the curtains fell, and the crowd dispersed out onto 45th Street, my dad and I followed the last trickle of audience goers. We wove our way through the stage door crowd, which was awaiting cast autographs. Isabel Keating had instructed us to ask for Kevin, the stage door guard. My dad informed him that Ms. Keating had sent for us and showed him the letter she wrote as proof. When we reached the top of the steps to the stage door, my dad motioned to one of the door tenders. "We are looking for Kevin," my dad said. The husky guard graciously nodded his head and went inside to find Kevin. When Kevin arrived, my dad said that Ms. Keating had invited us backstage. He showed Kevin the note she had written a couple of months back, and he said to follow him.

Kevin led us through the narrow corridors of the Imperial Theater's backstage and left us on the stage. He said to wait there while he went to get Isabel Keating from her dressing room. The view of the theater from the stage was spectacular, to say the least. The empty seats, the now semi-sleepiness of the house, the ghost-light had been brought to the stage, and all of the excitement of the finale number was hushed and tucked away until Tuesday when performances commenced again.

As I gazed over the orchestra to the mezzanine, out walked Isabel Keating. Casually dressed in jeans and a t-shirt, still in her stage makeup, hair still in her wig net, she greeted my dad and me with a big hug. Isabel Keating was very gracious and personable. I will never forget her warmth. She told us again how impressed she was by my project on Judy Garland, how she re-read it and how much it had captured her spirit. She talked about her year's run in *The Boy from Oz* and what it felt like to close in a couple of weeks. She said that she was grateful for the last year because she had not expected this show to be such a success. She credited this to her cast mates, especially Hugh Jackman, whose unapologetic charisma carried him through his run as Peter Allen.

Other visitors straggled on stage to speak with the cast. Ms. Keating asked if I would like to meet Hugh Jackman. I shakily said, "Yes." She mentioned that Hugh was signing autographs outside, and that she would ask him to meet us on stage. She said goodbye and reassured us that she would check in with Kevin to pass along her request to Hugh.

Now, with nerves on a new high, my dad and I continued to admire the view from the stage and discussed how much this show hit home to us, especially how Peter Allen dying of AIDS resonated with me. It seemed that minutes went by and still no sign of Hugh Jackman. My dad asked me to wait while he checked in with Kevin to see if Hugh might meet us. A moment later, my dad came back grinning saying that Hugh would arrive any moment now. I recall how my nerves buzzed and rattled in my body.

Hugh Jackman arrived with a welcoming smile. He gave my dad a firm handshake and thanked us both for coming to the show. I got a hug (wink!). I was speechless and paralyzed standing there, trying to believe that after all this, Hugh Jackman was there talking with us. My dad reiterated how much we enjoyed the performance and thanked him by giving him a cap from Baruch College. Hugh graciously took the hat.

"Would you mind taking a picture with my daughter?" dad asked.

"Absolutely not," he said. Hugh opened up his embrace and invited me for a side-by-side photo. Hugh jokingly shifted us a couple of steps to try to get the light right.

"There we go," he said cheekily. My dad snapped away on his digital camera, truly a moment captured forever, one I have hung on my kitchen wall to this day!

"Thanks, Hugh," I managed to utter.

"You're welcome, sweetheart," he said in his melodic Aussie accent. He wished me and my dad well and moved on to the other clusters of fans waiting for him on the stage.

That day, I felt that I had melted on the Imperial stage and would stay there forever! Friends and family of mine can attest to how much of a fan I am to this day.

The movie adaptation of *Les Misérables*, in which Hugh Jackman starred as Jean Valjean and one song, in particular, also had a profound effect on me. The musical is an operatic adaptation of Victor Hugo's 1862 novel of the disenfranchised Frenchmen fighting the government that followed the French Revolution. The story follows Jean Valjean's nineteen-year struggle to lead a normal life after serving a prison sentence for stealing bread to feed his sister's starving children. Valjean is later asked to take care of a young girl, Cosette, whose mother is dying and has turned to him to raise her child. Because Valjean's past prevents him from adopting Cosette, she goes to live with a couple of dysfunctional inn owners who are manipulative and selfish and who treat Cosette more like a chambermaid than a daughter.

Eventually, Valjean is able to gain custody of Cosette and raise her as his own. In the early stages of their relationship, Valjean sings "Suddenly." a song about his acceptance of fatherhood, the troubles of his past, and the surprising impact of what kind of love comes from a chosen parent-child relationship:

Suddenly you're here. Suddenly it starts.
Can two anxious hearts beat as one?
Yesterday I was alone.
Today you are beside me. Something still unclear.
Something not yet here Has begun.
Suddenly the world Seems a different place.
Somehow full of grace Full of light
How was I to know that so much hope was held inside me?
What has passed is gone.
Now we journey on through the night.
How was I to know at last
That happiness can come so fast? Trusting me the way you do.
I'm so afraid of failing you. Just a child who cannot know. That danger
follows where I go. There are shadows everywhere and memories I
cannot share
Nevermore alone

Nevermore apart
You have warmed my heart like the sun. You have brought the gift of life
And love so long denied me.
Suddenly I see What I could not see. Something suddenly Has begun.

—Music and Lyrics Copyright 2012 by Alain Boublil Music Ltd. (ASCAP)

The first time I heard "Suddenly" I was shaken to the core by Hugh's performance. Over the years, I have come to appreciate how much theater, stories, and the arts can nourish our minds and hearts. Hugh Jackman's performances, especially this song, spoke strongly to me because of the very unknown path of a new family. Claire had her heart set on taking me in and raising me as her own. With my dad, it took some coaxing and convincing for him to open up.

He has admitted to me that he did not know how to raise a daughter, after having raised two sons, and that he asked my mother for some grace during the process. He was admittedly a bit scared and reluctant to take on a new responsibility, but he always reminded me, that whenever he closed up, I was there to open him up again.

In the future, when I walk into rooms with my parents, and people are sizing me up and asking, "Where are you from?" I know this is not out of malice but out of curiosity, interest, and sincerity. This is especially so in New York, one of the great multicultural microcosms of the world, where race is a large part of one's identity. I have straddled the space of what it means to be "bicultural." I have playfully referred to myself as a "coconut," being brown on the outside and white on the inside.

My parents have encouraged me to learn and take pride in my Puerto Rican heritage. I have learned salsa dancing and how to cook homemade meals from Puerto Rico. When I look from the adopted side, there are still a lot of questions that remain. I love my adopted family so much and am grateful for them every day. I love breaking stereotypes and surprising people with my story. With every new person I meet, I am reminded just how unique my story is in so many ways.

Claire held me in her arms when I was just three months old, mothering me without realizing that's what she was doing, what she was destined to do. She cared for me by caring for me and my biological mother, Mommy Rosa, whose memory I cherish. And Mommy Rosa performed her most powerful act as a mother by placing me in Claire and Stan's care before she died.

Claire loved me before guardianship papers, social workers, and court orders became part of the fabric of our lives. And her love and commitment were so powerful that Stan, the only father I have ever had, grew to love me as well. You see, I had two mothers. But I have only ever had one father.

Adoption, taking a child into your home and heart by choice, loving, nurturing, and supporting them through all of life's transitions and challenges, is a powerful form of unconditional love that we are blessed to have experienced. In this, I truly was twice blessed.

# ACKNOWLEDGMENTS

OUR DEEPEST GRATITUDE goes to our beloved spiritual teacher Sri Sakthi Amma for her ongoing encouragement and spiritual guidance throughout the journey of writing this book.

Cathy and John Wenuk gave generously of their time and talent reading drafts of our manuscript and providing helpful edits and comments. They saw from the beginning that our story was more than about adopting Stefanie, but about the unconditional love that bound us together.

Our dear friend John Underkoffler was the first person to read an early draft of our book. His ongoing feedback, encouragement, and support kept us focused on telling our story.

We were fortunate to have many helpers in writing this book, including friends and family who read early drafts and provided suggestions: Helene Brezenski, Helene Bigley, and Josephine Brunoski. Then there were those who helped us in our search for a publisher: Mara Bergman, Stan Litow, Tony Wood, Jeannette Watson Sanger, and Brian Schwartz.

We are especially grateful to our friend and editor, Davida Siwisa James, who understood our story and helped us tell it more effectively, providing valuable suggestions for making it clearer and hopefully more engaging to read. We were surprised and pleased when Stephen G. Post offered to write the foreword to our book. Stephen's work on the power of love and service has always inspired us. Special thanks go to our friend Bob Callely, who as Stefanie's godfather, has been a guide for Stefanie and an important part of our family.

We are grateful to our attorneys: Ben Rosin, Mari Hinojosa, and Rebecca Mandel. We have learned a great deal from leaders in the child welfare field who provided us valuable guidance: Dr. Richard Dudley, Elizabeth Bartholet, Rosa Gil, Lilliam Barrios Paoli, Naomi Riley, David Hansell, Shirley Gabel Gatenio, and Ron Richter.

Individuals who played key roles in developing the Highbridge-Woodycrest Center, where this story began, include Bob Callely, Sterling Zinsmeyer, Dr. David Axelrod, and NYC Mayor David Dinkins. Persons who were important in Stefanie's development include Stefanie's soccer coach, Judith Stiles; her art teacher, Lisa Allen; her viola teacher, Lisa Whitfield; her riding coaches, Lorraine Roe, Rene Romeo, and Moira Roberts; her teachers—especially Jane Hsu; and our dear friends Dr. Kathleen Foley, Cathy Gaynor, Tashi Chodron, and Nathalie Latham.

Our thanks also to close friends and supporters whose memory we honor: Dr. Michael O. Smith, Dr. Alan Berkman, Dr. Mitchell Gaynor, Peter Britell, Joyce Bove, Helen Vanderbilt, and Angela Lansbury.

This story would not have been possible without the love and support from our family members as we became Stefanie's guardians and then her adoptive parents. Stan's dad, Jack Altman, our sons David and Jeffrey Altman and their wives Irma and Sara, our siblings Kathy, Jim, and Margie Haaga, and Anita Altman supported our raising Stefanie and writing this book from its inception.

The leadership and support of the team at Fordham University Press: Fred Nachbaur, director, who first believed in our book and has supported us every step of the way, Will Cerbone, Mark Lerner, Kem Crimmins, Kate O'Brien-Nicholson, Katie Sweeney Parmiter, and Teresa Jesionowski have all helped make our book a reality. Special thanks to our attorney Peter Smith, who has believed in this project from the beginning and has provided valuable guidance.

Finally, Stefanie, Stan, and I owe a huge debt of gratitude to each other for deciding to delve into our collective and individual memories to write this book together and work as a team to bring the story of our family to fruition.

# CHRONOLOGY OF CUSTODY/GUARDIANSHIP EVENTS

September 1995: Rosa, Stefanie's biological mother, asks Stan and Claire to become Stefanie's standby guardians. They agree.

March 1996: Rosa passes away.

June 1996: NYC Family Court certifies Stan and Claire's guardianship and their joint custody agreement with Rosa's female partner.

November 19, 2001: Rosa's partner and Stefanie's uncle are arrested in a "sting" operation for selling stolen goods from their apartment; Stefanie calls Stan and Claire to pick her up to "stay over at their house." Stan brings Stefanie back to their house.

November 20, 2001: Claire goes to NYC Family Court and obtains order of temporary full custody of Stefanie.

December 2001: Stan and Claire file motion for full permanent custody of Stefanie.

December 2001: Rosa's partner counters with claim for full custody of Stefanie and court orders weekly visitation by Stefanie with partner.

December 2001: Stan and Claire obtain order of protection for them and for Stefanie from her uncle, Rosa's bother, who has threatened all three of them.

January–February 2002: NYC Family Court assignment to Hearing Officer and court proceedings

March 2002: Official trial begins and continues through mid-July 2002 when it's adjourned until September 2002.

Late July 2002: Rosa's partner contracts pneumonia and dies.

August 22, 2002: Claire and Stan formally adopt Stefanie and she them. Family Court judge asked Stefanie if this is what she wanted. By then, Stefanie was eleven years old and able to decide matters for herself.

# SELECTED BIBLIOGRAPHY

Babicki, Elke. *Identity: From Holocaust to Home—A Memoir.* The History Collectives, 2022.

Bartholet, Elizabeth. *Family Bonds: Adoption & the Politics of Parenting.* New York: Houghton Mifflin, 1993.

Bartholet, Elizabeth. *Nobody's Children: Abuse and Neglect, Foster Drift, and the Adoption Alternative.* Boston: Beacon Press, 1999.

Boswell, John Eastburn. *The Kindness of Strangers: The Abandonment of Children in Western Europe from Late Antiquity to the Renaissance.* New York: Pantheon, 1988.

Cardaras, Mary. *Ripped at the Root: An Adoption Story.* New York: Spuyten Duyvil, 2021.

De Hartog, Jan. *Adopted Children.* New York: Adama Books, 1969.

Dunn, J. H. *Out of the Birdcage: Memoirs of an Adoptee.* North Haven, CT: CreateSpace, 2018.

Dusky, Lorraine. *Hole in My Heart: Love and Loss in the Fault Lines of Adoption.* Tempe, AZ: Grand Canyon Press, 2022.

Elliott, Andrea. *Invisible Child Poverty: Survival and Hope in an American City.* New York: Random House, 2021.

Emswiler, Mary Ann, and James P. Emswiler. *Guiding Your Child through Grief.* New York: Bantam Books, 2000.

Geballe, Shelley, Janice Gruendel, and Warren Andiman, eds. *Forgotten Children of the AIDS Epidemic.* New Haven, CT: Yale University Press, 1995.

Gibran, Kahlil. *The Prophet.* London: William Heinemann, 1926.

Goldstein, Joseph, Anna Freud, Albert J. Solnit, and Sonja Goldstein. *In the Best Interests of the Child.* New York: Free Press, 1986.

Hall, Elena S. *Through Adopted Eyes.* Wardrobe Media, 2018.

Heffron, Anne. *You Don't Look Adopted.* Self-published, 2016.

Herman, Judith. *Trauma and Recovery: The Aftermath of Violence—From Domestic Abuse to Political Terror.* New York: Perseus Books, 1995.

Hughes, Lynn B. *You Are Not Alone; Teens Talk about Life after the Loss of a Parent.* New York: Scholastic, 1995.

James, John W., and Russell Friedman. *When Children Grieve.* New York: Harper Collins, 2001.

Kranowitz, Carol Stock. *The Out-Of-Sync Child.* New York: Skylight Press, 1968.

Krementz, Jill. *How It Feels When a Parent Dies.* New York: Alfred A. Knopf, 1996.

Kübler-Ross, Elisabeth. *AIDS: The Ultimate Challenge.* New York: Collier Books, 1987.

Lifton, Betty Jean. *Twice Born: Memoirs of an Adopted Daughter.* New York: Penguin Books, 1977.

Massie, Robert, and Suzanne Massie. *Journey.* New York: Warner Books, 1976.

Morris, Kathy. *We Were the Morris Orphans: 4 Brothers, 5 Sisters, and Me.* New York: Post Hill Press, 2021.

Read, Shelley. *Go as a River.* New York: Spiegel & Grau, 2023.

Riley, Naomi Schaeffer. *No Way to Treat A Child: How the Foster Care System, Family Courts, and Racial Activists Are Wrecking Young Lives.* New York: Bombardier Books, 2021.

Towey, Jim. *To Love and Be Loved.* New York: Simon & Schuster, 2022.

Tucker, Angela. *You Should Be Grateful: Stories of Race, Identity, and Transracial Adoption.* Boston: Beacon Press, 2022.

Verrier, Nancy Newton. https://www.yourtango.com/experts/suzanne-jones/21-best-inspiring-quotes-for-parents-raising-kids-via-adoption. Accessed 11/18/24.

Williams, Mary. *The Lost Daughter.* New York: Penguin Group, 2013.

**Stefanie Mercado Altman** was born in 1991 to Rosa Mercado, a Puerto Rican woman suffering with AIDS, and was adopted by Stan and Claire Altman after her birth mother died. Throughout her life, Stefanie has been passionate about helping those less fortunate than herself. She earned a Bachelor's degree from Ithaca College in anthropology and a Master's of Science in Public Health from the London School of Tropical Medicine. Her first published work, a poem titled "Racing Heart," appeared in the *Anthology of Poetry by Young Americans* (2004). Stefanie continues to write poems, health promotion pieces, and now is co-authoring this book. Stefanie lives in Brooklyn, New York.

**Stan Altman** has served in higher education for over fifty years as an administrator and teacher. At the City University of New York, he served as the interim President of Baruch College and Dean of the Austin W. Marxe School of Public and International Affairs; currently at City College of New York he is a professor and Director of the Gaming Pathways Program. At SUNY Stony Brook, he served as an associate director and deputy to the President.

**Claire Altman** is a writer and consultant whose major work has been in developing innovative not-for-profit projects in affordable housing and support services, ex-offender re-entry programs, and senior programs. Claire has a BA from St. Louis University, a Master's in Public Affairs from NYU Wagner School of Public Affairs, and a JD from Fordham School of Law. Her work with individuals and families with HIV/AIDS led to her writing, with her husband and daughter, their story of adoption, *Twice Blessed: A Story of Unconditional Love.*

**Stephen G. Post** is Professor of Family, Population and Preventive Medicine and Founding Director of the Center for Medical Humanities, Compassionate Care and Bioethics (2008–present). Previously he was Professor of Bioethics in the Department of Bioethics of the Case Western Reserve University School of Medicine (1988–2008). He is a bioethicist who has studied the relationship between altruism, compassion, happiness, healing, and health to conclude that giving can lead to a happier, longer life. Post is a pioneer in publishing works regarding ethical aspects of diseases such as Alzheimer's, an important but neglected issue of the aging population.

Colin Davey with Thomas A. Lesser, *The American Museum of Natural History and How It Got That Way*. Forewords by Neil deGrasse Tyson and Kermit Roosevelt III

Wendy Jean Katz, *Humbug: The Politics of Art Criticism in New York City's Penny Press*

Lolita Buckner Inniss, *The Princeton Fugitive Slave: The Trials of James Collins Johnson*

Mike Jaccarino, *America's Last Great Newspaper War: The Death of Print in a Two-Tabloid Town*

Angel Garcia, *The Kingdom Began in Puerto Rico: Neil Connolly's Priesthood in the South Bronx*

Jim Mackin, *Notable New Yorkers of Manhattan's Upper West Side: Bloomingdale–Morningside Heights*

Matthew Spady, *The Neighborhood Manhattan Forgot: Audubon Park and the Families Who Shaped It*

Marilyn S. Greenwald and Yun Li, *Eunice Hunton Carter: A Lifelong Fight for Social Justice*

Jeffrey A. Kroessler, *Sunnyside Gardens: Planning and Preservation in a Historic Garden Suburb*

Ron Howell, *King Al: How Sharpton Took the Throne*

Phil Rosenzweig, *"12 Angry Men": Reginald Rose and the Making of an American Classic*

Jean Arrington with Cynthia S. LaValle, *From Factories to Palaces: Architect Charles B. J. Snyder and the New York City Public Schools*. Foreword by Peg Breen

Boukary Sawadogo, *Africans in Harlem: An Untold New York Story*

Alvin Eng, *Our Laundry, Our Town: My Chinese American Life from Flushing to the Downtown Stage and Beyond*

Stephanie Azzarone, *Heaven on the Hudson: Mansions, Monuments, and Marvels of Riverside Park*

Ron Goldberg, *Boy with the Bullhorn: A Memoir and History of ACT UP New York*. Foreword by Dan Barry

Peter Quinn, *Cross Bronx: A Writing Life*

Mark Bulik, *Ambush at Central Park: When the IRA Came to New York*

Brandon Dean Lamson, *Caged: A Teacher's Journey Through Rikers, or How I Beheaded the Minotaur*

Raj Tawney, *Colorful Palate: Savored Stories from a Mixed Life*

Joseph Heathcott, *Global Queens: An Urban Mosaic*

Francis R. Kowsky with Lucille Gordon, *Hell on Color, Sweet on Song: Jacob Wrey Mould and the Artful Beauty of Central Park*

Jill Jonnes, *South Bronx Rising: The Rise, Fall, and Resurrection of an American City, Third Edition*

Barbara G. Mensch, *A Falling-Off Place: The Transformation of Lower Manhattan*

David J. Goodwin, *Midnight Rambles: H. P. Lovecraft in Gotham*

Felipe Luciano, *Flesh and Spirit: Confessions of a Young Lord*

Maximo G. Martinez, *Sojourners in the Capital of the World: Garifuna Immigrants*

Jennifer Baum, *Just City: Growing Up on the Upper West Side When Housing Was a Human Right*

Davida Siwisa James, *Hamilton Heights and Sugar Hill: Alexander Hamilton's Old Harlem Neighborhood Through the Centuries*

Annik LaFarge, *On the High Line: The Definitive Guide, Third Edition.* Foreword by Rick Dark

Marie Carter, *Mortimer and the Witches: A History of Nineteenth-Century Fortune Tellers*

Alice Sparberg Alexiou, *Devil's Mile: The Rich, Gritty History of the Bowery.* Foreword by Peter Quinn

Carey Kasten and Brenna Moore, *Mutuality in El Barrio: Stories of the Little Sisters of the Assumption Family Health Service.* Foreword by Norma Benítez Sánchez

Kimberly A. Orcutt, *The American Art-Union: Utopia and Skepticism in the Antebellum Era*

Jonathan Butler, *Join the Conspiracy: How a Brooklyn Eccentric Got Lost on the Right, Infiltrated the Left, and Brought Down the Biggest Bombing Network in New York*

Nicole Gelinas, *Movement: New York's Long War to Take Back Its Streets from the Car*

Jack Hodgson, *Young Reds in the Big Apple: The New York Young Pioneers of America, 1923–1934*

Lynn Ellsworth, *Wonder City: How to Reclaim Human-Scale Urban Life*

Walter Zev Feldman, *From the Bronx to the Bosphorus: Klezmer and Other Displaced Musics of New York*

Larry Racioppo, *Here Down on Dark Earth: Loss and Remembrance in New York City*

Bonnie Yochelson, *Too Good to Get Married: The Life and Photographs of Miss Alice Austen*

David Brown Morris, *Ten Thousand Central Parks: A Climate-Change Parable*

Eve M. Kahn, *Queen of Bohemia Predicts Own Death: The Forgotten Journalist Zoe Anderson Norris, 1860-1914*

Miriam Chaiken, *Creative Ozone: The Artists of Westbeth*

Stephanie Azzarone, *Fabulous Fountains of New York*

**For a complete list, visit www.fordhampress.com/empire-state-editions.**